J.K. LASSER PRO™

SEPARATE ACCOUNT MANAGEMENT

AN INVESTMENT MANAGEMENT STRATEGY DESIGNED FOR HIGH NET WORTH INDIVIDUALS

**Larry Chambers
Ken Ziesenheim
Peter Trevisani**

WILEY

John Wiley & Sons, Inc.

Published by John Wiley & Sons, Inc., Hoboken, New Jersey
Published simultaneously in Canada

For general information on our other products and services, or technical support, please contact our Customer Care Department within the United States at 800-762-2974, outside the United States at 317-572-3993 or fax 317-572-4002.

Wiley also publishes its books in a variety of electronic formats. Some content that appears in print may not be available in electronic books.

For more information about Wiley products, visit our web site at *www.wiley.com*.

Library of Congress Cataloging-in-Publication Data:
Chambers, Larry, 1947–
    Separate account management : an investment management strategy
designed for high net worth individuals / by Larry Chambers.
        p.   cm.—(J.K. Lasser pro series)
    Includes index.
      ISBN 0-471-24976-9 (CLOTH: alk. paper)
    1. Portfolio management.   2. Investments.   I. Title.   II. Series.

Printed in the United States of America

10 9 8 7 6 5 4 3 2 1

Contents

Foreword

After decades of being pigeonholed, poorly defined, put down, and generally dismissed as a serious contender in the investment arena, the separately managed account has come into its own. An investment vehicle that has been up and running successfully since the mid-1970s is now achieving mainstream respectability. More than that, separately managed accounts are making a serious bid to become the core investment for high-net-worth individual investors, a subset of the investing market that controls, or will soon control, more than $40 trillion in investment assets.

Why has this happened? Why now? More important, what does it mean for your industry? For about 25 years, individually managed accounts, offered under a wrapped-fee pricing structure, were either ignored (the first 15 years) or attacked (the next 10). From the late 1980s to the mid-1990s, these programs were the favorite punching bag for the financial media. Articles about the so-called wrap fee and the wrap fee rip-off were the only press a managed account program could get. The cry was almost always the same: "It's too expensive, you can get the same thing cheaper in a mutual fund!"

But companies, mostly the major wirehouses, with broad enough vision (and deep enough pockets) continued to sponsor managed account programs, and quietly accumulated $100 billion in assets under management by 1995. Pretty small potatoes if you compare it with the trillions that were flowing into mutual funds, but respectable, if you believed that managed accounts were, and would continue to be, a niche product.

In the late 1990s, however, a mainstream shift began, powered by two important developments. Together, they have focused the attention of the financial press, the investment professional, and the affluent individual on separately managed accounts, literally tripling assets under management between 1995 and 2000.

The Pricing

The first development was in pricing. In the bad old days, the most frequent criticism of these programs was their cost. Typically marketed at a 3 percent annual fee, the managed account was vulnerable to critics who insisted that it was overpriced, and to those who wanted to know who was getting paid what, and what they were doing to earn their part of the fee. Also, as financial advisors migrated toward "fees" as a method of compensation, the "confined" fee became problematic.

Of all the stones thrown our way in those years, this was the one that hit hardest. The irony was that the wrapped fee, when it was instituted, was actually a better deal for clients than commissions. At the typical $0.85-per-share commission rate of the 1970s, it didn't take long for commissions to equal or surpass the wrapped fee. And getting paid for their best advice—whether it was to buy, sell, or hold—gave fee-based advisors the freedom *and* the incentive to recommend only what was in the client's best interest. It was the advice that generated revenues, not the transaction. But that was a hard concept to communicate in an industry that had a long tradition of compensation by commissions.

However, as transaction costs were forced down (and information was commoditized) by technology and competition in the late 1990s, the spotlight shifted to the value of unbiased advice.

As for pricing, in reality every program sponsor had a discount grid that enabled consultants to lower the fee in competitive situations. These discount capabilities were widely used, so we were getting bashed for a fee we hardly ever collected. In the face of this reality, a few companies began to pare down their pricing structures (see the section entitled "The Technology," which follows) and unwrap fees, creating lower, unbundled fee schedules that plainly identify each component of the separately managed account investment. Now, investors can easily find out how much they pay for research and consulting, how much the advisor is paid, how much the money manager gets, and what they're paying for clearing and custody. And, as we can see from the recent flows of new money into separately managed accounts, unbundling hasn't hurt business a bit.

Meanwhile, the investing public also began to understand that you couldn't get the same thing cheaper in a mutual fund. They realized that the critical differences between mutual funds and separate accounts, the ability to manage to an after-tax objective and the ability to customize the portfolio, were of significant value when added to their investing program. The closer separate account pricing got to average mutual fund expense ratios (never mind trading costs), the more attractive separate accounts became.

The Technology

The second development is the impact of technology. Advances in information management, analysis, and communication technologies, to name only the most obvious, have driven enormous changes in the investment consulting arena. Ours is an industry where you rise or fall on your ability to offer custom service.

Technological advances let us compete for business on an exponentially larger scale while maintaining the high level of customization and service our clients expect, and I believe we're just beginning to exploit the potential of technology to broaden our competitive horizon.

It was only 20 years ago that quarterly presentations of portfolio performance were done by hand. Fortunately, technology moved into this area long ago, with ever-increasing economies of scale in the account maintenance functions of separate accounts. In the same way that information management technology has revolutionized so many business applications, it has enabled our industry to do the trading, tracking, and reporting faster and more accurately than ever.

The New Breed of Client

Bringing prices down and unbundling fees eliminated the biggest single objection advisors encountered when they recommended separate accounts, and technological advances have enabled us to offer separate accounts to any investor who can benefit from them, introducing mass customization.

The long, strong bull market of the 1980s and 1990s triggered a phenomenon called the Wealth Effect. The corresponding bear market has educated investors about what they really need as an investment strategy.

Now, there's a new breed of client with wealth, and that fact is going to revolutionize the way we do business. These newly affluent investors are, on average, younger and more sophisticated about investing. They have high expectations about every aspect of their investing experience. They expect to make money; they expect excellent, personalized service; and they expect to understand what's going on in their portfolio.

It's all part of the lifestyle they're living. They go online to order upscale cars, defining precisely which motors, suspensions, and interiors they want. They expect, and get, broad selection, good service, and quality products. Even the vacation industry is now upscale, designing custom vacations for high-net-worth couples. Nothing has actually changed about the way the cruise is organized, but the cruise lines recognize that highlighting the customization capabilities of their services is a legitimate, effective marketing technique.

Today's investor has a new set of expectations. They already understand the benefits of professional money management—their positive experience with mutual funds taught them that. Mutual funds also made them familiar with key concepts of investing like diversification, expense ratios, and total return. They're comfortable with these concepts. But they are also beginning to understand the effect that taxes can have on a portfolio's growth. That understanding is driving a swelling demand for customized investments that address the individual's financial goals *and* tax situation. Now, its up to you, the advisor.

I want to introduce you to separate account management. It's complex, detailed, and will help you build your business, stay competitive, and help your clients.

LEN REINHART
CEO of Lockwood Financial
A subsidiary of the Bank of New York

Acknowledgments

The statistics, charts, graphs, data, and majority of information in this book have been collected over the past five years of interviewing, visiting, reading, and attending seminars and conferences. We wish to thank all those who have given us information, and a special thanks goes to Thornburg Investment Management (Brian McMahon, Leigh Moiola, Dale Van Scoyk, Steven Bohlin, George Strickland, Randy Dry) and Lewis J. Walker, CFP, CIMC, CRC; Chip Roame of Tiburon Strategic Advisors; Jack Rabun Cerulli Associates; and Len Reinhart, CEO of Lockwood Family of Companies.

PART

I

THE BASICS

In Part I, we will explain what a separately managed account is and how it works.

Chapter 1—Introduction

These accounts ultimately provide the same benefits as other investment packages—growing capital in a systematic process using professional investment managers to help people achieve their financial objectives—but they may do so with greater satisfaction. The real issue is not whether they provide benefits (they do), but how and for whom they should be employed.

Chapter 2—Separate Account Definitions

There is confusion in the marketplace regarding exactly what to call separate accounts. Are they separately managed accounts, managed accounts, individually managed accounts? Are they wrap accounts? What's the difference?

Chapter 3—The State of the Separate Accounts Industry

The five managed account segments, representing a total of $769.0 billion in assets, show a five-year growth rate of 32.1 percent, illustrating the stability gained through the advice and guidance that are inherent in managed accounts. The main sponsors and participants in the marketplace are discussed.

Chapter 4—Participants in the Separate Account Market

Private wealth is booming. Illiquid assets (e.g., small businesses, investment real estate) total approximately $46.5 trillion, of which approximately $17 trillion is investable assets—that's your market.

Introduction

Separately managed accounts have reached their *tipping point.* The tipping point is defined as the moment of critical mass, the threshold, or the boiling point (Figure 1.1). You need to prepare yourselves for the possibility that this product is about to get very big, very quickly!

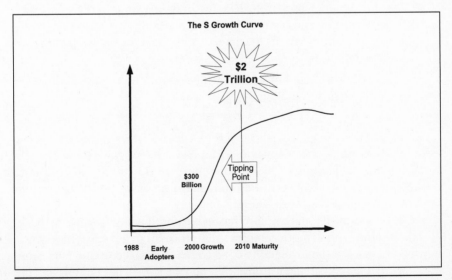

FIGURE 1.1 Tipping Point.

Mounting Evidence

- Assets totaling $752 billion are currently invested in five types of managed account programs.

- Technology continues to influence the evolution of the managed account industry.

- There's a higher degree of standardized automation between money managers and program sponsors.

- According to both Tiburon Strategic Advisors and Cerulli Associates, consultant wraps are the most popular investment vehicles among emerging affluent and high-net-worth clients.

- Currently, program sponsors report an average asset level in wrap account relationships of $500,000 per account.

- Fee-based program asset share as a percentage of overall brokerage assets has doubled in the past two years.

- The nation's financial product distribution powerhouses continue to dominate managed account assets, with the top 10 firms representing more than 80 percent of the industry.

- The traditional retail mutual fund companies are expanding into this market. Investment advisors, other than those who cater to institutional clients, must offer this product.

- The independent broker-dealers, fee-only investment advisors, insurance companies, and certified public accountant (CPA) firms are building fee account programs to compete with the in-house wrap programs of the wirehouses.

- The number of U.S. households with separate accounts will increase fivefold to nearly 5 million by 2010.

There is nothing magical about *separate accounts*—they provide the same opportunity as other investment choices for investors to grow capital but with certain unique capabilities. Chief among these are the ability to customize portfolios with individual securities, to manage tax liabilities better, and to control and manage cash flows better.

Acceleration in the marketplace has heretofore been governed by back-office limitations and a more complex sales process, but advances in technology have expanded the availability of separately managed accounts to more investors. While individual customization may be somewhat diminished, the fact that thousands of accounts can be administered and reported simply has enhanced the marketability of managed accounts.

However, managed accounts are not without controversy. Pundits question whether they provide adequate diversification when only one or two managers are employed, whether they are as cost-efficient as more traditional investment products such as mutual funds, and whether they actually deliver the degree of tax control advertised. There's also speculation that they may be just a passing fad in times of market turmoil. These are all reasonable questions that this book will attempt to answer.

In the end, it must be recognized that separate accounts are just another investment alternative—an opportunity that will be suitable for some but not for all.

These accounts ultimately provide the same benefits as other investment packages—growing capital in a systematic process using professional investment managers to help people achieve their financial objectives—but they may do so with greater satisfaction. The real issue is not whether they provide benefits (they do), but how and for whom they should be employed. This is why we have included a chapter on comprehensive financial planning.

The following material is designed for many different types of readers. It's a basic reference book for the financial professional with no previous experience in managing money as well as the advisor who has years of experience. It's for financial advisors who want to round out their knowledge about a product they already use. It's for the mutual fund wholesaler who recently switched to marketing separate accounts and wants to help the branch manager convince the corner office producer to start selling them. It's for the operational people reconciling accounts and the CPA wanting to move his practice into the world of investments.

We believe it will be useful to:

- Wirehouse sponsors and their financial advisors.
- Independent investment advisors.
- Elite producers who want to consider the independent investment advisory business to leverage their current client relationships.
- Producers in the growth stage of their career who aspire to be the best of the best. Some of these will want to go independent. We hope this book will help them make informed decisions.
- The corner-office producer interested in marketing financial services to the affluent.

The purpose of this book is to enable advisors to sit down with their clients and recommend a separate account program with confidence and knowledge.

When you complete this book, you will know more about separate accounts than 90 percent of your competition. It should take the mystery out of providing professional asset management services to a broad cross section of your clients. It will educate you about the opportunities and advantages of using separately managed accounts. It will provide you with information about how they work, how they operate, who should use them, and ultimately, how you can employ them in your financial advisory practice. Even though managed accounts have been around for several years, there is still much to learn and much to be developed. *Now* is the time for this book.

Yesterday and Today

Twenty years ago, separately managed accounts were reserved for the very sophisticated advisor who served only the wealthy. Today, separate accounts are the direction of the industry and are available to most advisors and to several layers of the affluent (Figure 1.2). It is our desire to introduce you to separate account management and how you can use separate accounts to build your businesses and help your clients reach their financial goals.

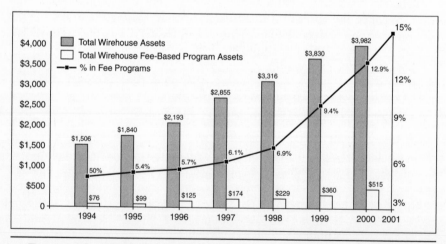

FIGURE 1.2 Wirehouse Assets in Fee-Based Programs (in $ Billions). Source: Company Reports, Cerulli Associates.

Why Should You Market Separate Accounts in the First Place?

There is an entire slate of different investment products available to you: individual securities, mutual funds, hedge funds, private equity, and others. Why use separate accounts?

There are three reasons. First, they serve your clients well.

Second, it's important to your business to keep the promises that you make to your clients. Using separate accounts can help you do that, especially if you have offered to assist your client in planning for tax liabilities. For instance, suppose that one of your clients has unrealized gains in some other investments. You can ask your separate account portfolio manager if there are any unrealized losses in the separate account portfolio. If so, those losses can be realized, offsetting the gains your client wishes to take. This gives your client control over timing of cash flows and the ability to take advantage of tax lot accounting, which increases your value in the eyes of your client and separates you from the competition.

Third, today's affluent are predisposed to using separate accounts. Affluence in America is exploding. According to the Financial Research Corporation (FRC), there will be 14 million millionaire households in the United States by 2004. Separate accounts give the affluent what are they looking for: direct ownership and prestige and personal attention.

All of your clients have unique tax considerations, which further complicates the investment process, not to mention your job. No single efficient market portfolio exists that can satisfy every investor's objectives. In reality, each of your clients' unique tax considerations results in a unique investment portfolio. And today, affluent investors expect you to understand their unique needs and how to solve their unique challenges.

Separate Accounts Can Help Streamline Your Business

When you build a business that grows to several hundred clients, you physically can't keep up. Here's a quick example of how you can get lost. Imagine that you bought an equity mutual fund for a number of your best clients. This particular fund was trading at $28 a share when your mutual fund manager decided to take profits in some big winners that ran up before you got your clients invested, resulting in $8 per share capital gains distribution at the end of the year. Your clients probably don't realize this act just diminished the total value of the fund.

Why? Because the mutual fund share price goes down by the exact amount of the now realized capital gain per share, $8. Therefore, your best clients' fund is now trading at $20 a share. This sounds okay because your clients have the $8, so they're even, right? But are they? They're going to have to pay tax on that $8 distribution, and even if the tax is at the lower 20 percent capital gains rate, your clients owe $1.60 in taxes. After taxes, there's a $6.40-per-share profit. However, when you add that $6.40 back to the $20 share price, it still spells *loss*. This could have been avoided in a separately managed account. And you can show them how. With separate accounts, you become an important part of their investment management team.

With a separate account you can, to some degree, customize the construction of your clients' portfolios well beyond the standard investment style differentiation. We will show you how in later chapters. You can restrict specific securities from their portfolios. This capability enables you to control the diversification of their overall investment plan.

Here's another challenge: Many of your clients own large positions in the stock of their employer, in their pension plan, in their 401(k) plan, or through stock options. Such investors may want to bar you from holding any of that company's stock or even from holding stocks of other companies in the same industry so the diversification plan stays on track. In a separately managed portfolio, managers may handle such restrictions as a matter of routine. This adds value and meets the client's need for customization.

You also may have clients who own large positions of low-cost-basis stock. For example, if they want to use that stock to fund a mutual fund purchase, the stock must be sold and capital gains taxes paid, regardless of how ill-timed that taxable event may be. Mutual funds can only be purchased with cash. In a separately managed account, however, the manager may accept the transfer of other securities *in kind* to fund the account.

These separate account managers will work with you. The new platforms are designed to examine your client's existing portfolio and balance the need for a disciplined investment approach with tax-efficient investing, depending on their financial needs. It is your clients' personal situations that dictate the handling of the securities, which also adds to your overall value.

Having a separate account can also free your clients, and therefore you, from the sometimes negative effects of the "herd instinct" that often drives market events. Everyone remembers October 1987 when anxious mutual fund investors redeemed shares in huge numbers. The managers of those funds reluctantly sold positions to fund the redemptions. They knew that they were selling into a great buying opportunity, but client redemptions left them no choice. Within months, the market had recovered and was higher than it was before the correction.

Similarly, the recovery from the stock market drop during the days that followed September 11 took only 19 days. Separate accounts can give your clients some control over their investment outcomes. They can elect to ride out, or buy into a downdraft in the market, going against the tide to take advantage of an opportunity. Mutual fund managers have to be sensitive to fund holder redemptions and may be forced to sell, as was the case in 1987.

Are you a financial planner? Your value may come from uncovering gaps and shortfalls in your clients' future planning. Your job is knowing how many dollars your client is going to need in future years and how to ensure that money will be there for him or her. The future dictates that you have a program that can work with *you* to keep them on track. You add value every step of the way. You can use this book to educate your clients, help them identify what strategies are appropriate, and continue to maintain the ongoing analysis and dialogue, as well as performance monitoring on the separate account money manager.

The consultative process of separate account management positions you as an expert. Instead of memorizing thousands of stocks or hundreds of funds, you can build expertise on after-tax management using a cadre of separate account money managers. This gives you more time to work with individual clients and to prospect for new ones. It also creates the opportunity to develop relationships and a deeper level of due diligence with the investment manager.

This book will give you directions and a template for your journey. It will help you avoid some of the potential hazards along the way. Without guidance, you can make the assumption (or get hung up on the assumption) that using separate account money managers is simply for beating the stock market averages as opposed to viewing your firm's separate account programs as a means to create an acceptable rate of return at the lowest possible level of risk. This is what we mean when we say separate accounts serve your clients well.

The majority of the money being managed in this country today is being managed based upon the investor's investment objective. This is contrary to what the popular investment press touts. If you read popular consumer magazines, you spend all of your time trying to match the performance of market averages or trying to beat the market. This media-induced perspective produces the belief in your client's mind that risk is not relevant. The real risk is not having the money you need *when* you need it.

Our goal is to keep you out of the dark and to allow you to make right decisions based on accurate information. For example, suppose that in 1995 you hired Nicholas Applegate, a mid-cap growth manager whose standard deviation back then was around 20 percent. The Standard & Poor's 500 (S&P

500) at that time had a standard deviation of around 10.1. Today, the S&P 500's standard deviation is around 15.24, or 50 percent more volatile than seven years ago. That means the market is twice as risky as it used to be in terms of volatility.

Unlike the S&P 500, though, Nicholas Applegate's standard deviation isn't five percentage points higher. The last we looked it was around 44. And, while it's true that they were one of the managers that went up the most from 1995 to 2000, they are also one of the managers that have gone down the most from 2000 to 2002. If you haven't been readjusting, monitoring, and explaining this to your clients, you are not adding value. Do your clients understand this? Most don't even know what you're talking about. Education and managing of expectations are critical aspects of a financial planner's job. The only thing your clients understand is that their account is down 50 percent, and now they want to sell it and have you send them a check.

Here's where we can show you how to really add value. We will show you how to shift your clients' focus away from past performance or so-called total return to help them see what their highest probability of achieving success is. It isn't finding the next best manager, but instead, it's shifting to a process that offers them more control, which includes the control of fees, taxes, and management of their investment expectations. They get this in separate account programs. The bulk of this book will focus on showing you how to take control and use these programs to your clients' advantage. We have no biases toward any one separate account management program. We believe they are all pretty much the same. They all can do a great job. What really makes them work is *you*. What makes a program great is your understanding of them and your ability to make them work in your clients' favor.

Separate account programs are built on a very sound foundation. That is, there are no tax gimmicks, no get-rich-quick schemes, and no loopholes in the law; no performance anomalies, no derivatives or synthetic securities. They are going to be around for a long time to come. Most separate accounts basically consist of fundamental long-term investing in stocks, bonds, and cash. This is plain vanilla, not the stuff of which fads are made.

What would happen if Congress actually eliminated estate taxes? On the one hand, this would devastate estate tax life insurance sales, one of the highest-netting insurance sales areas. (No wonder the insurance lobby is fighting so hard!!) On the other hand, it would simply enhance separate account sales. Just think, with no estate tax, the cost basis step-up at death would more than likely disappear. This means that while you're alive, you will want an investment strategy that slowly raises the cost basis of your portfolio, while producing competitive total performance. That's exactly the job of the separate account manager.

One last, but very important, consideration: Our goal is to prove that this is the right thing to do. There are, in fact, a lot of advisors out there doing the right thing, but who are having trouble selling the concept. We will show you how. Let's get started by defining the terms.

CHAPTER 2

Separate Account Definitions

There is confusion in the marketplace regarding exactly *what* to call separate accounts. Are they separately managed accounts, managed accounts, individually managed accounts? Are they wrap accounts? What's the difference, and who should use one?

The original wrap account was an account comprised of individual securities run by a professional money manager on a discretionary basis for the client. The term *wrap fee* came about after May Day in 1975, when Jim Lockwood realized that if commissions were negotiable, they could be negotiated to *zero*. In addition, if you charged a fee based on assets in lieu of commissions, it would put the broker on the same side of the table as the client for the first time. That was the idea behind the very first managed account that Lockwood put together for Hutton Investment Management.

At that time, it was very unusual to have a fee-based brokerage account as opposed to one that was transaction oriented. Mutual funds were usually identified by their fee structure—load funds, no-load funds, and back-end load funds. Hence, the managed account also became known as the *wrap-fee* account, since the total fee wrapped all the costs of the account. The name stuck in the press because they were accustomed to such terminology.

Although the money started to come in during the late 1970s, the big flows of money didn't really start until the late 1980s. By then, wrap programs were much more sophisticated. As the industry has grown, the wrap-fee label has become inadequate and inappropriate as a description of this investment vehicle. To name a professional service for the way you charge your fees is not really very professional.

What Is a Separately Managed Account?

A separately managed account is an investment vehicle in which the investor gives full discretion over cash and/or securities to an investment firm to manage according to the investor's specifications. Separately managed accounts have certain similarities to mutual funds, such as professional management, cost, diversification, and liquidity.

Inside a separate account, however, the investor directly owns the individual securities. Investments in a separately managed account are *not* pooled with those of other investors, as they are in a mutual fund. Plus, separately managed account programs routinely handle specific and unique requests, oftentimes pertaining to tax considerations. Because of their pooled ownership structure, mutual funds cannot take such individual preferences into consideration.

The term *separately managed account* is synonymous and used interchangeably with the term *individually managed account* or *managed account,* but for the purposes of this book and to avoid confusion, we're going to refer to them simply as *separate accounts.*

Other Definitions

individually managed account.   Synonymous and used interchangeably with *separately managed account* and *managed account.*

managed account.   Also used interchangeably with *individually managed account* and *separately managed account.*

multidiscipline account (MDA).   Very popular right now, specifically within Smith Barney. Acronyms are used to describe the packaging together of different investment disciplines managed by different investment managers in predetermined percentages—often with lower investment minimums. These are also referred to as *multiple style accounts.* An MDA manager is really a sponsor.

program sponsor.   The investment advisor, the entity responsible for establishing and maintaining the program.

Sponsors generally do not recommend an unlimited number of managers. They typically restrict each style category to 3 or 4 managers, with the total recommended list not exceeding 40 to 50 manager names. Our experience is that the sponsor-recommended lists turn over approximately 20 percent in a normal year.

multistyle account (MSA).   Cerulli Associates' umbrella term for the growing list of acronyms used to describe the packaging together of investment styles in predetermined percentages—often with lower investment minimums. Generally, each different style is managed by a different investment manager.

unified managed account (UMA). A centralized platform offered by brokerages to support a service offered by their financial consultants. This is a type of platform for wirehouse advisors.

client-directed, fee-based account. When the client directs the investments on a nondiscretionary basis and can trade as much as he or she wants, but is only charged one fee. These accounts are rising in popularity and usually contain trading restrictions to control the frequency of trading.

broker-directed account or personally advised account. When a stockbroker or financial advisor directs the investments on a discretionary basis. There is no independent money manager. Pioneered at EF Hutton, these programs are usually only available through a limited number of experienced, prequalified brokers or advisors.

guided managed account programs. Brokerage accounts that use their research departments to put together buy lists and give broker-advisors a choice of one or two securities in each category for the clients. These programs are some of the fastest-growing products at many firms.

fee-based brokerage account. Used interchangeably with *guided portfolio account* or client direct account.

wrap-fee account. The original wrap account was an individually managed account run by a professional money manager on a discretionary basis for the client, with one fee that covered all costs of the account.

mutual fund wrap (aka mutual fund managed account). Consists of a portfolio of mutual funds with an advisory fee overlay. This was the hottest product in the 1990s, but it cooled down, as diversified asset allocation did not perform well in the technology-heavy bull market. These are not separate accounts.

Over the past year or so, several fund complexes have rolled out tax-managed mutual funds that aim for significantly lower turnover and take advantage of tax lot accounting and other techniques. Although they are certainly a vast improvement over their non-tax-conscious counterparts, the very nature of a mutual fund will constrain this new breed of fund to, at best, an imperfect substitute for a tax-efficient separately managed account.

Names of Wirehouse Program Platforms

separate account consultant programs. These are programs in which unaffiliated institutional money managers manage investors' assets in separate accounts. High-net-worth investors, with account minimums of $100,000 to $250,000 or greater, are targeted. A bundled asset-based fee (often 2.5 to 3 percent before discounts from negotiation) covers money management, trading, and custody, as well as the advisor's fee, though sometimes this fee may be paid via directed brokerage commission.

proprietary consultant programs. This category is composed of discretionary fee-based separate account assets managed by a brokerage firm's internal asset management unit and gathered off-platform (i.e., outside of a brokerage's own consultant wrap program) via its retail sales force. High-net-worth investors, with account minimums of $100,000 to $250,000 or more, are targeted. A bundled asset-based fee covers money management, trading, and custody.

mutual fund advisory programs.   These programs are designed to systematically allocate investors' assets across a wide range of mutual funds. Services include client profiling, account monitoring, and portfolio rebalancing. An asset-based fee of 1.25 percent, for example, is charged instead of commission. Account minimums typically range between $10,000 and $50,000. These programs are generally discretionary.

fee-based brokerage.   A program in which active traders pay a flat asset-based fee (usually about 1 percent) for all trading activity instead of a commission for each individual trade. Historically, there has been no advisory element to these programs. However, to combat the growing popularity of online trading, many of these programs are now incorporating advice. These programs offer both mutual funds and individual securities, but individual stocks dominate.

sales representative as portfolio manager.   A program in which financial representatives act as money managers for their clients by taking full responsibility for selecting a portfolio of securities. Representatives go through rigorous internal training to qualify—only a small number are approved to participate in the program. There is often both a senior- and junior-level representative version of the program.

Other Terms to Know Before We Start

Proprietary programs include only investment managers inside the broker-dealer's own company. Raymond James and Merrill Lynch, for example, have their own proprietary program in separate account management: Merrill Lynch has Investment Management; Raymond James has Eagle Asset. Within Eagle, for example, there are 10 different strategies, including an aggressive strategy, a small-cap strategy, and a bond strategy, but the strategies are proprietary.

Both firms also have *nonproprietary programs,* in which they do the due diligence and hire outside independent money managers—but all managers use the same administrative platform that the proprietary managers use. Raymond James's program is called Investment Advisory Services (IAS). They have about 30 different money managers, and for those 30 managers, Raymond James performs due diligence on managers for the various asset class boxes, the reporting on private accounts, and the trading for those separate money managers. Overall, they serve as the investment advisor to the account and use the money managers as the *subadvisors.*

Merrill Lynch does the same thing; its program is called Consults. They hire independent money management companies as subadvisors—to fill in their style boxes—then all the trading, administration, and billing is handled by Merrill Lynch. The subadvisors just manage the money.

What Is a Subadvisor?

A subadvisory program is defined as one where clients' assets are invested among a sanctioned roster of money managers, in a separate account, as determined by the sponsoring brokerage firm. Some current examples include Legg Mason, Salomon Smith Barney, and Janney Montgomery Scott.

Minimums to access each asset manager typically range between $100,000 and $250,000. The investor usually pays one bundled asset fee for all managed account services, including trading, custody, clearing, money management, and investment consulting.

The subadvisor is the money manager. For example, under IAS, the client signs an investment advisory agreement with Raymond James, which serves as the *investment advisor,* and an independent money management firm serves as the *subadvisor.* In other words, the Raymond James investment advisory program hires the manager as a subadvisor to their program. Raymond James has the ultimate *fiduciary responsibility,* the reporting responsibility, and the trading responsibility.

Under subadvisory program processes, separate account investors have a single contract with a brokerage firm that covers the scope of the program, including the brokerage firm's arrangement with the money manager. That program is discretionary, but it is the investment manager that has the discretion, not the sponsoring broker-dealer. It is usually the broker-dealer's responsibility to pick the money manager for the client, though sometimes it remains the client's decision.

What Is Open Architecture?

Like separate account subadvisory programs, open-architecture separate accounts are invested in a separate account run by an asset manager. There are, however, several crucial differences between the two.

First, the investor, in conjunction with a financial advisor, can select virtually any money manager to manage his or her separate account portfolio, rather than be limited to a smaller approved list of 35 to 80 managers usually offered by subadvisory programs. Triangular contractual relationships typically exist where an investor has a contract directly with the money management firm that has advisory responsibility in addition to a contract with the sponsoring brokerage firm. That constitutes an *unbundled* program.

Most separate account providers offer versions of both the separate account subadvisory and open-architecture models. One brokerage firm, for example, has between 50 and 60 money managers in its subadvisory program, but also includes as many as 1,500 institutional money managers in an open-architecture version of its separate account program.

A major difference between subadvisory and open-architecture separate accounts is in pricing. Unlike a subadvisory program, which bundles together all pricing components such as trading, clearing, or management, investors in most open-architecture separate account programs have more options to pay for their services. There is generally an arrangement where they can elect to pay some sort of directed brokerage commissions or fee-plus-ticket charges instead of straight asset-based fees. In addition, the management fees are generally negotiable since they are outside the scope of the broker-dealer's sponsored programs.

This means that clients in an open-architecture program can pay for money management through either fees or commissions. Some open-architecture programs, like A.G. Edwards Private Advisory Services Program, allow multiple pricing options; others, like Merrill Lynch, do not.

The open-architecture structure is the older of the two program designs, but there are now more subadvisory than open-architecture programs. Subadvisory programs also dominate in terms of assets.

Platform subadvisors are outside money managers in a broker-dealer's program. For a list of providers, see Figure 2.1.

U.S. Large-Cap Value
  Sanford C. Bernstein & Co., Inc.—Deep Value
  Deutsche Asset Management—Core Value
  Iridian Asset Management—Relative Value
  LSV Asset Management—Contrarian Value

U.S. Small-Cap Value
  Artisan Partners—Deep Value
  LSV Asset Management—Contrarian Value
  Sterling Capital Management—Core Value
  DJ Greene—Intrinsic Value
  Chartwell Investment Partners—Relative Value
  Security Capital—REIT

International Developed Equity
  Morgan Stanley Investment Management—Non-U.S. Value
  BlackRock Financial Management—Developed Europe
  Capital Guardian Trust Company—Non-U.S. GARP
  Oechsle International Advisors, LLC—Non-U.S. Growth
  Martin Currie—Japan Value
  JF International Mgmt.—Pac. Basin x-Japan & Japan Gr

U.S. Large-Cap Growth
  Alliance Capital—Core Growth
  Peregrine Capital Management—Long-Term Growth
  Duncan-Hurst Capital Management—Earnings Momentum
  Transamerican Investment Mgmt.—Emerging Growth

U.S. Small-Cap Growth
  RS Investment Management—Aggressive Growth
  Sawgrass Asset Management, L.L.C.—Disciplined Growth
  Mazama Capital Management—Conservative Growth
  McKinley—Earnings Momentum Growth

U.S. Fixed Income
  Western Asset Mgmt.—Sector Rotation/Issue Selection
  BlackRock Financial Management—Mortgage Specialty
  Robert W. Baird & Co.—Enhanced Government/Corporate
  Thornburg Investment Mgmt.—Short-Interest Municipal

High Yield Fixed Income
  Nicholas Applegate—U.S. High Yield (Core)
  Nomura Corp. Research—U.S. High Yield (Concentrator)
  Shenkman—U.S. High Yield (Fundamental Value)

FIGURE 2.1 Example of Subadvisor List.

Name of Independent Program Platforms

Turnkey asset management programs (TAMPs) are used by independent practitioners, including independent advisors, CPAs, banks, and insurance agents for their separate account services. The TAMPs manage all of the components in the investment management process, including developing an investment policy statement, creating an asset allocation and style study, and manager selection and rebalancing. Large-cap equity is the dominant asset class in most programs. Almost 400 managers participate in the separate account wrap and TAMP market.

A User's Guide to TAMPs

Traditional turnkey platform providers include:

Assante (www.assante.com).　Emphasizes strategic asset allocation index fund portfolios; has added a "life management" offering, which includes insurance, personal CFO.

AssetMark (www.assetmark.com).　Offers mutual fund tactical asset allocation strategies; has added separate accounts; is about to launch eWealthManager online.

BAM Advisor Services (www.bamservices.com).　Emphasizes strategic asset allocation index fund portfolios; preparing to launch broader product offering; works primarily with accounting firms.

Brinker Capital (www.brinkercapital.com).　Provides separately managed accounts and related back-office and performance reporting services, primarily to insurance-oriented advisors.

Frank Russell (www.russell.com).　Advisory arm of pension consulting firm; emphasizes actively managed, proprietary mutual fund portfolios.

Greenrock Research (www.greenrockresearch.com).　Focuses on research and evaluation of separate account managers; provides related back-office and performance reporting services to financial advisors.

Investment Consulting Group (www.galleryworks.com).　Gives advisors access to traditional and nontraditional separate account managers and related back-office and reporting services.

Lockwood Financial (www.lkwdfncl.com).　Focuses on separate accounts; offers mutual fund and exchange-traded fund portfolios, and back-office and reporting services; annual Lockwood University training program.

Envestnet Portfolio Management Consultants (www.envestnetpmc.com). Offers separately managed accounts, mutual fund portfolios, and performance reporting services to financial advisors and institutions.

SEI (www.sei.com/iag).   World's largest provider of mutual fund managed account services uses actively managed proprietary mutual funds; limited, but growing separate account capabilities.

Web-based providers include:

Advisorport.com (www.advisorport.com).   Comprehensive separately managed account services for financial advisors, including back-office and reporting services.

Oberon Financial Technology, Inc. (www.mymoneypro.com).   Provides separately managed account services directly to investors or via financial advisors; assets held in custody at Fidelity.

Once you know the different program names and their characteristics, you will have mastered the first step to understanding separate accounts.

Who Should Use Separate Accounts?

Many investors open separate accounts because they are encouraged to do so by their financial consultants or because they are intrigued with the mystique and the supposed prestige that are attached. Normally, the argument in favor of separate accounts can be broken down to:

- Your client benefits from the individual attention of a portfolio manager.
- You can place restrictions around your client's account and the ownership of certain securities or types of securities.
- You have a lot more control over your client's tax situation.

Some investment management firms manage hundreds of thousands of separate accounts. Each account does not receive individual attention; rather, each account is matched to a model, and variances are eliminated by buying or selling securities for blocks of accounts with similar variances. Portfolio managers are usually focused on security selection and the performance of the product. The investment professional at a money management firm who has the most direct contact with an individual account is a trader.

The Trader

The trader's job is usually twofold: (1) to get the best execution for each trade, and (2) to minimize dispersion.

Best Execution

Best execution is an industry term referring to a trade or series of trades that optimize the trader's objective, which is not always solely best price. Since a trader or traders at the same firm will often execute trades in the same security for multiple products, minimizing market impact is also important. Some firms focus on the time element as well—the timing cost relates to potential returns lost due to slow trade implementation.

For example, a portfolio manager might want to buy ABCD, a moderately liquid mid-cap over-the-counter (OTC) stock, into a number of the products for which he/she is responsible. The first step is to inform the trading desk at his/her firm. In the best of all possible worlds, share counts are generated for every account, including any mutual funds, and then blocked together to form a single order. This order is worked by the trading desk. In the event that the entire position could not be purchased, it is typical for the shares bought to be prorated across all accounts. Whether the entire order is filled or not, every account receives the same price for its portion of the order.

Often, orders must be directed to certain firms for certain accounts. This occurs at either the client's discretion or because the domicile firm requires all trades be done through its own trading desk. For this reason, multiple orders need to be created—one for each separate firm that has directed brokerage, and then the aggregated block that represents the remaining accounts that have no restrictions. Unless otherwise disclosed in the manager's form ADV (an SEC-required filing that serves as a disclosure document for all aspects of an investment advisor's business), it is usual for the order of these trades to be randomly determined and then executed. Each block of accounts receives a different price. It is not always an advantage to be the first to buy or sell, especially with extremely liquid securities. The differences in purchase price create dispersion among the different groups of accounts, since the actual rate of return of each account is dependent upon the purchase and sell price of each security.

There is no benefit to deliberately directing a brokerage in order to be placed in a different group, or to be given your own spot in the random rotation. Most often the large block receives the best execution because it is usually worked by the trading desk. By working an order, the desk is giving the trade its full attention and the benefits of its skill. If a small account is directed, then it is usually routed to the relevant exchange to be executed at the market.

Dispersion

Dispersion refers to the variance in return among accounts in the same investment style. All accounts of a single style are aggregated together to calculate a composite return for a specified period of time. Certain accounts can be excluded from the composite due to large cash flows, inception date, or client-directed restrictions. Few accounts will achieve the exact return of the composite, but usually most are very close. Dispersion measures the grouping of returns around the composite return. High dispersion refers to the fact that several accounts have returns that are materially different from the composite return.

Dispersion can be caused by many different events, including directed brokerage, client-requested tax selling or account restrictions, time of opening, or time of cash flows into or out of an account. From the client's perspective, dispersion is not necessarily bad—in theory, their account is just as likely to outperform the composite as to underperform it.

Managers want to minimize dispersion for a variety of reasons. The primary reason is because it eliminates the question "Why did account A do better than account B?" Managers would prefer to avoid being asked this question, whether by the client, by the financial consultant, or by the Securities and Exchange Commission's auditors. Each brokerage firm has teams of people who evaluate managers, and one of the criteria is dispersion—obviously, brokerage firms want to eliminate the question as well. If dispersion is high, then a manager might not be able to establish new relationships with other brokerage firms, or may lose business at a current brokerage firm client.

The Portfolio Manager

The portfolio manager's job is to generate the best possible performance for the investment product, and create the model that is used by the trader to implement the portfolio manager's investment decisions. Unless your client's account is several million dollars or more, it will likely not be handled directly by the portfolio manager.

Account restrictions can be both a blessing and a curse. By restricting certain securities and preventing the portfolio manager from buying them if they are included in his/her model, you can be certain you are creating account dispersion—your client's account with restrictions will probably have materially different returns from other similar accounts. You may have better or worse performance, but it will be different over the course that the restricted securities are held in the composite accounts. Another potential issue is that by placing a restriction on an account, the account may be treated differently.

However, restrictions can be a valuable option for some investors. If you want access to a certain manager or a certain investment management firm, but are wary because their typical holdings might cause issues within your client's broader portfolio or for other reasons, then a separately managed account may offer the only real alternative to investing via a mutual fund. There are many reasons why you may want to have restrictions on your client's account:

- Your client already owns a lot of XYZ, because he/she or his/her spouse works for the company, and he/she doesn't want to own any more.
- Your client inherited stock that he/she doesn't want to sell for sentimental reasons, but that he/she doesn't need to own anymore. Your client has strong convictions about certain industries, such as tobacco or alcohol.
- One of your other managers has a large exposure to a certain stock, and he/she has no plans to sell it in the foreseeable future.

These are all legitimate reasons to use a restricted account. There are caveats, however. As a professional who has been hired to oversee your clients' assets, you want them to have as few limitations as possible.

Mystique or prestige are not great reasons for investors to have a managed account. As discussed elsewhere in this book in greater detail, the fee structure for a managed account is less favorable to the client unless he/she is receiving his/her ancillary benefits, such as tax management or use of restrictions. These are powerful tools in managing a complete portfolio, and their availability can be well worth the extra fees associated with these types of accounts.

Most managers are very good at implementing client directions, particularly when they are very explicit. If you want to place a restriction on an account, be sure to send the instructions in writing via e-mail, mail, or fax, and follow up to be sure it was received. This is particularly important regarding restrictions and tax management directives.

When communicating with clients, you need to have the right information. To restrict an account, keep the language as clear as possible. For example, "I want to restrict account X from ever buying Yankee Zebra Corporation (ticker: YZ)" is good. It is also helpful to tell the manager what to do if they ever do buy YZ into their other accounts. There are four typical options should this happen:

1. Keep the money in cash.

2. Increase every holding on a pro rata basis to compensate for the lack of YZ—the problem here is that this can generate a lot of trading turnover. This is a poor option if the average position size in the restricted account is a few thousand dollars—either because the account is relatively small or because the manager chooses to own hundreds of securities.

3. Replace YZ with a market proxy—for example, buying SPY (S&P 500 trust shares) instead of YZ, and thereby ensuring market or benchmark exposure from any extra cash.

4. Buy another security. Most managers will likely resist this, and recommend one of the other options. There are again a variety of reasons why a manager would prefer to stay away from this approach, although it seems the most obvious.[1]

Once an account becomes different from the composite, it can take a long, long time (or a lot of small transactions) to bring it back to a close match. If your manager uses 50 securities, then each of those 50 securities performs differently over any time period—which changes the mix of securities (as a percent of assets). This is why changing just one security can create meaningful dispersion in a managed account.

There is a good approach to managing your clients' taxes, and a bad approach. The bad approach is to pick up the phone on the afternoon of December 31, and hear your client say, "I need losses. Take losses!" Most managers cannot even guarantee this will get accomplished if they are informed in the 11th hour, although they will certainly try. The best approach is to follow your client's tax situation throughout the year, and guide him/her periodically. Again, it is best to be very explicit. Many managers can fax to clients forms that will walk them through the exact information the manager finds important.

Before proceeding, you should know exactly what you want to accomplish in the way of tax management. You want to follow your clients' directives as literally as possible to avoid any assumptions or misinterpretations—and possibly wind up being liable for a trading error. In the best of all possible worlds, clients will call you for clarification, but this is not always possible. The questions you should think about:

- Do I want to take *every* loss or gain? Will this raise an enormous amount of cash? Will there be a huge number of transactions?
- Do I want to take a certain dollar amount of gains or losses?
- What do I want to do with the cash being raised (see the preceding discussion)?
- Is there a certain amount of gain or loss in an individual security that I don't want to take? (For example, you might write: "Please take all losses in account up to $12,500 total. Please do not take any individual security losses of less than $500.") This will help control the number of trades placed in the account.

When you open a separate account in your client's name, he/she will own the individual securities. The client will sign a limited power of attorney that allows the investment manager to buy and sell securities in the client's account on his/her behalf. It does not allow the investment manager to transfer money out of the account or commingle your client's assets with anyone else's. The domicile firm will deduct fees for both the manager and itself directly out of the account unless instructed otherwise.

Because a separate account is a brokerage account and a limited power of attorney, your client will receive confirmations in the mail for every trade. If your manager owns a lot of securities or has high turnover, your client will receive a lot of confirmations in the mail. A benefit is that your client will know in almost real time what is happening in his/her account versus owning the average mutual fund, which will disclose its holdings on an annual or semiannual basis.

Periodically, an issue might arise. This may happen for a variety of reasons.

- The manager buys a stock and sells it a week later.
- The manager sells a security 10 days before it goes to a long-term gain.
- The investor becomes increasingly uncomfortable with the results generated in his/her account, or questions the approach.

When these issues arise, an investor should call and talk with his/her advisor. Often, the advisor will recommend a conference call (advisor, manager, client). Depending on the firm, the size of the account, and the advisor's clout, the conference will include someone from the investment department, whether a liaison, the portfolio manager, or someone in between. This person will likely not have the details of your client's individual account, but should be able to explain the rationale of any transaction or explain their investment philosophy.

Note

[1] The entire portfolio and the diversification within the portfolio are very important, so a manager cannot just add one utility infielder replacement stock that gets plugged to each whole—because then many portfolios will be riskier than others. It is often a lot of extra work to find additional names, and these are most often the most marginal names from an investment perspective.

CHAPTER

3

The State of the Separate Accounts Industry

The five managed account segments, representing a total of $752 billion in assets, show a five-year growth rate of 32.1 percent, illustrating the stability gained through the advice and guidance that are inherent in managed accounts (Table 3.1). The most popular vehicle for fee-based accounts in terms of overall assets is still the separate account. The two primary segments of the separate account space are composed of both separate account consultant and proprietary consultant programs, totaling a combined $422.1 billion at the beginning of 2002.

A comparable benchmark in professionally managed financial products is the growth in long-term mutual funds, which ended the year (2001) with $4.1 trillion in assets under management, representing –7.5 percent growth for the same year. Separate account and proprietary separate account consultant programs both finished the year posting growth of 6.8 percent.

The nation's financial product distribution powerhouses continue to dominate in managed account assets, with these top 10 firms representing more than 80 percent of the industry. The 60,000 financial advisors employed by New York wirehouses (firms 1 through 5 shown in Table 3.2) account for approximately 70 percent of the industry, with some of the largest regional, independent, and third-party firms rounding out the group. Several of these top firms have also taken advantage of the lucrative prospects of distributing

TABLE 3.1   Managed Account Growth Rates and Assets (in $ Billions)

	1998	1999	2000	2001	2002
Separate account consultant programs	$188.8	$249.9	$299.1	$319.4	
Proprietary consultant programs	—	—	$96.2	$102.7	
Mutual fund advisory programs	$66.0	$93.2	$124.8	$126.3	
Rep as portfolio manager	$36.2	$63.5	$71.8	$63.9	
Fee-based brokerage	$32.0	$101.5	$149.6	$154.6	
Total managed accounts industry	$323	$508	$741	$769	$752

Source: Cerulli Associates.

a proprietary asset management product through their brokerage force, as evidenced by the 5 percent or greater share of fee-based assets from proprietary consultant programs at 4 of the top 10 firms (Table 3.2).

Until recently, there was little need for innovation in the managed accounts industry, as tier I financial representatives (the highest tier of top-producing representatives according to Cerulli's market segmentation) historically generated the bulk of separate account consultant programs. However, this elite group is a small subset, accounting for only 1 to 2 percent of total wirehouse representatives. Looking forward, managed account industry growth will increasingly be dependent upon the larger ranks of tier II and tier III representatives embracing the managed account concept and selling it to their less well-to-do clientele. Most representatives want to be Tier I—you get there by using managed accounts and by attracting large clients. This is a self-reinforcing business.

Cerulli Associates believes that educating representatives who are new to managed account products on the attributes of managed accounts will be the cornerstone upon which the industry will expand to incorporate all tiers of representatives. Brokerage firms are promoting managed accounts from the top down and new-broker training is focused on managed accounts. Also, capital is being invested to simplify the managed accounts and investment consulting approach to assist in encouraging all tiers of representatives to embrace fee-based managed account business.

For the separate account consultant and mutual fund advisory program segments, 2001 reflects a deviation from the solid double-digit growth that both industries have seen in the past decade. Fee-based programs have shown resilience during down markets, attributable to larger trends, including advice

TABLE 3.2 Top 10 Program Sponsors, All Managed Account Segments

Firm	Market Share of Total Industry	Managed Accounts Program Asset Mix*					Total Firm Managed Account Assets ($ billions)
		Separate Account Consultant Programs (%)	Proprietary Separate Account Assets (%)	Mutual Fund Advisory Programs (%)	Rep as Portfolio Manager (%)	Fee-Based Brokerage Assets (%)	
1. Salomon Smith Barney	25.4	**42.1**	32.2	5.5	12.8	7.4	$194.7
2. Merrill Lynch	25.3	37.0	14.4	6.3	3.2	**39.1**	193.5
3. UBS Paine Webber	7.9	**51.2**	—	8.2	11.8	28.8	60.4
4. Morgan Stanley	7.4	**51.1**	7.2	6.2	0.7	34.9	56.6
5. Prudential Financial	4.6	**50.6**	2.6	16.1	13.5	17.2	34.8
6. SEI Investments	3.6	4.7	—	**95.3**	—	—	27.6
7. American Express	2.4	8.7	—	**91.3**	—	—	18.7
8. First Union Securities	2.4	**39.1**	—	16.8	18.0	26.1	18.3
9. Raymond James	2.2	27.8	34.0	—	0.7	**37.5**	17.1
10. Fidelity Investments	2.2	—	—	**100.0**	0.7	—	16.8

*Figures in bold denote each firm's top managed account segment.
Source: Cerulli Associates.

and guidance, distributor (brokerage firm) push for fee-based relationships, and the money flood of IRA rollover assets, all of which channel well into the construct of managed account programs.

Recent events have driven investors to realize their need for advice and guidance from professional financial advisors. One indication of this effect is evidenced by the transition of several mutual fund companies toward advisor-sold channels and away from direct-to-consumer efforts.

These firms are changing the way their brokers are compensated to drive more assets into fee-based accounts. The trend of asset flows from company-sponsored retirement savings to individual accounts in the form of 401(k) distributions is a phenomenon that aligns well for managed accounts when sponsoring brokerages are able to catch these assets. These sizable sums are appropriate for either mutual fund advisory or separate account consultant programs. Cerulli Associates expects the recent growth rates of the separate account consultant programs to continue (Figure 3.1). For separate accounts, this equates to 20 percent annual growth, or more than $680 billion in assets by year-end 2005.

Program Sponsors

Following are the top 20 sponsor firms based on assets gathered in separate account consultant programs. This is an important list for asset managers participating in or contemplating entry into the separate account consultant business, as these 20 firms are currently the gatekeepers to more than 95

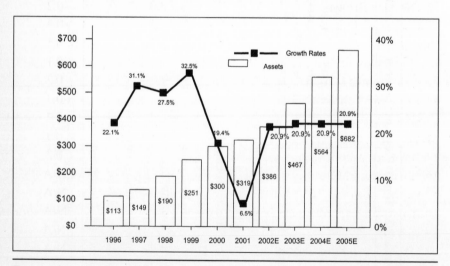

FIGURE 3.1 Projections of Separate Account Consultant Program Assets (in $ Billions).

percent of separate account assets (Table 3.3). (Note: This view does not include brokerage firms' proprietary separate account assets, as this channel is not available to outside money managers.) Beyond the 72.3 percent of assets controlled by the industry-dominating New York wirehouses, the remainder of the top 20 firms is composed of 9 regional brokerages, 5 third-party sponsors, and 1 independent broker-dealer (IBD). The low or nonexistent representation from independent and bank broker-dealers is explained by the coverage of the third-party sponsors, which supply separate account programs, technology, and marketing support to broker-dealers with limited infrastructure and resources.

TABLE 3.3 Top 20 Separate Account Consultant Program Sponsors

Firm	Market Share 4Q 2001 (%)	Market Share Change 2001 (%)
1. Salomon Smith Barney	25.6	−0.8
2. Merrill Lynch	22.4	1.2
3. UBS Paine Webber	9.7	−0.7
4. Morgan Stanley	9.1	−1.1
5. Prudential Financial	5.5	−0.8
6. AG Edwards	3.1	−0.5
7. DB Alex Brown	3.0	−0.2
8. Lockwood Financial	2.6	−0.3
9. Schwab	2.3	0.5
10. First Union Securities	2.2	0.1
11. CIBC World Markets	1.7	0.2
12. Raymond James	1.5	−0.3
13. RBC Dain Rauscher*	1.3	0.2
14. London Pacific Advisors	1.1	0.5
15. Brinker Capital	1.0	0.2
16. EnvestNet PMC	<1	N/A
17. Legg Mason	<1	N/A
18. American Express Financial Advisors	<1	N/A
19. Morgan Keegan	<1	N/A
20. US Bancorp Piper Jaffray	<1	N/A

*This includes recently affiliated Tucker Anthony Sutro program assets.
Source: Cerulli Associates.

TABLE 3.4 Largest Investment Managers of Separate Account Program Assets*

Manager Name	Organization Type	Total Consultant Program Assets	Portion Gathered in Proprietary Consultant Program Channel (%)
1. Citigroup Asset Mgmt. (PPG)	Proprietary	$70,660,000,000	88.8
2. Merrill Lynch Investment Managers	Proprietary	28,823,000,000	96.5
3. Brandes Investment Partners	Independent	20,623,000,000	N/A
4. John Nuveen Company	Holding Company	18,512,000,000	N/A
5. Alliance Capital	Independent	12,266,000,000	N/A
6. 1838 Investment Advisors	—	11,000,000,000	N/A
7. Lazard Asset Management	Independent	10,806,700,000	N/A
8. Allianz	Holding Company	9,807,607,077	N/A
9. Affiliated Managers Group	Holding Company	9,316,000,000	N/A
10. Lord Abbett & Co.	Independent	9,303,878,383	N/A
11. AMVESCAP	Holding Company	7,023,555,771	N/A
12. The TCW Group	—	6,897,000,000	N/A
13. Old Mutual	Holding Company	6,478,469,431	N/A
14. Mellon Financial	Holding Company	6,450,134,757	N/A
15. Phoenix Investment Partners†	Holding Company	5,812,000,000	N/A
16. Eagle Asset Mgmt/Raymond James	Proprietary	5,800,000,000	100
17. Davis Select Advisors	Independent	4,800,000,000	N/A

TABLE 3.4 *Continued*

Manager Name	Organization Type	Total Consultant Program Assets	Portion Gathered in Proprietary Consultant Program Channel (%)
18. Roxbury Capital	—	4,771,066,850	N/A
19. Kayne Anderson Rudnick LLP†	—	4,700,000,000	N/A
20. Calamos Asset Management	Independent	4,591,086,000	N/A
21. Morgan Stanley Investment Advisors	Proprietary	4,115,000,000	99
22. John A. Levin & Co.	—	4,033,000,000	N/A
23. Franklin Resources	Holding Company	3,645,420,025	N/A
24. Navellier	Independent	3,177,000,000	N/A
25. Neuberger Berman	Independent	3,050,000,000	N/A

*Asset totals include combined traditional consultant program and proprietary consultant program assets.
†Recently acquired interest in Kayne Anderson by Phoenix Investment partners not included in the holding company total.

Source: Cerulli Associates.

Asset Managers

Table 3.4 looks at the aggregated broker-dealer separate account assets under management by the largest participants in this industry—including assets gathered in both separate account consultant and proprietary consultant programs.

All managers that are affiliated with larger *holding company* structures (two or more subsidiaries managing consultant program assets) are rolled up to the holding company level. Firms that are part of a corporate structure affiliated with large retail financial advisor networks (Merrill Lynch, Salomon Smith Barney, Raymond James, etc.) are deemed *proprietary* managers. *Independent* firms—as the name suggests—are not owned by any other firm. (A firm can also be classified as independent if it is publicly traded.) The organizations shown here represent the 25 largest investment management corporate entities that control investor assets through separate account consultant programs (Figure 3.2).

Cash Flow

Figure 3.3 recaps separate account consultant program cash flows, which reflect actual reporting firms plus Cerulli's estimates for nonreporting firms.

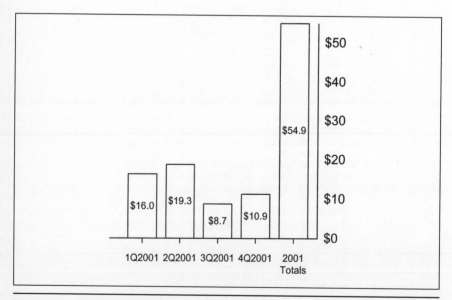

Figure 3.2   Separate Account Consultant Program Cash Flows (in $ Billions).

Fourth-quarter 2001 yielded $10.9 billion in industry cash flows, putting the estimated total for 2001 just shy of $55 billion. Notice that the net assets of the industry grew only by roughly $20 billion during 2001 (from $299 billion to $319 billion in assets). The gap between cash inflows and asset growth is easily explained by negative market returns. An industry that is roughly 50 percent weighted to large-capitalization stocks is not immune to underperformance when the S&P 500 index posts –13 percent returns for the year. In contrast to the separate account consultant industry's growth during 2001, long-term mutual funds lost a net 7.5 percent in assets during the same period. If one assumes differences in asset allocation and investment performance to be a neutral factor between the two products, then this can be taken as clear evidence of stronger demand for individually managed separate accounts versus pooled mutual funds by the end investor.

Note in Figure 3.3 that separate account consultant programs outpaced flows into long-term funds in the third quarter of 2001, even though the long-term mutual fund business is more than 10 times the size of the separate

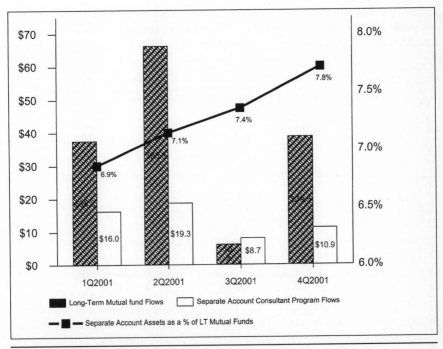

FIGURE 3.3   Gaining Ground: Separate Account Consultant Program Assets and Cash Flows versus Long-Term Mutual Funds (in $ Billions).

account consultant program industry. As the line in the chart illustrates, separate accounts have been steadily gaining ground on mutual funds in terms of aggregate industry assets over the four quarters of 2001. When coupled with the additional $102.7 billion in proprietary separate account consultant assets, broker-sold separate accounts represent an industry that is slightly more than 10 percent of the size of long-term funds at year-end 2001.[1]

The Independent Side of Separate Accounts

What about the independent world where separate accounts are booming? This group consists of independent advisors, CPAs, banks, and insurance agents. The group as a whole is not as well reported, and most all use turnkey asset management programs (TAMPs). Therefore, it is harder to get your hands around their statistics. There is more room for interpretation, and it's easy to count the same dollars twice if you're not careful.

TAMPs are the independent advisors' version of wirehouse wrap programs. These widely available, fee-based programs (which include separate account *and* mutual fund programs) allow independent broker-dealer representatives, fee-only financial advisors, insurance agents, certified public accountants (CPAs), and banks to compete in the growing market of fee-based advice. TAMPs generally provide four services:

1. Technology for client profiling, asset allocation, investment policy statement creation, and proposal generation
2. Assistance in investment selection
3. Management of the ongoing monitoring, rebalancing, and reallocation processes
4. Performance measurement, performance reporting, and billing services

The first TAMPs emerged in the mid-1980s, and the number of TAMPs has grown steadily since then to 57 at year-end 2001. Assets of these TAMPs have likewise grown steadily to $78 billion, but this is still far smaller than the brokerage channel wrap market (Figure 3.4).

The independent markets are moving quickly to embrace separate accounts, though, and several new platform-oriented TAMPs have emerged. At this point, separate account TAMP assets are showing similar concentration to the overall market; Lockwood and five other separate account TAMPs control 83 percent of the separate account TAMP market.

Charles Schwab has gradually—and without much fanfare—hit the charts.

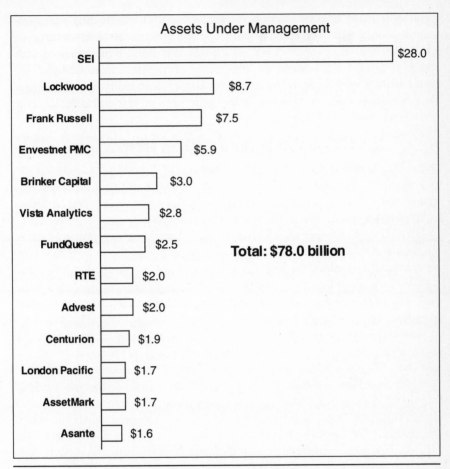

FIGURE 3.4   Market-Leading TAMPs in Terms of Assets.
Source: Tiburon Strategic Advisors.

Schwab's managed account program was launched just three years ago. They ranked 10th with $8 billion, or 2.2 percent of the market, as of September 30, 2001. That puts Schwab ahead of such well-established independent players as Brinker Capital, one of the oldest providers of managed accounts. Schwab has tied with First Union Securities and is within striking distance of Lockwood Financial, which has a 2.7 percent share.

The average separate account TAMP uses 59 managers and 111 products. Leading wrap account programs listed Brandes, Rittenhouse, and Alliance

Capital as their favorite managers (Figure 3.5). Other leading managers include Rorer, Roxbury, Lazard, and Lord Abbett. The wirehouses can only work with the largest money managers, who can handle their flow of new assets. Wirehouses also need to have many of the same managers as their peers as they attempt to recruit representatives from each other. Forcing a client to move assets from a manager simply because it is unavailable at the new firm can be a recruiting deal killer.

Tiburon Strategic Advisors surveyed TAMPs for their favorite managers. They received a long list of candidates including Capstone Asset Management, Holdsmith & Yates, McKinley Capital, MJ Whitman, National Asset Management, Systematic, and Tom Johnson. While more traditional choices like Brandes and Lazard were also mentioned, none of these other firms are on the top-10 list of separate account wrap managers.

It has long been speculated that there is a pending departure of many wirehouse representatives to the land of independence. This would have significant impact on the structure of separate account independent TAMP programs. If we see a flood of fee-oriented wirehouse brokers leaving for the ranks of independent advisors, we would expect to see the TAMPs' lists start to mirror those of the wirehouses.

Across TAMP programs, the descriptions of separate account manager and mutual fund selection processes are consistently complicated. Many follow some version of the four *ps*: process, performance, people, and philosophy. Key members of the decision-making process vary. Nearly two-thirds of mutual fund wrap and TAMP sponsors have a formal committee or informal group who decides which managers to include in their programs. Prudential, for instance, has a group of analysts who rely on a 10-step process to assess portfolio managers, although only 14 percent of programs use an outside consultant.

Screening is the dominant way of finding new separate account managers. Some databases are very comprehensive, but their accuracy may be questionable, because managers give information to them voluntarily.

Checkfree's Mobius offers the most popular technology used to screen separate account managers. Other popular choices include PSN/Effron, and Nelson's Directory.

Style adherence was the most highly rated selection criterion among TAMP programs. Style consistency was also ranked as an important criterion. Comments included: "The most important criteri[on] for us is for the manager to have a well-defined, clearly articulated, and systematically implemented process." And, "For us, the experience of the portfolio manager is the most important criteri[on]."

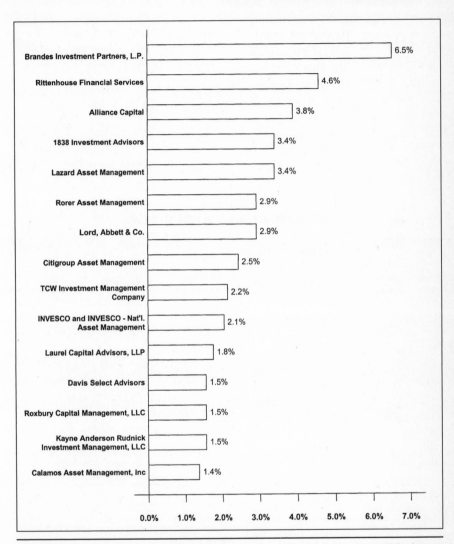

FIGURE 3.5 Example of the Top 15 Managers of Separate Account Wirehouse Consultant Program Percentage of Assets. These 15 Managers Represent $320 Billion in Assets, First Quarter of 2002.

Source: Cerulli Associates.

On the flip side, manager turnover was the most important criterion for being eliminated. Manager turnover and style drift can cause serious problems. Loss of key investment personnel was cited as an important reason for dropping a manager.

A wide variety of mutual fund companies are just now starting to make moves to enter the separate account wrap and TAMP business. Fidelity, Vanguard, Putnam, American Funds, MFS, Oppenheimer, T. Rowe Price, and American Century are all long-awaited entrants. Although well known, these firms could find it more difficult to penetrate the separate account wrap preferred manager lists due to their overcrowded nature.

The Transformation of Mutual Funds

Most mutual fund companies are starting to home in on the lucrative market of separate accounts, but so far they're barely a blip on the radar. Fund companies, particularly the latecomers, are fighting for shelf space alongside the well-established separate account programs of the wirehouses. They're going to look to the third-party programs; they're going to look to the independent broker-dealers; and they're going to look to the banks and insurance companies where shelf space isn't as much of an issue.

Mutual fund companies are going to redouble their efforts to go after the markets that have traditionally been underserved by the wirehouses. They have massive marketing muscle, top portfolio managers (PMs), lavish advertising budgets, and access to wholesale and retail distribution. They are well positioned to carve out a chunk of the separate account business.

Resources that were previously committed to selling mutual funds are getting shifted to helping brokers sell separately managed accounts. Message to the wirehouses: To the extent that you are on the separately managed account bandwagon, expect the funds to come along with you and to be even more aggressive by the middle of the decade.

Fund companies certainly have the motivation: The mutual fund business is experiencing some signs of maturity. At $4.4 trillion (excluding money market funds) in net assets, mutual funds have become too much of a behemoth to continue experiencing rapid growth.

The number of U.S. households with separate accounts will increase fivefold to nearly 5 million by 2010, predicts Forrester Research. By then, separate account investments should top $2.6 trillion. Half of that tally may come from mutual fund liquidations.

Add to that the push by brokerage houses to get the most desirable high-net-worth clients out of mutual funds and into the annuity streams provided by fee-based managed accounts, and it's easy to see why mutual fund companies are wading into the new market.

The problem for most funds is their traditionally abysmal record in retaining assets in a rollover. The best fund families are somewhere around the low–20 percent range for retaining assets in a rollover situation. For a mutual fund company, this is a frightening statistic! The current generation holds the largest amount of assets ever seen. If you're a fund family, you can basically assume, as we have, that 80 percent of those assets are going to go to someone else.

Soon, separately managed accounts will be offered inside a 401(k) with no account minimum. Whether it's Fidelity or Vanguard or any of the other large plan administrators, you'll see them create these accounts in an effort to retain those assets.

Separate accounts are going to be big, maybe even end the mutual fund dominance in the marketplace. Not that mutual funds or mutual fund companies will go away, but the mutual fund is really the only packaged product there is, whether it's inside an annuity or in a taxable account.

Mutual funds are really the only investment product being threatened by this new breed of products, namely, separately managed accounts. It would appear that about one-third of this generation's large accumulation of assets is going to head into separately managed accounts. The end result? You've got a mutual fund industry that could end up owning less than half of all long-term investable assets.

Putnam Investments, MFS, Phoenix Investment Partners, and Delaware Investments are among the fund families that have launched separately managed account programs over the last year or so, while others, such as Oppenheimer Funds and Pioneer Investment Management, are promising to enter the managed account business this year. "You can't afford *not* to be in this business," says Daniel Geraci, Pioneer's CEO.

The industry is counting on the fund companies to make separate accounts consumable to the investing public.

Operations

Although the big wirehouse sponsor programs are very determined *not* to lose the control they currently have, they inevitably will. The big sponsors are fighting the movement to improve operations because the poor state of that side of separate account functionality is distinctly in their favor.

Ultimately, however, this will change. We'll see trading move away; we'll see a custodial shift back to the fund companies. The fund companies will handle separately managed accounts the way they currently handle mutual funds, and the operational problems will slowly disappear into the background.

The bad news is that the operational mess in the back offices of some of the firms with which we've talked recently, along with some of the technology that's currently being developed, could certainly lead the independent firms to challenge the status quo. They could challenge the dictatorial terms of the big-sponsor firms in terms of how a separate account is created. The same process is used to create a packaged mutual fund.

The typical pattern for technological development in this industry is that first, someone dips their toe into the water. Everybody else waits for a while, then they *all* jump on the bandwagon.

Eventually, the sponsor firms start losing their lock on control, the product becomes a little cheaper to create, the operations problems begin to go away, and all of that contributes to the ballooning assets. The independent firms are then able to contribute more dollars and more resources. It becomes economically viable for them to make a significant commitment to the separate accounts business.

The Biggest Challenge

The biggest challenge for the fund companies is operational, because there is no single standard for clearing in separate accounts as there is in the mutual fund industry. Also, fund companies have to learn how to provide individual attention to clients and to the representatives that put them into managed accounts. They will need to move from a transaction-based approach to a consultative approach.

Fund companies have learned that they can't make a separate account mirror a current mutual fund they offer. For one thing, managed accounts hold fewer shares than similar mutual funds and often must be customized for the client. Managed accounts are meant to be tax efficient and, in general, hold fewer stocks.

On the side of the money managers themselves, there are things they are just now learning, such as true after-tax customization. Case in point: Suppose that a manager in today's climate is successful and gets in all the right sponsor programs. All of a sudden, the manager has 50 custodians, 50 new account procedures, 50 closing account procedures, and 50 trading desks with which to deal. Then the manager has all the error accounts with which to deal, and the list goes on and on. It's going to be a nightmare!

This is where standard operating procedures step in. Lockwood's Len

Reinhart refers to the current landscape as a *fiefdom*. He likens it to *Jurassic Park*—"Life finds a way." One broker moves to another firm. A manager gets into another program. All of a sudden, it gets all mixed up. And we're left with this archaic system supporting these new fiefdoms.

There are no standard operating procedures and nothing in the way of infrastructure compared with all of the other financial products in the industry. *These* are the issues that the industry continues to tackle and which it will work through.

Note

[1] This information was used with permission from the Cerulli Report™ Series. Cerulli Associates' latest report, *Asset Management: Operations and Profitability Benchmarks for Separate Account Consultant Programs,* presents the managed accounts industry with a comprehensive benchmarking study on the operations, technology, and profitability of the separate account consultant program business.

Participants in the Separate Account Market

nvestors whose needs can be fulfilled by separate accounts are usually characterized as *high net worth*. This generic grouping is often separated into at least three segments:

1. *Semiaffluent.* Investors with roughly $200,000 to $500,000 in investable assets.
2. *Affluent.* Investors with roughly $500,000 to $5 million in investable assets.
3. *Superaffluent.* Investors with multimillion-dollar portfolios, at least $5 million in investable assets.

The ideal target client is between 45 and 70 years old, has a net worth of $1 million or more with at least $500,000 of assets to invest, and needs comprehensive financial planning.

Of this high-net-worth market, 95 percent falls into the semiaffluent category, which includes 48 percent of U.S. investable assets. This market is where many financial advisors have placed their focus. Unfortunately, mass advertisement has inundated this group, making it very difficult to have a compelling story of differentiation.

The affluent category represents the fastest-growing area, comprising about 4 percent of the market. This category continues to be a sweet spot, although competition is significantly increasing.

Three years ago, the superaffluent segment represented 0.1 percent, or about 100,000 households. Today, it numbers 200,000 households and is still growing.

Affluent investors are noted for being less price- and performance-sensitive than either general retail or institutional investors. Financial and investment management for the affluent is more of a relationship business. The high-net-worth client wants to develop a face-to-face, interpersonal relationship with an advisor who can provide turnkey financial management, problem solving, and peace of mind.

How Big Is the Affluent Market?

Despite the last year of stock market declines, private wealth is booming. Illiquid assets, which include assets like small businesses, investment real estate, and so forth, total approximately $46.5 trillion. Of that amount, about $17 trillion is considered as liquid investable assets—that's your market. Whether you look at the aggregate amount of assets or the aggregate number of wealthy people, the numbers are way up even with the current downturns in the market.

The money management industry is currently experiencing some of the most exciting investment opportunities of a lifetime. The affluent portion of the population is growing in assets faster than it is growing in people, and this growth is resulting in a boom market for investment advisory services.

It's even bigger when you consider that, in our judgment, most of these numbers actually underestimate the case. There are several reasons for this. First, the wealthy seek to minimize their taxable income, and so will appear—statistically—less well off than they actually are. The source of wealth for many is a privately owned business, and private business ownership provides many opportunities to accumulate assets outside of the "private wealth" label.

Many financial advisors are going independent because there are relatively low barriers to entry. The transition to independence can be brought about with a loyal affluent client following, a handle on back-office procedures and product technology, and skill development in such areas as practice management and marketing.

Investment management with the affluent is also a knowledge business. It revolves around *whom* you know as well as *what* you know. The *whom* you know is critical to prospecting. For this reason, the independent investment advisor of the future will be very much like the traditional European private banker—a friend, a counselor, a financial advisor, an investment psychologist, and an entrepreneur.

Affluent investors want customized, sophisticated investment advice. Thus, advisors see opportunity. This translates into a sense of confidence in the future.

The Downside

Today, separate accounts can be sold by almost any financial advisor. The affluent investor knows they can obtain them from any number of sources. Translation? You need to add value in addition to your sponsored programs.

One point of differentiation can be your expertise. Expertise involves specifying the investment needs of affluent individuals, selecting the right investment products, and ensuring that the affluent client's investment needs are being met over time.

The Competition

One could be easily overwhelmed by the number of separate account competitors targeting the affluent market (Figure 4.1), but the competitive advantages favor the advisor willing to develop strong interpersonal relationships with affluent clients. As a matter of fact, industry competitors view the independent investment advisory firms, with their demonstrated ability to build and nurture client relationships, as their most competitive threat.

As larger, well-capitalized competitors enter the affluent market to provide financial planning and turnkey asset management, there will be greater pricing pressure and commoditization of service, which will bring the profits of the smaller, independent advisors under pressure. The Internet will become a communication medium that will revolutionize the financial business. The proliferation of financial information available on the Internet is already creating the perception that financial information alone has little inherent value. Clients will continue to focus on building a relationship with an advisor who will be able to provide comprehensive problem solutions and overall financial management. One of the societal trends that will ensure the seeking of advice and professional management by the vast majority of seniors and boomers is their need to develop an increased quality of life as they mature. As their affluence and account sizes grow, few will opt to risk their financial well-being by becoming their own part-time financial managers using the Internet.

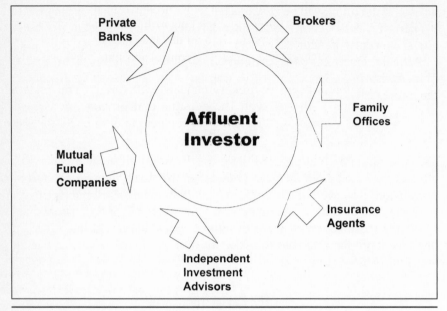

FIGURE 4.1   Competitors in the Affluent Investor Market.

The segment of the financial services industry that caters to the affluent investor can also be separated into subsegments. This segmentation often depends on the distribution channel. For example, national wirehouse advisors might be segmented into fee-based, fee-only, and corner-office. Registered Investment Advisors (RIAs) could be segmented into asset manager, wealth manager, and market timer. Independent advisors could be segmented into financial planners, certified public accountants (CPAs), and investment advisors.

Wirehouse Brokers/Advisors

Historically, the affluent have often turned to brokers in wirehouses, as well as regional and smaller brokerage firms for investment advice. The *average* brokerage client is well below the affluent investor threshold. Industry statistics show the typical broker does not have many affluent investors with $1 million or more in a discretionary investment account, wrap account, or similar product. The average broker will have just 5 to 15 percent of his/her clients at this level. The majority of clients will have fewer assets to invest.

Firms are taking the initiative to create specialty wealth management groups to assist brokers in finding and working with the affluent. Such groups bring a highly sophisticated approach to money management, offering more intricate products such as hedge funds and control accounts, plus estate planning services.

These initiatives will enable brokers to meet a wide variety of the financial needs and wants of the affluent. The question that brokers are asking is, "Does the brokerage house offer sufficient compensating value for the share of revenue they receive?"

Part of the wirehouse share offsets administrative costs, costs of recruiting and training new brokers, developing new products, positioning the firm and its brokers, and so forth. This group has tremendous back-office support and years of experience. Some of their separate account platforms will be based on legacy technology, and will struggle to meet clients' needs in the rapidly evolving separate account environment.

As a general rule, their marketing budget is bigger than most financial advisors'. Individual financial advisors just won't be able to compete with them on marketing. As a matter of fact, one of the reasons Merrill Lynch and Charles Schwab are growing so quickly is that they've become the default investment source for investors who don't know where to go. Merrill Lynch's advertising budget is greater than some countries' gross national product!

The Independent Advisor

The asset management industry is one of the few industries in America today in which an individual can get started with almost no capital. In a short period of time, an investment advisor can build a substantial income and a lucrative business, establishing the foundation for personal wealth and family security. This means you are going to continue to have strong competition coming into this industry. There are around 45,000 RIAs, of which only about 24,000 are active. If we subtract the 7,583 who earned commissions and other income, we find 16,427 who are fee-based or fee-only. Separate out the 1,376 institutional managers, and we find that there are 15,051 managers of fee-compensated, individual assets.

These 15,051 financial advisors control $870 billion of assets under management. These assets are not evenly divided. Only 175 advisors have assets under management of more than $1 billion. A larger number, 812, have assets totaling between $200 million and $1 billion. Together, these advisors control 72 percent of the individual managed assets. The remaining 14,064 managers, with up to $200 million of assets under management, share a total of $240 billion in assets. This averages approximately $17 million per advisor in the below–$200 million group—certainly nowhere near what it takes to run a successful business.

So why is the majority of the individual managed assets under the control of so few? The successful advisors have targeted the affluent investors and follow a focused plan to reach that market. Most advisors don't; their approach is bird-shot at best and reactionary at worst. They sell separate accounts the same way they sell a mutual fund, not realizing their full potential.

Accountants/CPAs

Accountants are also moving into the investment management business. Most accountants stop short of wanting to perform the direct investment management tasks. Nearly all of the accountants surveyed (91.8 percent) report that they do not see themselves as portfolio managers in the sense of selecting specific securities (AICPA meeting Jan. 2003).

Those who enter this field will do so as independent investment advisors. Because of their training and professional culture, accountants generally see themselves as impartial advisors and consultants. Rather than become directly involved in portfolio management, accountants would prefer an advisory status, allowing them to still participate in the flow of fees.

For most accountants, the investment management business is appealing because their current business is not as profitable as it once was. They are coming under considerable competitive pressure for some of their core services.

Accountants are the most trusted advisors that most business owners, professionals, and affluent individuals have. Accountants measure their relationships with their clients in decades. Nearly two-thirds of the accountants who are interested in participating in investment management service (64.6 percent) cite a secondary reason based on demand from their affluent and business clients.

Some accountants will find that they can enter the investment advisory business directly because of the ready availability of turnkey asset management programs (TAMPs). These services manage all of the components in the investment management process, including developing an investment policy statement, creating a portfolio, and rebalancing a portfolio. While the accountants eventually master the mechanics of investment management, these TAMPs eliminate a considerable amount of the work.

The most control, as well as the most work, occurs when the accountant brings in people to perform as investment advisors. Still, it provides the accountant with the greatest command over the process as well as over the relationship with the client.

In many states, the easiest way for accountants to be in the investment management business is to refer clients to investment advisors. In return, they could collect a finder's fee for the effort. Accountants can lower their exposure by recommending a number of investment advisors and insisting that the client make the final advisor selection decision himself/herself. However, this is not an option for many accountants, who are barred by regulations. This option also generates lower revenues.

Insurance Agents

There is a strong push by the insurance industry to enable agents to become fee-based advisors. It's important to note that it is not the insurance companies that are driving the trend among insurance agents to become fee-based investment advisors. The insurance industry is responding to market demand and competitive pressures. The majority of insurance agents want to be in the investment advisory business, and many have already taken steps to expand their business. This has been relatively easy for insurance agents, as investment advice is a complementary service to what they provide currently.

Anecdotal evidence shows us that the elite insurance agents are exceptional asset gatherers, possessing the marketing expertise and, more important, the contacts among the wealthy, to build a $100 million investment advisory business relatively quickly.

Insurance companies have been creating loyalty for quite some time. The insurance industry is structured so that high-end insurance agents are very likely to use the services and products of a number of different carriers.

Insurance companies are already taking action to support agents who want to do more in the investment management field. Many carriers already provide producers with a wide range of products to sell. The goal of insurance companies is to be chosen by agents for business. Forward-thinking insurance companies will continue to take steps to help their agents be effective.

Many high-end insurance agents have a well-developed, affluent clientele that can be leveraged into an investment advisory relationship. They know from experience that it is far easier to sell an existing client a new product than it is to find a new client. With the right products and services, they can go back to their book of business again and again. For some insurance agents, it makes good sense to sell separate accounts in order to leverage those client relationships even further. The crossover between the insurance and investment fields has been building over the past decade. Increasingly, insurance agents want to sell investment management services (Figure 4.2).

Younger insurance agents are more excited by the investment management business than older agents. Agents who are 45 years old and younger (84.4 percent) are much more interested in the investment management business than agents who are over 45 years old (35.5 percent). Younger agents tend to be more comfortable with the nature of investments and less intimidated by the necessary education and licensing requirements.

Insurance agents need to be able to offer a similar lineup of separate account products. By doing this, they can compete head-to-head with all other financial services providers. The front-loaded nature of the insurance business means that they must always be looking for new sales. Moreover, once a sale is made, that particular affluent client is unlikely, in the near term, to need more life insurance. A steady stream of revenue coming in can be very attractive.

The basic hurdle faced by many insurance agents is just how to enter and work in the fee-based investment management business. They have to take

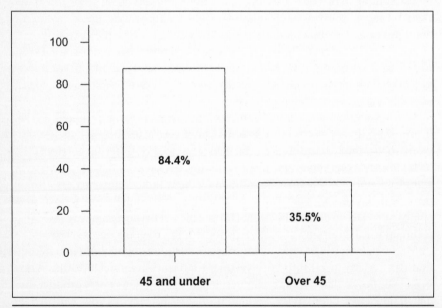

FIGURE 4.2   Younger Agents Are More Interested in Investment Management (Based on a Survey by Russ Prince & Associates of 494 High-End Insurance Agents).

steps to incorporate investment management services into their current business.

If you are a high-end insurance agent seeking to become a fee-based investment advisor, you have a number of options. One approach is to work through your primary insurance company (i.e., the insurance company you use most). Insurance companies have broker-dealers and increasingly are accommodating successful insurance agents who want to work to provide fee-based investment management services to their affluent clients.

Another option might be to affiliate with a producer group or insurance brokerage network that is able to deliver these services. An increasingly popular option is for insurance agents to go independent and affiliate with an independent broker-dealer and/or service firm. Most insurance companies already have broker-dealers. A significant number have their own investment management units. Cerulli counted close to 52,000 independent insurance representatives at the end of 2000.

Bank Representatives and Bank Trust Departments

These entities have been experiencing the slowest growth of all. They recognize that they must make competitive offers because the credibility of the bank and the brand is simply no longer enough. They are making those changes, and they're coming after your clients. And they are doing this successfully!

Bank trust departments are *not yet* significant players in any part of this market, because they have failed to reach critical mass in assets under management. For whatever reason, consumers do not see bank providers as having the sophisticated tools. Now, each one is trying to reinvent itself to address these issues. Before we close this section, the Bank of New York stepped up to become a real player by acquiring the privately held parent company of the Lockwood Financial family of companies (Lockwood). Based in Malvern, Pennsylvania, Lockwood is the industry's largest provider of individually managed account services to independent financial advisors (Table 4.1).

Media

There has been a dramatic increase in access to information. The Internet and the personal finance media give consumers access to information that was previously only available to professionals. Many a financial advisor previously made a great living by acting as a facilitator. This was accomplished by

TABLE 4.1 Competitive Analysis: How Does Your Firm Rank against Competitors?

Category Rank 1–10 (1 = low, 10 = high)	Your Firm	Financial Planners	CPA Firms	Wall Street Brokers	Banks
Financial resources	3	6	10	9
Marketing program	4	3	10	8
Technological competence	6	4	8	5
Access to distribution	3	2	10	9
Access to other professionals	3	5	10	9
Economies of scale	1	4	10	9
Operational efficiencies	5	4	8	5
Sales process/competence	8	5	7	3
Consulting menu breadth	6	6	7	5
Strategic partnerships	3	4	10	7
Company personnel	6	7	7	5
Knowledge level	8	8	5	3
Certification/regulatory	6	4	9	5
Patents/trademarks	1	1	7	5
Industry contacts	4	4	10	8
Other:				
Total points	67	67	128	95

making this information, as well as products and services, available to the consumer who could not otherwise obtain them. That was all the advisor needed to do. Today, the Internet is the best facilitator ever created. It has displaced you as a facilitator and has removed that function as a value-added service for you.

The New Value Added

Study after study shows that individuals want to work with a knowledgeable and trusted professional who can integrate their investment business, financial, and estate matters consistently with their life goals in a tax-efficient method utilizing a comprehensive investment approach. The catch is that they are not willing to pay much, if anything, for this but expect it as part of the ongoing relationship.

The only viable choice for most financial advisors is to compete on value in the relationship. Fortunately, most are well equipped to dramatically increase value by coming full circle and offering financial planning services— which many advisors abandoned due to their success with gathering assets under management.

One solution for you is to reintroduce financial planning as a high-quality experience so that clients perceive greater value from *you* than from your competitors. The challenge is to deliver this experience systematically to each one of your clients every time, while maintaining profitability.

In traditional manufacturing environments, companies consider their products successful if sales continue to rise. Likewise, successful mass financial services must be weighed by how well these services are received by clients.

Establish a feedback loop with your clients to understand what they truly want, need, and value. The key to being effective requires not only getting the right information about what the client wants, but also applying this information intelligently, especially in this highly competitive separate account industry.

Investors are confused with the many products and options available to them. It is your job to help them make smart choices about their money, not to just be a facilitator. The choices that you provide to your clients should be consistent with your management of all their financial affairs, which points in the direction of the control account.

To effectively differentiate yourself from your competitors, you are going to have to provide value-added services and relationships. You must, however, have a clear, delineated process. This is the subject of Part II.

Your job should be to help your clients get their financial house in order. This service provides your clients with a tremendous sense of comfort because they have had no one to work right alongside them in the past. You need to position yourself as a financial problem-solving expert and trusted advisor. We believe the keys to client retention are integrity, education, and managing the client's expectations.

The big question will be whether your clients have sufficient assets to achieve their goals. The best-performing separate account is meaningless if your clients don't reach their financial goals.

In Part II, we'll look at the separate account process, including Chapter 6, "Start with Financial Planning."

THE PROCESS

Affluent investors should have financial advisors who help them create and execute an individualized, long-term financial plan. To do this, the advisor must be willing (and able) to grapple with every aspect of such a plan, from wealth accumulation through protection and distribution. He/She must dedicate the time and effort necessary to understand the broad, as well as the specific, financial goals that apply to each client.

It's a Process, Not a Product

The process covers the most overlooked aspect of separate account management, which is *financial planning*—how to set investment objectives and how the separate account process is a natural extension of planning. You will begin to see how the various types of managers work with each other and their process; which manager's style fits best. Where you go to get help, what a multidiscipline account is, and how to build a simple core investment portfolio using separate account managers are the scope of this part of the book.

Part II will help show you:

- What to do next
- How separate accounts work in your planning
- How to set investment objectives
- How to write an investment policy statement
- How to choose separate account managers
- How to build a core portfolio

- How to use a control account
- What all of this costs
- How to use taxes to your advantage

Chapter 5—The Investment Management Consulting Process

Many advisors rush into the sale of the separate account like it's a new product. The problem is that at this point your chances for success are based solely on your asset allocation and investment strategy. You're still leaving too much to chance. What top advisors do is assess their client's long-term dollar needs and evaluate the probability of achieving those goals.

Chapter 6—Start with Financial Planning

Every aspect of the investment planning process is inherent in the overall financial planning process. The process of financial planning follows the same basic track as the investment management consulting process.

Chapter 7—Asset Allocation

The purpose of asset allocation is to create an insulating effect around an entire portfolio so it doesn't move up or down too rapidly. A number of studies have concluded that asset allocation decisions have the greatest impact on the overall long-term performance of a portfolio.

Chapter 8—Understanding the Different Styles and Types of Managers

Too many choices sometimes confuse advisors; too few may not allow for a successful long-term investment.

Chapter 9—Building a Core Investment Portfolio

Your firm may do this or you may be required to select someone to manage your client's account. Nevertheless, you should understand how to create an investment portfolio even if this is not your full-time job. A core investment strategy is the basic structure of an investment portfolio that supports growth while giving it stability the same way a tree grows efficiently upward, outward, and downward, all at the same time. The stronger the core, the more solid the foundation.

Chapter 10—The Creative Process of Writing an Investment Policy Statement

An investment policy statement is a written statement that sets forth the investment *objectives* of an investment portfolio and general guidelines for specific investment decisions.

Chapter 11—Selecting Separate Account Managers

Your next decision in the separate account process is to pick the appropriate money manager for your client's asset allocation. Your selection starts with the screening process.

Chapter 12—The Control Account

Using the separate account as a control account dramatically alters the separate account sales process. Asset allocation and picking the best manager take a back seat to customizing the separate account to fit neatly and efficiently into the investor's overall investment strategy. Creating the highest probability of meeting the investor's objectives on time with net dollars should always be the highest priority.

Chapter 13—What Does a Separate Account Cost?

Actually, pricing in the securities industry is a mess due to the never-ending quest by financial institutions to hide fees. Find out what the unbundled costs of a separate account really are.

Chapter 14—Tax Management in the Separate Account

The erosion of returns from taxes happens so gradually over the years, that it escapes the notice of many investors. However, the impact is there all the same, and it can be significant—even for those investors who are not in the top tax bracket.

The Investment Management Consulting Process

I n Part I, you got a glimpse of the industry, how it relates to you, and how fast it's growing. Before getting down to the nuts and bolts of separate account structure, however, we'd better take a general look at how some of the top financial advisors work—or ought to work.

They start by gathering pertinent financial information about their clients using a specially designed questionnaire that, unlike those typically in use in the industry today, is detailed but not cumbersome. The questionnaire asks clients to describe their future real-dollar needs, retirement plans, and any major financial transactions such as the sale of a home or business.

The advisor works with the client to identify all known variables (e.g., the time period until retirement, required cash flows, investment saving pools [401(k)s, IRAs, taxable accounts, applicable tax rates, social security benefits, etc.]).

The goal of the consultant at this point is to uncover what the client truly wants. Some advisors set a *target* goal and a *fallback* goal. A target goal is what the client would *like* to have (if everything goes right), and a fallback goal is what the client *must* have. Next, the advisor converts the client's financial goals into future liabilities—viewing them as money the client owes to himself/herself at some point in the future. By setting these dollar goals and understanding the risks that are inherent with various investments, the consultant can determine the probability of reaching those specific goals (Figure 5.1).

If this sounds to you like financial planning, that's because it is. This doesn't mean that you have to be a financial planner, but you may want to consider forming a partnership or strategic alliance with one.

After all data are gathered, the consultant looks at the *absolute dollars* required to satisfactorily meet the client's financial objectives at specific periods of time in the future. Only after this information is laid out does the advisor attempt to solve for unknown variables such as the combination of assets that will provide the best future capital market returns. As the advisor works with the client, he/she uses the information gathered to determine the probability of achieving financial goals using various investment allocations. The advisor is continually adjusting all known variables to approach as close to 100 percent probability of success as possible. The goal of the advisor/consultant at this point is to focus on the investment strategy that has the highest probability of achieving the stated result.

In most cases, this evaluation will indicate a shortfall. If it does, you will have to explain to your client that he/she will need to take more risk, the larger the size of that shortfall. Can you see why this step has nothing to do with any risk tolerance questionnaire you had your client fill out? What if you discover that your client has no tolerance for risk? Your job is to explain that *real* risk is not having enough money at retirement, and there is no way to make enough money unless he/she takes more risk. It may be an uncomfortable conversation, but it may be one of the most important in your client's life.

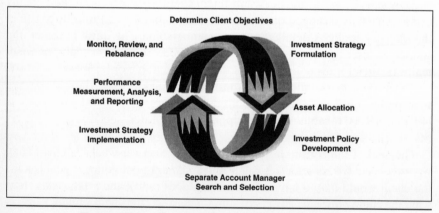

FIGURE 5.1 The Investment Consulting Process.

This also takes the responsibility out of the realm of how good your manager selection was and puts it back squarely on the client's shoulders. You just show the client the facts.

Once the client understands that he/she will have a money shortfall, you can look at optimal asset allocation and recommend a strategy. (Do you see why we are including financial planning in the next chapter?)

You should have a series of market charts that you can show at this point to help your client see what the market has done over different time periods. Show him/her how, by adjusting the asset allocation percentages, he/she can meet his/her future financial goals and stay within his/her risk tolerances. Include your client in this step of the process. Together you may discover that optimizing his/her asset allocation is still not enough to bring the probabilities of success to acceptable levels. Now what?

Work with your client to adjust more of the *known* variables (e.g., savings rate, expenditures rate, and/or time allocated to achieve his/her goal). The client may need to extend his/her retirement date by 5 or even 10 years to make things come into line. This makes him/her think. He/she may also bring in more assets. At this step you are building trust.

This is the most important step of the process because it establishes realistic expectations and begins the educational process. Including this step will impact the probability of your client reaching his/her target financial goals. Explain that the ultimate decision between the downside volatility versus the promise of a higher probability of success is based on the fine-tuning of all known variables, such as time horizon, savings, and expenditures. Keep putting responsibility back in the client's court. Help your client fine-tune these variables, and he/she will see where you are going.

Once your client understands and accepts the risks, it's time to create a detailed asset allocation within the major asset classes. This becomes the long-term strategic investment plan with the highest statistical degree of probability of reaching your client's goals.

Discuss Taxes

Because top advisors understand that taxes can reduce wealth accumulation significantly, a critical step in the process is to optimize the allocation of investment styles between taxable and tax-deferred portfolios.

Be sure to look at each pool of savings on a stand-alone basis (i.e., IRA; 401[k]; taxable savings). Neglecting to do this is a common advisor error in designing an investment strategy. Your objective should be to get each pool of your client's assets in concert with one another, thus creating an efficient strategy on both an investment and tax basis.

Only after this aspect of the client's plan is complete should you initiate an investment vehicle search. This search is conducted for each style in each allocated pool of assets. When all of the information is known, then the universe of possible investment products—including mutual funds, index-type investments, and separate accounts—can be examined objectively. Explain what is to be expected and what is not.

Realistic Expectations

- Investment style and discipline are clearly defined.
- Separate account manager adheres to that style and discipline under all market conditions.
- The manager outperforms the benchmark over the long term.
- The separate account manager agrees to communicate in a timely and ongoing fashion.

Unrealistic Expectations

- The manager will make a profit on every investment. (Some selections will decline in value or may be sold at a loss.)
- The manager will perform in line with or better than the market in every period.
- The manager will be in the top quartile of managers in every period.
- The manager will change style to perform at the top of each market.

Long before the clients see these managers, the smart advisor puts recommended investment vehicles through an intensive qualitative and quantitative screening process. The process makes sure that the separate account or mutual fund consistently adheres to stated discipline and style, providing quality results with minimal surprises. In addition, with taxable accounts, investment vehicles are screened to find those that create the fewest taxable events. An ongoing step is *rebalancing,* or bringing the percentage of assets back to meet the client's target dollar goals.

As you follow the process, your client will see how value is continually added each step of the way. On a quarterly basis, your client will receive a report depicting his/her progress. If done correctly, these reports should keep him/her concentrating on long-term goals rather than on short-term capital market swings. If capital market movements cause the strategy to drop below the agreed-upon probability of attaining the goal, the report will recommend changes in strategy to get it back on track.

This process can set you apart from the competition. Overlay your original investment policy with your client's current situation. Show him/her statistical models that back up your method using proven investment principles. If you do this, you will rise head and shoulders above your competitors. Follow this process, and you also can achieve the highest probability of future business success. You will become a very valuable member of your client's team and get him/her to stop concentrating on past performance and look at the resources needed to reach his/her goals and financial expectations. Your client will feel like he/she is part of the process, not an outsider ready to switch advisors the second something goes wrong.

The 10-Step Separate Account Process

1. Information gathering
2. Financial planning
3. Fine-tuning of known variables such as time, savings, and expenditures
4. Asset allocation
5. Style allocation and tax considerations
6. Written statement of investment objectives (client goals)
7. Selection of appropriate investment vehicles (manager search)
8. Measurement of progress (monitoring)
9. Rebalancing
10. Ongoing communications

Next, let's break down each step starting with information gathering and financial planning.

Start with Financial Planning[1]

very aspect of the investment management consulting process depends on
the answer to critical financial planning questions. As an example, a simple
question like how to title the accounts depends on an understanding of the
estate plan, not just as it exists, but as it should be. Trust planning is becoming
a big issue, and we see major errors being made. Warning! This doesn't mean
that you now have to start doing financial planning, or become a Certified
Financial Planner (CFP), you just need to understand what the top advisors
are doing and why. If you simply wish to sell separate accounts as a product,
skip this chapter.

Knowing Your Client

Every aspect of the investment planning process is inherent in the overall
financial planning process. The process of financial planning follows the same
basic track as the investment management consulting process.

The first step is to analyze the client's situation. What does your client
need? What are his/her priorities? What are the client's current resources, net
worth, liquidity levels, earning power, tax status, health and longevity assumptions, and other relevant factors that should be considered in determining the
probabilities of meeting his/her goals, needs, and priorities? You've got to
have this information before you can assist him/her in making an informed
decision. Have you spelled out responsibilities for implementation, monitoring, and reporting?

Information Gathering

There is a big difference between consulting to institutions compared with advising to a higher-net-worth individual or couple. With individuals there may be fuzzy goals (i.e., uncertainty as to concrete objectives or disagreement among family members as to specific needs). There may be tax issues (income and estate taxes), varying time frames related to multiple objectives, ownership issues, risk management questions, insurance matters, legacy and succession concerns. Asset management decisions and investment policy statements must be framed within an overall financial planning context.

Data gathering can be a daunting task. As a financial advisor you must know "where and what all of his/her stuff is." Often the client does not know. You have to have a method in place to organize data and the patience to wade through it.

In many cases, no single advisor "owns the client relationship." Money, securities, and other assets may be on deposit at multiple institutions. No one understands the big picture. What you are selling is a *process* to accomplish that objective.

Many advisors employ an abbreviated data sheet up front, which is completed by a potential client and submitted prior to the first meeting or brought to the first meeting. Initial data is a *first cut,* used to get a sense whether the counselor and the client have a basis for a long-term mutually satisfactory relationship. Most financial planners offer a no-obligation initial interview. The objective is to gather enough information to determine the scope of the engagement as well as to get an opportunity to define and sell your process.

Often, a more detailed data sheet is completed once the engagement has been accepted and construction of the financial plan has begun. Clients are given checklists and questionnaires. Staff members, associate planners, and interns often work with clients to assemble the data. Patience is required, especially when affairs are complex. *Scattered assets* are the norm, and at times it may take more time to gather data than it does to do the planning.

Basic data gathering would encompass but should not be limited to:

- Family census: names, residential and business addresses, contact data (phone, fax, e-mail), names of children, ages and dates of birth for all family members, Social Security numbers. Are children married? Grandchildren? Health status? Special needs?

- Net-worth statement: determine ownership for all assets (i.e., ownership by client, spouse or partner); joint ownership (define such as jointly owned with right of survivorship [JTWROS], TIC, community property, etc.); trust (define); other (define, such as accounts held for minors). Request copies of all statements.

- Accounts: checking, savings, money market, CDs (show maturity date).
- Stocks, bonds, mutual funds (list or provide brokerage or custodial statement): include data on U.S. Savings Bonds. Obtain tax basis for all securities.
- Annuities (fixed and variable): obtain copy of policy and recent quarterly and annual reports. Determine owner; annuitant; primary and contingent beneficiaries; tax status.
- Life insurance: request copy of policy, original proposal, last annual report. Determine type of policy, face amount, the insured, owner, beneficiary (primary and contingent), premium payments, adequacy of payments (how long will the policy carry given current assumptions?), purpose of the coverage, cash values if applicable (current value, surrender value, loans outstanding). Include data on group insurance and any coverage tied to employer benefits or business arrangements such as buy/sell agreements. Determine all sources of death benefits.
- Real estate, including residence, vacation home, rental properties: identify owner, purchase price, current value, mortgage terms and current balance, cash flow from rental properties.
- Partnership investments (obtain copy of recent quarterly or annual report): determine cash flow, tax benefits, estimated values, liquidity, if any.
- Business interests: name; type of business; form of ownership (C corp., S corp., sole proprietor, partnership, LLC); percentage of ownership; value of interest; buy/sell agreement or succession plan?
- Personal assets: description (car, boat, aircraft); value; debt. List value of other assets such as jewelry, household furnishings.
- Retirement plans: obtain statements for all pension/profit sharing plans; IRAs; 401(k); 403(b); 457 plans; deferred compensation plans, and so on. Specify primary and contingent beneficiaries.
- Stock option plans: obtain complete description; type of options; number of shares; exercise price; current stock price; vesting.
- Education planning: Section 529 Plans, Education IRAs, other.
- Tangibles: type of asset (precious metals, gems, coins); date of purchase; original investment; current value.

- Other insurance: copies of homeowner, rental, auto, umbrella liability policies; personal and group disability policies; long-term care.

- Copies of legal documents and other key documents: will(s); trusts (including revocable or irrevocable living trusts, charitable trusts); durable powers of attorney for assets and health care; divorce decrees, alimony and child support agreements; prenuptial agreements; stock purchase agreements; business buy/sell agreements; family limited partnerships; most recent tax return.

- Advisory team: you want to know the name, address, and contact information for other key advisors such as a CPA or other tax advisor; attorney, banker, trustees, insurance agents, brokers, and so on.

- Anything else the client(s) thinks is important to his/her life and future.

Beyond the Financial

To most of your affluent clients, investing and financial planning isn't just about making *money*. It is about the meaning of money as it relates to one's psyche, one's mission in life and final legacy.

For example, it is easy to run a retirement planning calculation targeting X dollars by a certain date to fund retirement. You may use linear assumptions or Monte Carlo simulation to come up with a hypothetical result. But is that enough?

What does *retirement* really mean to the client? Or to him *and* her, if a couple? Will one or both work part-time? Will a hobby become a source of income? Do they want to sell a home and relocate? Rent or buy a boat and sail away? Travel? What are their longevity assumptions? Do the husband and wife agree? (Is there harmony or conflict?)

The client may have achieved financial success. Is there more to it than that? Bob Buford, in his meaningful book, *Half Time: Changing Your Game Plan from Success to Significance* (Zondervan Publishing, Grand Rapids, MI, 1994), noted: "One of the most common characteristics of a person nearing the end of the first half (of the game of life) is that unquenchable desire to move from success to significance."

Significance reflects the client's vision of a legacy during his/her lifetime and after one transcends at death to, hopefully, a higher order where character counts and net worth means nothing. A man or woman of true depth recognizes that all earthly blessings are merely loans. All must be left behind. Significance is a desire to give back now and beyond death, to make a difference.

You start to become his/her trusted advisor. You may not want to go this route, but if you do, you're going to need to know more. What does the client want to do in terms of lifelong learning, a second career, spiritual or ministerial goals, charitable desires, legacies for survivors and as yet unborn generations? A client may wish to fund trusts, endow causes, build cultural edifices, create foundations, educate, enlighten, or inspire. Addressing these issues will make your separate account program significant in his/her life.

These are the *soft issues* regarding money. It is questioning and probing in the deeper areas beyond money and surface simplicities that will set you apart from other advisors and from those looking for quick sales. Matters of significance require money, but money is not the point.

Beyond the Questionnaire

Information gathering means going beyond the data sheet. An understanding of the client's core values and objectives comes out of face-to-face conversations over coffee or other refreshments, over lunch or dinner, in relaxed atmospheres, in unguarded moments. It is an exercise in human communication, verbal and nonverbal, that leads to important discoveries and creative solutions. Furthermore, do not be surprised if the client becomes a true friend.

"What if?" Questions

As you approach the formulation stage of writing an investment policy statement for your client, you should explain the three phases of money life: (1) accumulation, (2) preservation, and (3) distribution.

In similar fashion, here is a simple template that Walker uses for an effective approach to strategic estate planning based on only three possibilities. The client is:

1. Okay
2. Not okay
3. Dead

Clients often find the preceding statement to be amusing, but it does help to clarify thinking. When most prospective clients come to talk with you initially, they are okay, at least from a health standpoint. They may be under stress from a divorce, death of a spouse or other loved one, or a forced retirement or other job loss. They may be looking to the future in a positive mode, wanting to better deploy capital, set goals, operate from a defined plan. The point is, they are not incapacitated. They can think, study, learn, and make logical and informed decisions.

However, what if at some point they cannot make good decisions? They are incapacitated due to illness or accident? They are comatose or suffering from a mental impairment? Who is empowered to make decisions for them?

Often, clients will say, "My executor will make decisions."

"Wrong, dear client. You are not dead. Your will is not effective. Your life insurance has not paid off. You are suffering a 'living death,' which may or may not be permanent."

Go to an extreme to make a point. Paint a grim picture. "You have been in an accident or had a stroke and you are in a coma. Who has the authority to deal with your investments? Your rental properties? Business interests? If an asset is titled in your name, your spouse, your adult child, your business partner does *not* have the authority to act in your behalf. There is a legal proceeding that can be invoked to have a court declare you incompetent, but do you really want to put them through that?"

This opens the door to a discussion of the pros and cons of durable powers of attorney for assets, revocable living trusts, and strategies to protect business interests.

One note of caution: You are touching on legal matters. If you are not an attorney, you may not offer legal opinions or legal advice. You must avoid the unauthorized practice of law. Do not give your client samples of legal documents that he/she could copy.

In every plan or memo touching on legal matters, add a disclaimer:

(Your name) is not an attorney and may not give legal advice. Nothing in this plan should be construed as legal advice. Legal advice may be rendered only by a qualified attorney, and action should be taken only after consultation with said attorney. My role as an advisor is to assist you in organizing data, help you to define your goals and objectives, and to help frame questions for discussion with legal counsel.

You should be working in concert with an estate and tax attorney in the client's behalf. First, strive to preserve existing relationships if the client has an attorney that he/she values. There may be an opportunity to get to know an allied professional who could become an important member of your strategic alliance group. However, many clients do not have an attorney and want your referral. Here, again, is an opportunity to build your cross-referral network.

Continuing your probing of "what if?" questions, in the case of incapacity, "who has the authority, dear client, to make decisions regarding your most precious asset—your body?" This statement triggers a discussion of durable powers of attorney for health care and living wills. How does the client feel about endgame intervention, about being kept alive artificially?

Discussions with "Not okay" clients may touch on insurance matters, such as personal or group disability insurance, long-term care insurance, umbrella liability coverage, funding of business disability buy/sell agreements. If you are not an expert in these matters, here again is an opportunity to extend your network of strategic alliances.

A Will Is Not Enough

It is very common for people with significant wealth to have no wills, old wills, or inefficient wills. Estate structures that *maximize* taxes and administrative costs are the rule, not the exception.

Estate Tax Changes

As you are already aware, President Bush has signed into law the Economic Growth and Tax Relief Reconciliation Act (EGTRRA) of 2001. One of the hallmarks of the new law is the eventual elimination of the federal estate tax in 2010, and prior to that, the law increases the estate tax exemption and reduces the top estate tax rate (Table 6.1). For many investors, this will be

TABLE 6.1 Summary of New Law

Year	Exemption	Top Tax Rate
2001	$675,000	55%
2002	$1,000,000	50%
2003	$1,000,000	49%
2004	$1,500,000	48%
2005	$1,500,000	47%
2006	$2,000,000	46%
2007	$2,000,000	45%
2008	$2,000,000	45%
2009	$3,500,000	45%
2010	Estate tax repealed	45%

the first time anyone has shown this to them. This chart can open up new discussions and even give you the opportunity to work closely with a client's estate attorney. This creates added value. And, if you don't understand what this means to your client, maybe you'd better sit down with an estate attorney.

The uncertainty and complexity of EGTRRA merely added to the confusion. EGTRRA has increased the need for quality financial advice and in-depth planning. As a value-added consultant, you can demonstrate value and increase fee income by helping clients to structure their affairs to:

- Minimize income and estate taxes
- Increase legacies to loved ones
- Increase social capital to support philanthropic goals

A will is only *part* of an estate plan. Everyone has a will. If the client has not drafted a will, his/her state of residency has done it for them. It's called *intestacy,* and it is a poor substitute for planning.

A will governs distribution of property. You need to know with what you are dealing. Is the will a simple "I love you" will (i.e., "I give it all to her, she gives it all to me," or vice-versa)? Are the wills more complex, containing various trust provisions? Is the will tied to a living trust (i.e., a pour-over will)? Define the functions of all trusts in the will or independent of the will.

However, some property may not be subject to the will. If property is owned jointly with right of survivorship (JTWROS), unless disclaimed, the property goes to the survivor at the death of the first owner to die.

In a similar fashion, contractual designations (beneficiary designations on insurance contracts, annuities, retirement plans, benefit plans, buy/sell agreements) govern distribution. If the beneficiary is not the "estate of the decedent," the asset will pass to the named beneficiary independent of the will.

It is not uncommon where most investments are held jointly (JTWROS) and where the primary beneficiary on insurance policies and retirement plans is the surviving spouse, to see the bulk of postmortem liquidity pass outside of the will. In other words, dear client, "you may have a will that is legal and valid, but it will not work because of the way you own assets and have designated beneficiaries." Explain this to your client, and you will be impressing him/her each step of the way.

Ask about trusts that own property (living trusts or testamentary trusts from previous estates, revocable or irrevocable, also govern the distribution of property).

Before you help your client make the second largest purchase in his/her life—his/her separate account—you need to understand the scope of estate planning, you should have a working knowledge of various types of wills and common provisions, the impact of ownership forms and contractual beneficiary designations, and the uses of trusts as stand-alone entities or as part of a will. Work with a qualified attorney. When a client is opening a $1 million separate account with you, the question as to how the account should be registered is not an idle query. The estate and income tax ramifications may be significant, depending on the efficacy of your answers. Estate planning is not just about estate taxes—it is also about *distribution*.

Who Gets the Money?

Tax issues cloud rational thinking at times. Ask the client to forget tax laws. Make believe that there are no ordinary income taxes, capital gains taxes, or estate taxes. "If there were no tax laws, Mr. and/or Mrs. (Ms.) Client, what would you like to do with your money and your assets?"

"Once we figure out your true wishes and core values, I as your advisor, will work with other members of your advisory team, your CPA, and attorney (or other advisors) to minimize taxes and maximize your legacy."

How does the client feel about his/her children as heirs? Are there minors in the picture? If heirs are adults, are there health issues, immaturity factors, spendthrift concerns?

If you are planning for a noncitizen spouse, note that to qualify for the marital deduction at the death of a spouse, the surviving spouse must be a U.S. citizen. Specialized trust planning is called for a relative to a spouse who is not a U.S. citizen.

Well-off clients who are double-income, no kids (DINKs) may want to set up trusts for aging parents. Because they do not have children, more thought may be called for as to final distribution at the death of the surviving spouse.

As baby boomers age with prospects of greater longevity, albeit with an increased likelihood of old-age infirmities, a greater emphasis will be placed on trust planning, both living trusts and testamentary (postmortem) trusts. It is an area worthy of study.

For the larger estate, advanced estate planning strategies may be called for. Life insurance will continue as a tool to leverage legacies. Your role as an advisor, in concert with technical specialists who are well versed in advanced planning alternatives, is to help the client achieve his/her goals in the most efficient way possible. How can you propose investment strategies for significant monies without a deep understanding of the client's quest for significance—in life and thereafter?

An Integrated Consulting Process

What sets you apart from your competitors? What makes you unique? Lewis Walker landed a $4 million account because the competing advisor never asked about the client's will and living trust.

Your firm's separate account programs do not distinguish you from the crowd. Everyone sells separate accounts. The number of choices and distribution channels are overwhelming.

Not long ago, separately managed accounts were the purview of the experienced broker or advisor who dealt with an exclusive clientele. With an explosion in the number of vendors offering separately managed accounts and with lower minimum investments per account, separate account management is trending toward commodity status.

Now everyone from Wall Street to Main Street sells advice. Has advice become a generic product? Fee-based services and products are no longer unique.

Clients want an integrated, holistic financial planning and asset management process. The key word is *process*. It is your process that will set you apart, how you blend the precepts of estate, tax, and investment planning into a strategic overlay. It is your process that distinguishes your initial client presentation, fact finding and data mining, formulation of a plan and actionable recommendations, plan execution, and monitoring.

Your mission should be to enhance the client's probability of achieving defined goals and objectives—both the quantifiable and unquantifiable. There are numbers and there is *life*.

Family (or individual) security and estate planning issues, as we have described, may be viewed as the first part of a two-part strategy. Once you fully understand the structure required to actualize security and legacy objectives, you may move to the second part, investment planning.

Again, your data mining process is useful in organizing information to allow you to see the big picture. You have all of the client's statements. You know where all of the money is.

Organize your client's accounts within two buckets based on ownership and tax status as follows:

Taxable Monies	*Tax-Deferred Money*
1. His	1. IRA (traditional or RO)
2. Hers	2. Roths (tax-free)
3. Jointly held	3. SEP-IRA
a. JTWROS	4. Pension plan
b. TIC	5. Profit sharing plan
c. Other	6. 401(k)
4. Community property	7. 403(b); TSA
5. Living trusts	8. 457 plan
6. Kiddie accounts	9. Education IRA
a. Under age 14	10. Section 529 plan
b. Over age 14	11. Nonqualified annuities
7. Sub–S corp/sole prop. Partnership	12. Life insurance cash value
8. Other trusts	13. Nonqualified deferred comp.
	14. Stock option plans

It is also useful to discuss each registration to determine the client's original objective in setting up the account. Are those goals being served? What has been the experience with the account? Is the client happy with it? If a change is being contemplated, why does the client feel the need for change? An understanding of subjective issues can be useful in establishing the investment policy.

Does the client even know what he/she has? A common problem is *scattered assets* (i.e., accounts and securities acquired over time with little thought as to an overall strategy). Or perhaps the assets were inherited and the portfolio was designed to meet a decedent's needs and no longer fits the objectives or tax status of the inheritor.

It is unusual to find a defined investment policy driving the portfolio. As a value-added advisor you can render a service by analyzing the portfolio as it is. You may use tools from companies such as Zephyr Associates, Morningstar, or others to generate a portfolio analysis. How much risk is the client taking? Are there concentrated positions? Growth or value bias? Underweighted or overweighted by asset class, subclass, or sector? Often the unwritten investment policy surprises the client.

Moving from the "policy as it is" to "the policy as it should be" is based on a decision-making matrix. Do the personal accounts, by registration and size, square with the defined estate plan? With married persons, do estates need to be balanced? Should assets be transferred from one spouse to another or to a trust? If so, which positions or holdings?

Will assets serve social capital objectives and be donated to a charity, charitable trust, family foundation, or supporting organization? If so, which securities?

Does the client have sufficient personal liquidity outside of tax-deferred accounts? Based on projected cash flows and expenditures, how much money should be held in working capital reserves like money market funds?

Identify *sleep-at-night* money. Identify *no-risk* or *low-risk* alternatives. What are the current yields on Treasury bills and shorter-term government paper, money market accounts, CDs? Is that enough? What are the real-return needs over and above inflation and taxation? Answers will depend on a variety of factors, including the client's age and longevity assumptions, sources of cash flow independent of investments, size of the capital pool, and psychological factors relating to risk/reward trade-offs.

If the client has sizable fixed-income positions, you may wish to submit the portfolio to the appropriate bond manager for analysis. Once you determine the ratio of fixed income to equities, discuss with the client whether he/she/they wishes to keep the same ratio or alter it based on newly defined risk/reward parameters and rate-of-return requirements.

Consider whether the fixed-income allocation should be placed within one or more of the tax-deferred buckets such as a retirement plan or nonqualified tax-deferred annuity. The goal is to defer ordinary income events on the retirement side of the ledger; on the personal taxable side, the goal is to capture and harvest gains and losses employing a tax-efficient separate account manager. This is a simple but powerful idea. How often have you seen a tax-sensitive client with a portfolio of tax-free muni bonds owned personally, and with a relatively tax-efficient equity manager positioned within a retirement plan?

Do not assume that the client understands the interest rate yield curve and the inverse relationship between interest rate movements and bond prices. In 2001, a leading mutual fund group surveyed investors in their bond funds. Less than 30 percent understood that when interest rates rise, bond values decline, and vice versa.

Clients often do not understand *total return* and the difference between *income* and *tax-efficient cash flow*.

A Matter of Safety

Most advisors have a way to explain risk, using various measures of historical volatility to classify asset classes and managers. However, as we saw in the rocky markets of 2000, 2001, and 2002, linear projections of wealth accumulation based on a specific assumed rate of return are spurious. Because the future is an unfunded liability, various disciplines such as a Monte Carlo simulation or other mathematical and statistical machinations are being used to estimate a range of probabilities relative to success or failure of a strategy.

If *reversion to the mean* has more relevance following the growth stock and Nasdaq drubbings of 2000 and 2001, and we wish to factor in periods of low performance as a possibility, clients will have to increase contributions to savings and/or lengthen time horizons.

The wisdom of prudent diversification was proven again in the southeastern drift of hot dots in 2000 and 2001. Trendy gurus trumpet *thinking outside of the box.* Perhaps our job as advisors is to keep people *in the box,* maintaining discipline and sticking with a policy while other investors are chasing chimerical fads and the story du jour.

Concentrated Wealth

Are there any sacred cows in the portfolio? Does the client own stocks that carry emotional baggage? Perhaps the stocks were gifts or bequests from a spouse, parent, grandparent, or other relative and the client feels guilty about selling. Or the stock may have a very low tax basis, and the client is intimidated by the tax liability.

One key question is useful in creating a resolution. Ask the client if, instead of the stock, he/she had cash, would he/she buy the same stock today? If the answer is no, liquidation alternatives should be discussed.

By engaging managers who employ covered call writing strategies, significant cash flows can be generated from sacred cows and low-basis stocks. By letting stock get called away at defined higher prices over time, a phased-diversification element can be introduced while controlling tax events.

The collapse of Enron and dot.com stocks illustrated the hazards of *concentrated wealth.* However, you as an advisor can point to numerous mainstream large-capitalization New York Stock Exchange (NYSE)-listed household names that saw jarring declines in price of 50 percent or more in recent years.

Suppose that a client has amassed significant wealth by *not diversifying.* He/she bought into a stock that in hindsight has been a winner and it dominates his/her net worth statement. The stock constitutes from 50 to 90 percent or more of their liquid net worth. They succeeded because they rode a winning horse. How do you tell them to dismount and trade their trusty steed for a herd?

For clients who have achieved success, especially clients nearing retirement or who are already retired, they may have sufficient assets under prudent assumptions to last the rest of their lives. In fact, in the estate planning discussion you and they have considered gifts and other legacy issues.

Pose the question: "If your liquid wealth increased by 50 percent, would that have a major impact on your lifestyle?" Most likely, the answer will be no.

"But if your wealth *decreased* by 50 percent, would that have an impact?" Quite likely, such an event would be disturbing, or perhaps, devastating. Strategies to deal with the risks associated with concentrated wealth are increasingly important.

Executive and management compensation schemes continue to involve significant measures of stock options, stock bonuses, and restricted stock. In the 1990s in particular, a boom in stock-for-stock mergers also created unprecedented equity wealth concentration. Risks associated with such holdings include concentration in one company and one industry sector, in some cases limited liquidity, and tax ramifications relative to low basis and alternative minimum tax exposure. Concurrently with the growth of personal, concentrated, and taxable wealth, the past decade has witnessed the creation of innovative strategies for hedging and monetizing restricted and low-cost basis stock positions.

Private hedging strategies could include a protective put option, sale of a covered call option, a costless collar, a participating collar, costless put spread collar, purchase of a 1-by-2 call spread, short against the box.

Monetization strategies combined with a hedged stock position can provide capital for diversification purposes while deferring a taxable event. The three most popular techniques involve (1) a costless collar plus a loan, (2) a variable prepaid forward sale, and (3) a private sale relative to restricted and control securities.

Other techniques may include public sale hedging and monetizing strategies and exchange funds.

All sophisticated wealth management solutions require an experienced team of professionals who have mastered the complexities of various techniques. If you are dealing with high-net-worth clients, you should have a strategic alliance with a group that can evaluate various solutions and clearly explain the pros and cons to you as the advisor, the client, and other advisory team members such as a tax advisor and attorney.

Today's affluent like the idea that there is one source from which we can seek solutions to our problems or fulfillment of our needs. The financial planner and investment advisor of the future may indeed be as much a concierge as a consultant. Our practices may resemble a family office. As managed money, whether separate accounts or other formats, becomes more commonplace, value will be added through an expansion of services beyond the traditional. Certainly, as the age wave rolls on, elder care advisory services and lifestyle maintenance services will be more important.

Those advisors who concentrate solely on asset management risk losing accounts to planners/advisors who effectively combine comprehensive financial planning with fee-based asset management. Increasingly, clients demand an integrated, holistic financial planning and asset management process. They want education and customized advice. They want ongoing counsel and oversight with clear communication and accountability. Do you have a plan in place to deliver this type of service?

Your goal is to formulate, propose, and execute a consulting process that will:

- Meet and exceed the client's expectations
- Set you apart from your competitors
- Uncover hidden needs
- Add value to the client's financial and psychological bottom line
- Add value to your bottom line and business model
- Enhance the quality of your life

It isn't about being able to sell the most products anymore. It is about *process,* and a full recognition that investment management consulting and wealth management tools are part of a bigger picture.

Note

[1]Mr. Lewis Walker, CFA and Certified Investment Management Consultant, is responsible for this chapter.

Asset Allocation

You don't have to sell clients on asset allocation these days. After the last couple of years, they are all in favor of it.

The purpose of asset allocation is to create an insulating effect around an entire portfolio so it doesn't move up or down too rapidly or harshly— which will, in turn, provide a more consistent return over any long time period (5-, 10-, 15-, or 20-year time frames). Asset allocation can level the peaks and valleys of the effects of volatility on the value of a portfolio. A number of studies have concluded that asset allocation decisions have the greatest impact on the overall long-term performance of a portfolio.

Asset allocation is not simply a pie chart illustrating the categories of a portfolio. It should be a formal ongoing recorded process based on the advisor's considered evaluation of each investment portfolio and the principles of modern portfolio theory.

Four variables enter into every asset allocation decision:

1. Assumed risk tolerance or variability of returns
2. Expected rate of return
3. Time horizon of the portfolio
4. Selection of asset classes

Clients don't need a tremendous amount of explanation to feel comfortable with a complex subject, but when you explain complex information to them, it's important that you cover all the steps.

When trying to convey complex material, assume that your clients are going to need some coaching. For example, most investors are confused by the industry or investment jargon when their advisor tries to explain the concepts of risk. During a discussion such as this, you might find that explaining Sharpe ratios or even standard deviation is too much for many clients to absorb. As a general rule, you'll have to tailor your explanation to each individual investor.

Risk

The first step in the asset allocation process is to determine your client's risk tolerance. How many clients *tell* you they want to invest for maximum growth, but are really only willing to risk a 10 percent decline in their portfolio? You need to establish the maximum risk exposure with which your client will be comfortable over different time periods.

Risk should be spoken about in absolute terms—not to scare clients, but to ensure that they aren't surprised when their investment goes down. When a client walks in and says, "I want to buy XYZ Internet fund," many advisors respond by saying "But, XYZ fund has a Beta of 1.5." or "You should be aware that the fund is 50 percent more risky than the market." However, this seldom makes sense to the client until the inevitable decline happens. Once the storm hits, they are often shocked by how much a fund can drop. To make the point in layman's terms, you need simply to say, "That investment regularly drops 40 to 50 percent." In that way, you are preparing the client for the magnitude of the potential decline (though, after this recent drop, you may not have to explain!).

The traditional measures of risk in our industry have always been Beta and standard deviation, which are very effective when looking at investments over a lengthy time frame. However, individuals don't have a long-term view; long-term to many investors is *tomorrow*.

Institutions use tools such as Beta to measure risk because they are comparing a money manager with a benchmark. For example, if an institutional investor has hired a money manager whose Beta is 1.5 (or 50 percent riskier than the benchmark), when the benchmark is down 10 percent, and the manager is down 12 percent, an institution would be very pleased with this result. Why? Basically, because the manager had a Beta of 1.5, he should have been down 15 percent. Instead, the money manager was only down 12 percent, which essentially indicates superior risk-adjusted performance.

Of course, that's not the way a typical individual thinks! An individual would say, "The benchmark's down 10 and I'm down 12—you're fired." So Beta is only a useful tool if a client understands it.

There is a difference between Beta and standard deviation. Where Beta is a good measurement for one investment style or one stock or fund, it's not a very good measurement for a separate account portfolio. Standard deviation is a far better gauge of how much risk an investor is taking. However, to most investors, this measurement is even more confusing.

Risk is about absolute loss. We find the best thing you can do for investors is help them understand how much *actual decline* they are really willing to absorb with their money. If you do this in the beginning of the relationship, then when their investments approach that level of decline, you can at least remind them that they said they were willing to withstand that drop.

Following is an exercise (thanks to Joe Duran) for clients called the Lifeboat Drill, which measures the lowest decline clients can tolerate before they abandon their investment ship.

The Lifeboat Drill

Assume for a moment that you put all of your money (we'll use $100,000 for simplicity) in an investment. In the first month, your investment goes up 3 percent. You feel pretty good, right? In the next month, it goes up 2 percent. You're feeling even better. But what if your money starts to decline? What percentage decline could you withstand? Your ship is taking on water—how low in the water will you let the boat sink before you abandon ship?

What if, on your monthly statement, you see that your $100,000 has become $97,000. Are you still on board? The next month, you're down to $94,000; then it drops to $92,000. How are you feeling now? Are you still okay with doing nothing or are you getting your lifeboat ready? The month after that, it drops to $90,000. Then it goes down further: to $85,000, $77,000, $65,000, and eventually to $50,000.

At what point do you jump ship? At a 15 percent drop, nearly everybody wants out, but when it isn't related to a specific dollar amount, almost everyone will say they are willing to accept a greater percentage.

Clients need to have an understanding of the risks that are involved in investing. You must help them invest in such a way that they will sit tight when the water gets choppy and not jump ship. Additionally, if clients have a good understanding of their risk tolerance, they will realize that their investment performance is directly linked to it (Table 7.1).

This drill can also serve as a reminder. For example, if your client wants to move to a new hedge fund, you can review the lifeboat drill, and tell your client, "If you're willing to watch this investment drop from $100,000 to $50,000—which you *will* experience—I'm more than happy to buy it for you. But don't tell me, when it's down $50,000, that you want to sell it." This keeps investors from blaming you if they do decide to jump ship.

TABLE 7.1 The Lifeboat Drill

Potential Quarterly Decline	Original Investment—$100,000	Check the Box Where You Would Take Action
(3%)	$97,000	☑
(6%)	$94,000	☐
(8%)	$92,000	☐
(10%)	$90,000	☐
(15%)	$85,000	☐
(23%)	$77,000	☐
(35%)	$65,000	☐
(50%)	$50,000	☐

The biggest mistake investors can make is to go beyond their risk tolerance, or threshold of comfort, get in the lifeboat, and then not make their destination; because when the investment picks up steam again, it will leave them behind.

Expected Rate of Return

After establishing the client's risk tolerance, the next step is to determine the client's expected rate of return. For any given expected rate of return, an optimal mix of asset classes could be determined that will yield the expected rate of return with the least amount of volatility or risk. Conversely, for any given level of assumed risk, a higher expected return may be obtained by mixing different asset classes than by investing in a single asset class.

The percentages can also be broken down to determine how much money goes into each asset class. The concept of Modern Portfolio Theory has helped in this process. Harry Markowitz won the Nobel Prize in Economics in 1990 for this contribution. He states that for every level of risk, there is some optimal combination of investments that will give you the highest rate of return. The range of portfolios exhibiting this optimal risk-reward trade-off form what we call the *efficient frontier* (Figure 7.1). The efficient frontier is determined by calculating the expected rate of return and standard deviation for each asset class.

By plotting each percentage combination of the various asset classes, we are able to view the efficient frontier curve. In this example, we see that a portfolio of 60 percent stock and 40 percent bonds gives us a higher expected

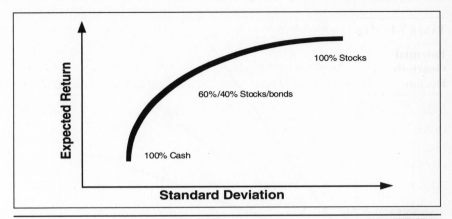

FIGURE 7.1   Efficient Frontier Curve.

return than cash, without the volatility of 100 percent stocks. As investors assume more risk, they are rewarded with higher returns, but at the expense of a higher standard deviation (greater volatility).

What's a Reasonable Growth Rate of Return?

A general rule of thumb is that if you take the decline level with which you are comfortable as a quarterly decline and divide that percentage in half, the result is a reasonable rate of anticipated growth over a three- to five-year period. If the result is less than seven, add a conservative money market rate of 3 to 4 percent. We do this to account for the fact that risk is nonlinear. This can give a simple overview of expected return.

For instance, if you are willing to take a 10 percent decline quarterly, divide that number in half (5 percent) and add 3 to 4 percent; a reasonable rate of growth that you can expect to capture is 8 to 9 percent annually over a three- to five-year period with a properly structured investment portfolio.

Example: If you discovered from the Lifeboat Drill that your client's high-risk money can take up to a 25 percent decline, then your goal would be an investment that would capture 12.5 percent (Figure 7.2).

$$\frac{25\% \text{ decline}}{2} = 12.5$$

It is important to note that sometimes there will be periods when you will experience declines in excess of this amount, and your returns might be

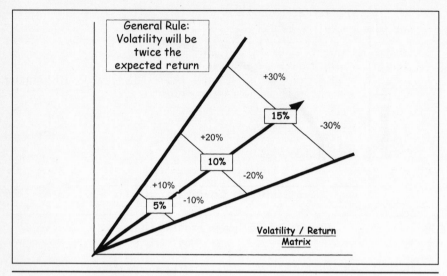

FIGURE 7.2   Risk Increases as Reward Increases.*

*Investors should never rely solely on this or any chart to make investment decisions. Data by: Ibbotson (1926–1994).

superior at other times. This is just an oversimplified example of explaining risk to your client.

What is a reasonable expected return based upon your decline level? Table 7.2 shows what a reasonable expected return is based upon your decline level (column one) over a three- to five-year period. In essence the growth expectations are developed relative to the risk that an investor is willing to assume. Even sophisticated investors tend to focus on their rate-of-return objectives rather than on risk. Your growth rate, however, is going to be a direct result of your willingness to take risk and the realization of the long-term nature of the investment objectives. As you target higher growth, results become much less predictable.

Time Horizon

The ascertainment of the available investment time horizon for each client is basic financial planning. You will need to define how much money your clients are going to need to live the lifestyle they want for the rest of their

TABLE 7.2   Investment Objectives

Level of Decline (%)	Target Growth Rate (%)	Approximate Time Frame	Core Strategy	Riskometer
0	3–5	0–6 months	CDs, money markets	
3	5–6	3–12 months	Bond manager, money markets, CDs, cash	
8	6–8	6 months–2 years	Conservative balanced portfolio, Portfolio 1	
10	8–9	18 months–3 years	Balanced managers, Portfolio 2	
15	9–11	3–5 years	Conservative equity manager, Portfolio 3	
23	10–13	5–7 years	Equity manager, Portfolio 4	
35	11–14	5–10 years	Equity managers, Portfolio 4	
50	12–15	5–10 years	Equity managers, Portfolio 4	

lives. Once you understand what specific goal is in their minds, your investment objective should correspond to those goals. The amount of money they'll need in the future becomes one of their investment objectives. Now, how do they fund this need? That decision becomes their investment policy.

If your client's investment objective is to have $3 million, the question you should ask is: How much risk does he/she have to take to get to $3 million over the prescribed time period? How concentrated does your client need to be in his/her investments?

It's at this point that you're going to match up the expected returns with appropriate investment vehicles based on what you have discovered about your client's risk levels and the time they have to meet their financial and investment objectives.

The Impact of Taxes

Before we can accurately calculate the necessary growth rate for a client's money, we need to calculate the impact of taxes, especially when investing nonqualified money (e.g., money that is not in an IRA or a 401[k]).

If your client wanted to capture 10 percent after taxes, you would need to target different levels of growth depending upon the taxes the client would be realizing. For example, if you were turning the portfolio over and 100 percent of the gains were short-term in nature and your client was in the maximum tax bracket, you would need to capture a 16.5 percent return for your client to end up with 10 percent after taxes. If, however, you wanted to end up with 10 percent and you managed to defer all of the gains so they were long-term in nature (over 12 months), you would only need to capture 12.5 percent. Obviously, by reducing the tax handicap, you can invest more conservatively and have a higher probability of capturing desired after-tax returns.

Owning individual stocks in a separate account portfolio puts control of taxes in your hands. After you've explained risk, time, and the impact of taxes, it's time to discuss why the client should allocate his/her assets.

Selection of Asset Classes

The objective when combining asset classes is to select ones that exhibit low correlation to one another. The concept is to select asset classes that do *not* move lockstep with one another as the financial markets change. In statistical terminology, this implies a low *correlation coefficient* (Figure 7.3).

Here's an example of how this works: Let's examine the period from 1982 to 2001 and track the best-performing sector, and then match it against the

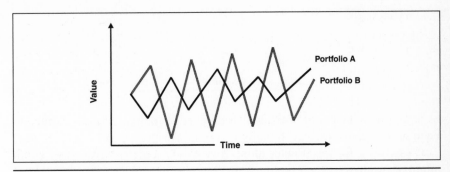

FIGURE 7.3 Portfolios That Have a Negative Covariance. The Two Portfolios Move Inversely.

worst-performing sector in each year. This is an interesting period of time because in 1982 foreign stocks were the worst-performing sector, but in 1983, they were the best sector. Government bonds were the worst-performing sector in 1983, but the top category in 1984.

If you'd been 100 percent invested in stocks over the 1982 to 2001 time frame, you would have averaged 11.2 percent, and you would have had seven down years. If you'd been 100 percent in bonds, you would have averaged 8.7 percent and you would have had six down years. But had you allocated your assets 60/40 percent in stocks and bonds, respectively, you would have averaged 10.5 percent, with only three down years. If you'd been invested one-third each in stocks, bonds, and cash, you'd have averaged 9.6 percent and had two down years.

This is one way of explaining asset allocations and how it can remove some of the bumps, or down years.

This raises the question of what percentages in what asset classes? This is where experience helps. Yes, it depends on risk tolerance, time horizon, and all the millions of little nuances, but sometimes it just comes down to filling a gap (why we do financial planning). If your client says he/she needs to accumulate more assets to retire and can stomach it, you'll have to add more risk to achieve greater returns.

The following are two basic approaches to asset allocation: (1) the style box approach, and (2) the core/satellite approach. Equity style boxes have been popularized by Morningstar, the ubiquitous mutual fund rating organization. Morningstar's style box, started in 1992, features nine boxes in a tic-tac-toe grid, as shown here.

Large value	Large blend	Large growth
Mid value	Midblend	Midgrowth
Small value	Small blend	Small growth

Unless a client's total portfolio is well over $1 million, it is difficult to get adequate diversification with the style box approach unless either (1) mutual funds are used for the smaller allocations, or (2) some categories are eliminated or combined (e.g., creating a small/midgrowth allocation).

Using the style box approach creates numerous questions: What happens when a manager drifts into a different style box? How often do I rebalance? Do I need to use all nine boxes? There is little that can be done with a manager who drifts into different boxes other than replacing that manager with one who is more style adherent. Or, as an alternative, you could use a core/satellite approach.

A core/satellite approach entails creating a portfolio that has as its foundation a core equity fund or strategy that serves as the anchor. This core equity position generally includes both value and growth-type investments, and focuses primarily on the highest quality of companies with the least amount of risk. After the core position is established, the other, more aggressive equity strategies can be added as satellites to the portfolio.

Either approach requires relatively large asset positions in order to properly fill all the boxes or satellites. In many cases, by using a combination of funds and separately managed accounts, you can have access to virtually every asset class while also retaining some level of control over the clients' tax situation. For many advisors, this is the best of both worlds. Some great fund managers do not offer separate accounts or have extremely high minimum account sizes, but their product can be accessed through mutual funds. Some managers specialize in the separate accounts business, and do not have a fund offering. In some cases, a desirable manager may run a fund with a lot of imbedded tax gains, but a comparable product is offered on the separate account side of the business without built-in tax liability.

The obvious way to combine boxes is to collapse the small and midcapitalization categories together, leaving the advisor with six boxes to fill. The result, assuming the managers are well selected, should give the client most of the benefit of the style box diversification without the additional resources required to fill all nine boxes.

There are multiple methods to eliminating boxes. The easiest is to simply remove the center column (i.e., the "blend" column) and allocate assets to the remaining six boxes. If the center column *and* the center row are eliminated, the result is the original style box, which has been used informally for decades:

Large value	Large growth
Small value	Small growth

This is an excellent approach for clients with fewer assets. Many investors have a bias toward growth or value, which can be incorporated into the asset allocation by eliminating a couple of boxes from the "value" or "growth" columns. For example, if Mr. Jones tells you that he is a risk-averse value investor, you might use "Large value," "Small value," "Midblend," and "Large growth." This allocation favors his bias, while insuring participation in the growth part of the equity market (albeit the least volatile of the growth sub-categories).

The core/satellite approach is based on the philosophy that managers should manage the money the best that they can, and advisors monitor the managers. The premise of this approach is that each client has a core portfolio allocation, and then some satellite allocations. Constructing a core portfolio is challenging, but rewarding (see Chapter 9). The core portfolio is characterized by diversification, low volatility, and market participation. Managers are more likely to describe their own investing philosophy in terms of style ("growth" or "value") rather than size ("small cap" or "large cap"). With this in mind, the core of an asset allocation would include a fixed-income portion, a growth portion, and a value portion. Usually, the equity managers used are the go-anywhere type of manager (i.e., a manager who does not follow the capitalization constraints inherent in the style box approach.

The satellite aspect of the allocation can be used in a variety of ways. Some advisors like to tilt client portfolios toward certain asset classes at different times, and use a relatively active asset allocation strategy. The core/satellite approach supports this approach by allowing an advisor to create smaller satellite allocations that can be used to add value to the overall portfolio. By maintaining the bulk of the assets in the core allocation, both the client and the advisor are protected in the event of a poor timing decision. Often, the client or the advisor strongly favors a certain manager or market niche. This could prove to be an excellent complement to the core holdings, providing additional diversification.

For instance, a client might receive a recommendation of:

60% Equities	30% Large Cap Value
	20% Large Cap Growth
	10% Small Cap Core
20% International	15% Developed Countries
	5% Emerging Markets
20% Fixed Income	Muni-Management

Multiple separate account managers could be recommended for each capital market segment. If the investor has adequate assets, up to six different separate account managers might be recommended to properly diversify. If the investor has fewer assets, the recommendation would probably roll up the segments into the three broad categories using three different separate account managers plus a few mutual funds.

The Fixed-Income Allocation

We have discussed how to properly allocate the equity portion of a client's portfolio. To allocate the fixed-income portion, it is first important to determine the desired outcomes. For most investors, the desired outcomes are safety of principal, low volatility, and liquidity. Higher returns are obviously desirable, but it does not make sense to reach for yield unnecessarily. Seeking additional yield generally requires the assumption of additional risk, and most of the time, the additional return does not warrant this additional risk. Simple mathematics reveals the truth of this statement. Assume a 40 percent fixed-income allocation, 60 percent equity allocation. Expected fixed-income return is 4.5 percent, blended equity return is 10 percent. A riskier fixed-income return is available at a 5 percent expected return.

The original expected portfolio return is (40 percent fixed income × 4.5 percent) + (60 percent equity allocation × 10 percent) = 7.8 percent total return for the portfolio. The riskier portfolio has an expected return of 8 percent: (40 percent fixed income × 5.0 percent) + (60 percent equity allocation × 10 percent). An increased risk of principal loss is simply not worth the extra 20 basis points of total return.

Junk bonds, or low-quality bonds that are rated below investment grade, are deserving of their name. Buying junk bonds is definitely an example of reaching for yield. Historically, junk bonds have generated lower returns over time with greater volatility than intermediate-term investment-grade bonds. This has been especially true in the late 1990s and early 2000s. Default risk and high principal volatility make this asset class unsuitable for almost all individual investors.

Figure 7.4 illustrates the risks in below-investment-grade (junk) bonds. The left-hand scale shows the probability of default given the rating of the bond at time of purchase/issuance over the specific time periods noted. Investment-grade bonds are rated AAA, AA, A, or BBB by Standard & Poor's (S&P). In this case, for example, if you had purchased the highest-grade junk bonds (rated BB by S&P), you would have lost, on average, almost 10 percent of your client's principal over a 5-year period and over 15 percent of principal over a 15-year period. And, this chart does not reflect the fore-gone interest rate payments on the bonds that defaulted.

Unless you are an expert in fixed-income securities and can absorb rela-tively high rates of risk on below-investment-grade bonds, we recommend

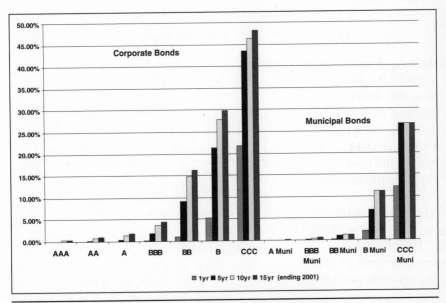

FIGURE 7.4 Cumulative Default Rates.
Source: Moody's

that the majority of your clients' fixed-income exposure be limited to basic strategies using high-quality bonds. Among the primary benefits of fixed income investing are predictability and safety of principal. Trying to generate too much income can compromise these benefits.

How should this be accomplished? As a general rule, separate account minimums for fixed-income portfolios are higher than the average equity portfolio. In addition, fixed-income separate accounts are operationally more difficult. In terms of strategy, we generally recommend finding managers who use only short and intermediate investment-grade bonds. These factors are explained in *The Laddered Bond Portfolio: An Efficient Bond Strategy for Managing Risk and Capturing Market Returns*. This booklet was written by Thornburg Investment Management, Santa Fe, New Mexico, which focuses exclusively on laddering portfolios. For a copy of the booklet, call 800-847-0200.

The historical data clearly demonstrate the superiority of intermediate-term government bonds versus the AAA alternatives of short-term Treasury bills or 20-year long-term government bonds.

In data collected by Ibotson Associates and shown in Table 7.3, you can see that high-quality intermediate-term bonds generate a slightly better return than long bonds with significantly less volatility.

A common strategy often employed in the management of fixed-income securities is *laddering*. This requires buying and holding equal amounts of

TABLE 7.3 Summary Statistics of Annual Returns (40 Years, 1962 to 2001)*

Standard Investment	Mean Return	Standard Deviation of Return
Treasury bills: total return	6.11	2.57
Intermediate-term government bonds: total return	7.52	6.60
Long-term government bonds: total return	7.26	11.54

*All numbers are percentages.
Source: Ibbotson Associates.

fixed-income securities with different maturity dates designed to mature regularly over a defined period of time that can range from 1 to 20 years. When the shortest security matures, it is replaced with a purchase of an equal amount of the longest maturity in the ladder. Laddering tends to outperform other bond strategies because it simultaneously accomplishes two goals: (1) captures price appreciation as the bonds age and their remaining life shortens, and (2) reinvests principal from maturing short-term bonds (low-yielding bonds) into new longer-term bonds (high-yielding bonds).

Laddering also reduces interest rate risk because it shortens the average maturity of a portfolio, which reduces the portfolio's reaction to changing interest rate conditions.

Building the Portfolio

After you've determined the amount of money representing core holdings, you can begin adding other asset classes. This raises the question of *which* asset classes to invest in and in *what percentages*.

For illustration, we have constructed four model portfolios (Figures 7.5 through 7.8), ranging from conservative to aggressive, to serve as guideposts using only very basic allocations of equity and fixed income. We blend a large-cap growth and large-cap value strategy to create effective diversification, and do the same for small-capitalization stocks. Mathematical probabilities of past success determine the mix for each.

The portfolios are rebalanced annually, based on the weight that is assigned to each asset class. The best and worst annual returns for each portfolio are calculated by compounding 12 best or worst months during a calendar year. The average annual return is an arithmetic average during the

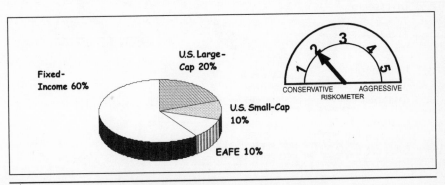

FIGURE 7.5 Portfolio 1—Conservative.

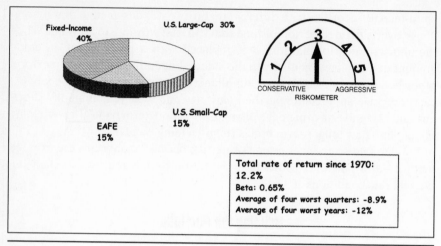

FIGURE 7.6 Portfolio 2—Balanced.

designated time period. The asset class weightings of each portfolio are listed in Tables 7.4 and 7.5.

The following performance is based on a buy-and-hold (with annual rebalancing) strategy since 1970 and does *not* include the impact of taxes or expenses of any kind.

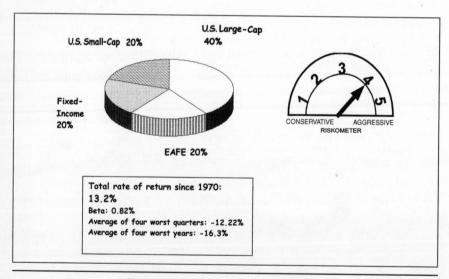

FIGURE 7.7 Portfolio 3—Growth.

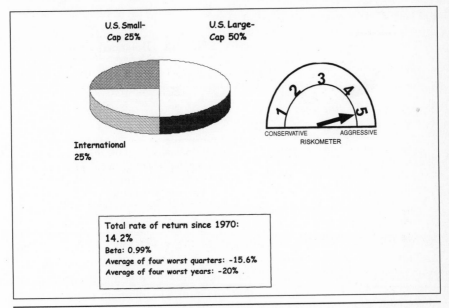

U.S. Small-Cap 25%

U.S. Large-Cap 50%

International 25%

CONSERVATIVE AGGRESSIVE
RISKOMETER

Total rate of return since 1970:
14.2%
Beta: 0.99%
Average of four worst quarters: -15.6%
Average of four worst years: -20%

FIGURE 7.8 Portfolio 4—Aggressive. The U.S. Large Cap and Small Cap Should Be Equally Weighted between Growth and Value.

By averaging the worst four quarters and years (Table 7.6), the extreme results of any given period are eliminated. However, in point of fact, there were declines of greater magnitude than are illustrated here. It is therefore necessary to fully understand the range of available returns to accurately assess your risk tolerance.

It's very surprising to notice how a small increase in the internal rate of return creates significant increases in risk. If you notice that your level of

TABLE 7.4 Portfolio Weightings*

	Large Stocks	Small Stocks	International Stocks	Bonds
Conservative	20	10	10	60
Balanced	30	15	15	40
Growth	40	20	20	20
Aggressive	50	25	25	0

*All numbers are percentages.

TABLE 7.5 Returns of the Portfolios

	Aggressive	Growth	Balanced	Conservative
Rate of return	14.2	13.2	12.2	11
Beta*	0.99	0.82	0.65	0.48
Average worst 4 quarters	−15.6	−12.22	−8.9	−6
Average worst 4 years	−20	−16.3	−12	−8.3

*Beta measures a stock or portfolio's volatility compared with the market as a whole. The S&P 500 is used as the benchmark for measuring the beta of a stock or portfolio. If the benchmark is 1.0, a beta of 1.1 indicates that your stock is 10 percent more volatile than the market. A beta of 0.9 indicates that your stock is less volatile than the market as a whole.

decline tolerance exceeds the average of the worst four quarters, please remember that we're not taking a snapshot of what happened through the quarter, and that certainly there were periods where you were down a lot more in the course of the quarter than the number you see in Table 7.5.

The final step of the asset allocation process entails quarterly performance reporting on the total plan as well as each separate account manager. Specific indices for comparison are selected by the sponsor and recommendations to keep or fire the separate account managers are made periodically.

TABLE 7.6 Individual Asset Classes

	Rate of Return	Beta	Average of Worst Four Quarters	Average of Worst Four Years
Large-cap growth	12.9	1.13	−29.7	−29.7
Large-cap value	15.6	0.83	−17.6	−10.9
Small-cap growth	8.97	1.4	−29.5	−28.8
Small-cap value	17.6	1.1	−23.2	−18.4
EAFE	13.2	0.75	−19.5	−17.8
Long-term government bonds	8.94	0.25	−10.3	−5.8
Short-term government bonds	7.78	0.0	−.4	3.8

Source: The data is from Ibbotson Associates, Inc., from 1970 to 2001.

Most of your clients assume one style will always be in favor. This is not the case. Every manager style has its rotation or cycle. Some say a typical capital market cycle is 45 months from trough to trough, and that no manager style will perform well for more than two-thirds of that cycle, or 2.5 years. Others say a manager performs well for six to eight quarters (1.5 to 2 years) and poorly for eight quarters (or 2 years). Whatever the amount of time, the key is to understand that manager performance among various investment styles goes in cycles.

How can you maintain the same percentages in your asset allocation to maintain proper diversification? You rebalance. Many large pension funds rebalanced their equity positions down to their allocation targets as the bull market pushed equity values upward. Then, during the last two years or so, they increased equity positions as the declining markets dropped those positions below targets. As a result, they have been selling high and buying low. See the logic? When the price is down, you are able to buy more shares. Plus, you're reinvesting the money you've made along with your principal, and *compounding* your growth.

Although the mechanics of rebalancing are fairly straightforward, there are an infinite number of methods that could be used to reach that optimal portfolio goal of maximizing returns while minimizing risk. From a theoretical standpoint, two questions arise: Is rebalancing effective? And, how often should one rebalance?

These are five techniques using 23 years of data (the Russell Indices) to compare their effectiveness and the differences between the frequency of rebalancing annually and quarterly.

"Let It Ride."   This is a passive rebalancing strategy. Under this strategy, the investor simply sits back and allows the style rotation to occur without interference; the market cycles do the rebalancing.

"Back to the Start."   This strategy involves rebalancing all styles back to the original allocation. In the case of diversification equally across six styles, each would be rebalanced to 16.7 percent every time rebalancing took place.

"Tolerance."   This strategy is similar to "Back to the Start," but it allows a predefined tolerance level around the original allocation percentage. For example, a 2 percent tolerance level would allow each style to vary between 14.7 and 18.7 percent. At each rebalancing interval, only those styles that had declined below 14.7 percent of the overall portfolio or increased to greater than 18.7 percent would be rebalanced.

"Robin Hood."   Just as Robin Hood stole from the rich and gave to the poor, this strategy involves taking the gains from the style with the highest weight (highest proportion of the overall portfolio) and giving those gains to the style with the lowest weight at the time of rebalancing. This strategy results in rebalancing only two styles: the one with the highest weight and the one with the lowest weight.

"Reverse Robin Hood."   This is the strategy unknowingly applied by most individual investors. They usually reduce their holding in the style that has declined the most and increase the style that has recently gained the most. This tactic is known as "chasing the hot dot." (See Figure 7.9.)

When comparing the risk/return matrix for each of the five strategies based on rebalancing annually, three strategies produced similar results: "Let It Ride," "Tolerance," and "Back to the Start." However, the other two stand out. The "Robin Hood" strategy improved returns and reduced the standard deviation. The "Reverse Robin Hood" strategy detracted from performance and increased volatility. (See Figure 7.10.)

When increasing rebalancing frequency to quarterly from annual, the passive "Let It Ride" strategy did not change its results. The two strategies most similar to the passive strategy produced similar results. "Tolerance" and

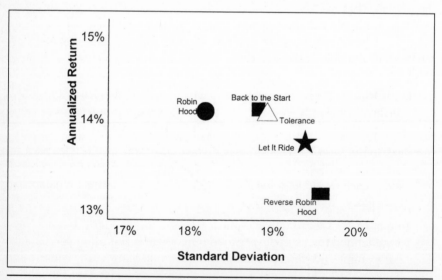

FIGURE 7.9   Rebalancing Annually.
Source: FactSet.

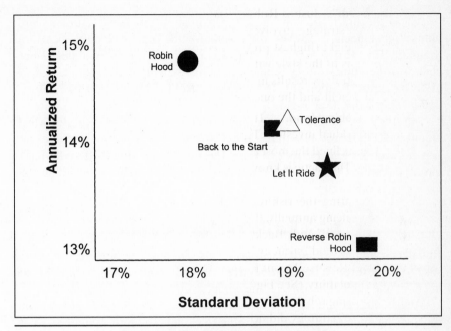

FIGURE 7.10   Rebalancing Quarterly.
Source: FactSet.

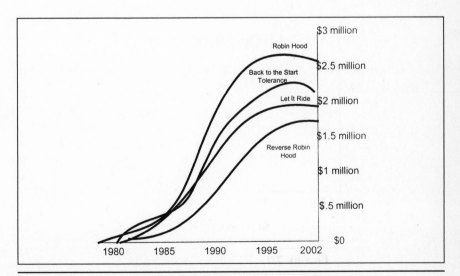

FIGURE 7.11   Growth of $100,000.

"Back to the Start" both offered approximately the same return as with annual rebalancing. However, the results for the other two strategies were dramatic. The "Robin Hood" strategy improved the return by almost 1 percent over the same strategy rebalanced annually, and reduced standard deviation by almost 0.5 percent. The "Reverse Robin Hood" *decreased* returns and *increased* risk. (See Figure 7.11.)

The study shows that more frequent rebalancing improved results, which would indicate that a style that is outperforming the broad market does not stay in favor for long periods of time. The same holds true for a style that is underperforming the broad market: Its out-of-favor status does not sustain for long periods of time.

How to Use These Results to Add Value

Rebalancing an investment portfolio seems simple on the surface, but as you start to think through the method, frequency, tolerance limits, fees, and commissions, the subject becomes quite complex and without easy answers.

You should become knowledgeable about the various issues surrounding rebalancing and, ideally, should be able to explain them to a client in a way that makes the desired method acceptable and persuades the client that *value is being added* to the consulting process. Once you've decided on the asset allocation, then you're ready to look at which management strategy should be employed.

Additional Reading

Roger C. Gibson, *Asset Allocation—Balancing Financial Risk,* Irwin, Burr Ridge, IL, 1990.

Understanding the Different Styles and Types of Managers

T oo many choices sometimes confuse advisors; too few may not allow for a successful investment strategy. If this is too basic, just skip on to the next chapter. It's good for explaining to clients.

Following is a description of the types of separate account managers and what they do.

Separate account managers generally fall into one of following asset class subcategories: growth, value, balanced, international, global, income (taxable or tax-free), money market fund, and specialized. From here it can get confusing. The terms that most programs use are elementary descriptions of the various types of asset classes.

Your clients read terms like *small-cap, mid-cap,* and *large-cap* and may not understand what they mean. The word *cap* is an abbreviation for *market capitalization.* Capitalization indicates the size (the value of a corporation as determined by the market price of its outstanding stock) of the companies that are being invested in. Cap is calculated by multiplying the number of outstanding shares by the current market price of a share. It is important to note that the definition varies by market conditions and by practitioner, but the concept is universal.

Small capitalization.

Stocks with a median market cap of up to $2 billion.

Medium capitalization.

Stocks with a median market capitalization between $2 and $7 billion.

Large capitalization.

Stocks with a median market capitalization of more than $7 billion.

Growth Management Styles

The goal of growth managers is to purchase companies that are growing earnings per share (EPS) at a rate above the market average. Typical sectors include finance, technology, energy, health care, and retail. Many of these companies possess high returns on equity, high sales growth, and low yields due to reinvestment of profits. Debt is occasionally used, but usually remains less than 40 percent of capital. Investors typically pay a premium in terms of price to earnings or price to book in order to buy companies with higher-than-average EPS growth. One of the risks is that the price of a growth stock is capitalized by revenues alone, because valuation is not supported by a stream of dividends or earnings. If actual earnings are less than are expected by analysts, the price may falter significantly. Growth stocks often exhibit high volatility, even in low-volatility market environments. Growth stock investing usually performs better in a slow to moderate growth economy, as investors will pay a premium for above-average earnings growth. In times of a rapidly expanding economy, the premium paid by investors for growth stocks may expand significantly, thereby incurring greater price risk and volatility.

Growth Substyles

Momentum-based growth.   This is a more aggressive approach focusing on earnings acceleration, relative price strength, and earnings strength.

Earnings surprises and revisions are often very important and may trigger purchases and sales. Portfolio turnover will likely exceed 200 percent annually, and may be several multiples of that. Momentum managers are buying high-expectations stocks that are extremely susceptible to earnings disappointments. Examples of momentum growth managers include Driehaus, Sirach, Bjurman, Navillier, IBD.

Pure growth. Investors usually focus on long-term projected growth rates (3 to 5 years). Fundamental research plays a very important role in identifying those companies that have a catalyst for growth. Accurate prediction of future growth in EPS is critical, as is identifying the key company-specific risks. PIC and HBSS are examples.

Conservative growth. The portfolio will contain companies that could be considered *blue-chip* in nature. The portfolio generally includes stocks with lower price/earnings (P/E) ratios and should generally be more diversified with less sector over- or underweights relative to the benchmark. There is often more of an emphasis on consumer goods companies with stable earnings histories and low debt serviced by good cash flow. This strategy will usually have a lower portfolio turnover. Examples of these types of managers include Voyageur and Baird.

Value Style Characteristics

The goal of value managers is to purchase stocks when they are priced low relative to the market, or when their (P/E) ratio or price-to-book ratio is low relative to other companies in the same industry. In essence, the managers are looking for value-priced securities when considering everything else. Value stocks generally are less volatile than growth stocks, generally have higher yields than growth stocks, and represent more mature established companies.

Value Substyles

Yield. Above-average income stream through higher-than-average dividends. An example of a firm that focuses on yield is Domino & Delaware.

Contrarian. An extreme form of value investing focusing more on searching for companies or industries with excessive negative psychology. A manager example is MJ Whitman.

Asset and private market value. The main analytical tool is free cash flow analysis of the separate divisions and the company as a whole.

Off-balance sheet or undervalued assets are the prime sources of the discrepancy to realize the value. A manager example is Roxbury.

Low P/E.   This is the most common approach when analyzing multiples. The critical factor is the definition of the earnings component. A manager example is Lazard.

Low price to cash flow.   Cash flow is preferred by many investors over EPS as a measure of profitability of the company. A manager example is Oppenheimer.

Multifactor approaches.   Dividend discount models, P/E versus growth (earnings surprise, return on equity (ROE), etc.). Manager examples are Boston Co. & NWQ.

Value Managers

Value stocks have low book-to-market ratios, which means the stock is trading at a low price compared with its book value. Book value is defined as the company's assets on a balance sheet, less its liabilities, and is often figured on a per-share basis. If a company has a book value of $15 per share and the stock trades at $12, it may be perceived as a bargain.

Large-cap value.

An investment strategy that invests in stocks of large companies with an average capitalization of approximately $7 billion or greater.

Mid-cap value.

An investment strategy that invests in stocks of mid-sized companies with an average capitalization of between $2 billion and $7 billion.

Small-cap value.

An investment strategy that invests in stocks of smaller companies with an average capitalization of less than $2 billion.

Value and growth stocks tend to behave differently. There are market cycles when value stocks outperform growth stocks, and other periods when growth stocks outperform value stocks. In general, a growth investor's returns are more volatile than a value investor's returns. Both styles in a portfolio can even out performance over time. When one group is underperforming the market, the other is generally outperforming it.

Each of these styles represent varying attributes—they can be used separately or together. It is your job to properly fit each style given the risk profile of your client. You can begin to determine that allocation by answering two essential questions:

1. What is the time period until your client will need his/her money?
2. What percentage of decline in a given quarter can they tolerate without panicking?

Clients with a longer time frame until they retire or otherwise need their money can afford to have a larger allocation of growth stocks with longer time periods between rebalancing. Investors with shorter time frames, such as three to five years, may need to review and rebalance core holdings every six months.

Value and growth investments rarely perform in lockstep. In some years, growth performs better. In other years, value comes out on top. By blending these two very different styles, you balance your risk and enhance your opportunities for reward.

Value managers seek their returns by buying low-priced stocks that are currently overlooked or out of favor, but are expected to come back into fashion. If you've ever booked discount airfares during off-peak travel times, you've already practiced what value managers preach.

On the surface, buying out-of-favor stocks may appear to be a risky proposition. But when you look deeper, you'll see that value stocks feature two characteristics that help reduce their volatility:

1. *Below-average prices.* Because value stock prices have already been heavily discounted, additional market downturns generally result in less downside risk.
2. *Above-average dividends.* Value stocks normally pay higher dividends, which help to cushion the impact of any negative returns.

Growth managers prefer the stocks of already fashionable, fast-growing companies and are willing to pay a premium for such accelerated growth. Put another way, value aims to buy low and sell high, while growth is content to buy high if it means selling even higher.

Both value and growth styles have their merit, which is why a core equity portfolio strategy blends both value and growth, again depending on the risk profile of the client (Figure 8.1).

Table 8.1 tracks three portfolios for 10 years. Notice the significant difference between the returns of the all-growth and all-value portfolios in 1999. Except for the period of 1994 to 1997, one style strongly outperformed the other. However, when you look at the 10-year cumulative returns, all three portfolios resulted in 17 percent–plus returns. Maybe the middle portfolio smoothed out the year-to-year volatility somewhat, but bottom line is that they're all pretty close.

You will notice that these results are quite high, since we have gone through an amazing market where both bonds and stocks have done extremely well.

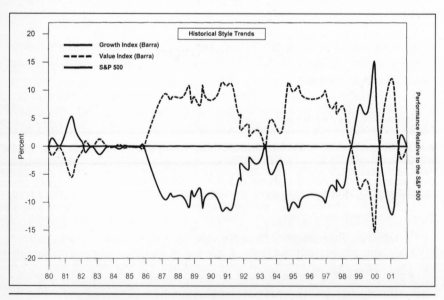

FIGURE 8.1 Core Blends Value and Growth Chart.

TABLE 8.1   A History of Three Portfolios

Year	Growth 100 percent	50/50 Blend	Value 100 percent
1991	41.16	32.76	24.61
1992	5.00	9.41	13.81
1993	2.90	10.51	18.12
1994	2.66	0.35	−1.99
1995	37.19	37.77	38.35
1996	23.12	22.43	21.64
1997	30.49	32.86	35.18
1998	38.71	26.81	15.63
1999	33.16	20.25	7.36
2000	−22.42	−7.69	7.02
10 yr (Annualized)	17.33	17.68	17.38

Source: Frank Russell Company. Growth and value returns are that of the Russell 1000 Growth and Russell 1000 Value indices. Past performance is no guarantee of future results.

International Managers

Subcategories of international managers include:

Diversified international.

Typically leaves control in the hands of the manager, and with investments diversified across developed countries and industries.

Diversified emerging market.

Focuses its investment on those economies that are still developing and growing. These are some of the most volatile managers.

International growth.

Focuses their portfolio on stocks of high growth international companies.

International value.

Focuses the portfolio on stocks of undervalued companies worldwide.

International investing. Investors could miss over 50 percent of the world's equity investment opportunities if they don't consider investments outside of the United States.

World Equity Market Capitalization

- United States: 46.7 percent
- Canada: 2.1 percent
- Europe: 32.7 percent
- Japan: 9.0 percent
- Pacific, excluding Japan: 3.2 percent
- Emerging markets: 6.3 percent

American depository receipt (ADR). May improve diversification and help boost overall return while reducing overall volatility. ADRs are the vehicle of choice:

- They are U.S. securities.
- Eliminate the need for currency transactions.
- Portfolio of ADRs can correlate fairly highly to the MSEAFE Index.
- Cost effective way to invest overseas.

For example, a client who would like to mimic the Morgan Stanley Capital International benchmark, MSEAFE, can purchase 50 names and attain a tracking error of less than 3 percent.

Balanced Managers

A balanced separate account manager includes two or more asset classes other than cash. In a typical balanced manager, the asset classes are equities and fixed-income securities.

These portfolios stress three main goals: (1) income, (2) capital appreciation, and (3) preservation of capital. This type of manager balances holdings such as bonds, convertible securities, and preferred stock, as well as common stock. The mix varies depending on the manager's view of the economy, market conditions, and the prospectus.

Most balanced managers hold between 40 and 60 percent bonds, between 40 and 60 percent stocks, with the remainder in cash in their portfolios.

Fixed-Income Manager

The investment objectives of fixed-income managers are safety and income, rather than capital appreciation. Income managers invest in municipal bonds, corporate bonds, or government-insured mortgages; if they own any stocks at all, these are usually preferred shares. The danger is chasing higher yields and not looking at the risks.

Subcategories of fixed-income managers include:

U.S. fixed-income.

These managers invest in U.S. government and corporate. They will typically invest in higher-quality investments with little risk of default. This strategy is used in both taxable and nontaxable investors.

High-yield.

These managers typically invest in low-quality debt and are subject to a high risk of default. Therefore, they tend to offer a higher yield, but your risk increases significantly.

Municipal securities.

These managers invest in a portfolio of municipal securities that generate tax-free income. These portfolios are appropriate only for taxable investors including individuals and specific industries.

Government.

These managers invest in debt from the U.S. government. By their nature, they are quite conservative, depending upon the maturity of the underlying bonds.

International fixed-income.

These managers specialize in investing in bonds of international governments and are usually riskier than U.S. investments since they also suffer from currency shifts.

Global-bond.

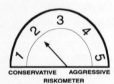

These managers invest in foreign, as well as in U.S., bonds. Historically, global-bond managers have outperformed domestic managers, but you do assume additional risk.

Money Market/Cash

Money market funds are the safest type of mutual funds if you are worried about the risk of losing your principal. Money market funds are like bank savings accounts.

Summary

The goal is to find managers that complement each other. By properly diversifying a portfolio between value and growth, domestic and international, equity and fixed income, the overall portfolio will experience less volatility.

Building a Core Investment Portfolio

Your firm may have guidelines in place for building client portfolios, or you may have the primary responsibility merely to select a manager for your client's accounts. Regardless of responsibility, you still need to understand the process of building the core portion of a portfolio.

Structuring a portfolio is like painting a picture: You combine different factors to create an overall effect. You put together specific managers to generate an expected return with an expected rate of risk based upon consistent investment manager styles.

The following is an established example of how you could build a core investment portfolio inside your separate account program. The goal of creating a core portfolio strategy is to confirm that a designated portion of the portfolio is designed to perform well in all market environments. This gives both the client and advisor confidence that the risks are understood and that a certain level of comfort is attained.

The foundation of functional investment activity is to build a base starting with a core objective; it is the basis upon which all asset management strategies are built. Regardless of the ultimate mandate of the portfolio, whether its focus is risk control, income generation, or seeking capital appreciation, it is critical to build and maintain the core of the portfolio *first*.

A core investment strategy within an investment portfolio generally supports growth while providing stability the same way a tree grows efficiently upward, outward, and downward all at the same time. The more solid the core, the greater the strength and confidence level in the total portfolio.

Establishing and adopting a core philosophy is the first thing an advisor or individual investor does—whether the investor has $100,000 or $10 million. A typical financial planner may be using multiple style boxes: small-, mid-, and large-capitalization equities on one axis; value, growth, and blended equities on the other axis, in addition to multiple classes of fixed-income securities. However, most individual investors' core portfolios need only contain the broader asset classes—growth and value equity investments and fixed-income investments.

By acknowledging the concept of core investing, and recognizing how other investment strategies can be implemented around this core, a healthy relationship between advisor and client is created. It is therefore essential that both advisors and clients understand the theory of core investing because it represents the platform from which all comprehensive investment strategies spring.

The Process of Developing a Core Portfolio

Even though most financial advisors explain *core* as the center of the style box, or a central investment strategy around which other, more style-specific funds or sectors can be built, it must be recognized that a core investment strategy is different for every investor (Figure 9.1). The portfolio's core positions should be representative of a proven investment strategy employing stocks, bonds, and cash strategically allocated based on certain factors such as investor objectives, return requirements, and risk profile.

Our philosophy is to hold higher-risk-type investments outside of the core. As a result, if there are negative, unanticipated consequences associated with a risky investment, there is minimal, if any, effect on the core of the portfolio. By following this type of strategy, the amount of money representing core holdings is identified; similarly, the amount of money at significant risk is also identified.

Your job at this point is to help your clients find the optimal balance between risk and reward for their assets. Younger investors can afford to have a larger allocation of growth stocks with longer time frames before rebalancing, but older investors who are three to five years away from retirement or already in retirement may need to review their core holdings every

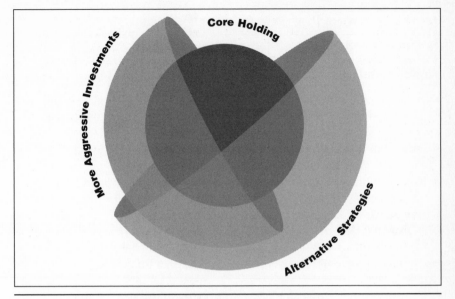

FIGURE 9.1 Chart of Three Rings.

six months. Also, considering lengthening life expectancies, the traditional rules of financial planning regarding the shift from equities to bonds may very well be altered. In this sense, the core portfolio may be very different among these different investors.

As an individual investor gets closer to retirement or to his/her predefined money goal, the core asset class percentages may shift between equity and fixed income, but the ultimate goal of the core remains the same: protecting against both actual loss and loss of purchasing power. Thus, the core is built around what an investor cannot afford to lose within any specified time parameter.

An uninformed investor might claim that a core strategy, which employs both stocks and bonds, is nothing but a guarantee of mediocrity. The portfolio will never be concentrated in the top-performing asset class, but that is okay. Every study shows that nobody can forecast which asset class will represent the winning strategy with any indication of reliability. Therefore, to avoid the probability of being wrong most of the time, the objective is to build a diversified core portfolio, and build it with an understanding of the investor's psychology (Table 9.1).

The initial balance within the core portion of the portfolio between equities

TABLE 9.1 Investor Psychology and Core Investments

Serious Investors with Informed Core Portfolio Strategy	Day Traders and Speculators with No Core Investment Strategy
■ Focus on long-term success (building wealth).	■ Focus on short-term or daily success (desire for overnight wealth).
■ Individual investments are part of a larger system.	■ Investments are viewed independently.
■ Rules around investing require accountability.	■ Rules around investing require exactness.
■ Relationship with investment advisor, planner, or brokerage firm involves dialogue.	■ Relationship with investment advisor or brokerage firm is always in jeopardy.
■ Ability to repair and recover—not replace.	■ No room for error.
■ Growth through expansion of the system.	■ Growth through independent investments.
	■ Emotional insecurity.
	■ Lack of commitment.

and fixed income is determined by the overall risk tolerance of the investor. Mathematical probabilities of past success, historical patterns of volatility, and correlation analysis among various asset classes are reviewed to determine the actual asset allocation and relative percentages between the fixed-income and the equity components. Because the purpose of the fixed-income portion of the portfolio is to reduce risk and provide liquidity, that portion should represent relatively stable asset values with reliable and predictable income streams, whereas the equity portion represents opportunity for capital appreciation and dividend income growth, albeit with greater risk and volatility. The goal is to achieve an acceptable balance, which over time will meet identified financial objectives. Only after this core allocation is established will the effort be directed to establishing investment positions outside and beyond the core.

There are various attributes of an investment discipline or investment manager that contribute to achieving the level of confidence required to qualify the designated equity and fixed-income securities as the core of the portfolio. Some of these attributes may differ for the equity and fixed-income markets, but they are all similar in that they form the basis for building confidence in the core portion of the portfolio.

Core Equity Attributes

A primary belief of a core equity manager is that the ultimate method of controlling risk is through excellent stock selection. For example, if a company is high quality, reporting a growing stream of earnings and the price paid for the stock is reasonable, by definition, the stock should have less risk relative to other stocks.

If the portfolio is full of these *excellent* stocks, the relative risk of loss or volatility should be less than other noncore stock portfolios, where the objective will differ. This rule applies equally to both growth and value equity managers because excellent stocks can have either or both growth and value attributes. In essence, *growth* is not necessarily a dirty word to a core value equity manager, and *low price* is not necessarily an impediment to a core growth equity manager. In the case of separate accounts, this mission can be accomplished with both a core growth and a core value manager working together to achieve the overall objective.

A core equity strategy is generally not bound by capitalization or geographical constraints, because these inherently restrict investment opportunities or cause early forfeitures of gains or forced loss realization if strictly applied. In addition, strict application of these constraints may require a manager to avoid a capitalization range or specific country that is in favor while requiring participation in either a range or geography that is underperforming.

Core equity managers generally do not believe in momentum investing, which in many cases, is based on emotion or market psychology rather than investment fundamentals. Momentum investing also often leads to the application of specific investing or selling rules with little or no flexibility to adapt to unique circumstances. A stock that is sold solely because it has doubled may not become a success story if it thereafter continues to appreciate but at a slower rate.

An experienced portfolio management team is a necessary component in building confidence in the core portion of an investment portfolio. Some of the more significant experience factors include a philosophy of investing only in businesses that are understood by the managers as well as the ability to recognize, and then correct, mistakes early. Oftentimes, the first sale is the best sale, thereby affording the opportunity to move on to other opportunities.

Other attributes of character include a natural reluctance to follow the crowd, a tendency to engage in independent thinking, adherence to a fundamental investment philosophy despite changes in market sentiment or falling security prices, and recognizing that the importance of a sell discipline is equal to that of a buy discipline.

Finally, within the core portion of any portfolio, tax management is an important objective. Regardless of the rate of portfolio turnover, the ultimate result should be a high degree of tax efficiency relative to realized gains and losses.

Core Fixed-Income Objectives

There are four fundamental objectives that all investors expect from the fixed-income portion of their portfolio:

1. Return of principal
2. A predictable income stream
3. Minimized market price fluctuations
4. Liquidity

Of these four objectives, return of principal is the top priority. Obviously, because fixed-income securities are really debt instruments whereby one party lends money to another, the credit quality of the borrower and the ability of that borrower to repay is the most significant consideration. Within the core, the lowest-risk fixed-income securities often are debt instruments with short and intermediate maturity ranges and high credit quality ratings.

Because an objective is not to maximize capital appreciation within this segment of the portfolio, absent are high-yield bonds, emerging market debt, and other fixed-income securities with enhancement options. Portfolio managers typically concentrate more on credit quality than yield; they create broadly diversified portfolios with multiple holdings, thereby increasing the odds of preserving the principal value of the portfolio.

The predictability of the income stream, while primarily dependent upon the credit quality of the borrower, is also dependent upon the length of the maturity of the securities. While it is common for longer-term bonds to pay a higher rate of interest than shorter-term bonds, there is little to be gained by extending maturities beyond the intermediate maturity range since the higher market risks of the longer-term bonds are not offset by a significant or proportional increase in income. For the core portion of the fixed-income portfolio, it is much more desirable to sacrifice minimal amounts of income in return for less market price volatility. Portfolio managers of core fixed-income portfolios generally understand that the future level of interest rates cannot be predicted with any significant level of accuracy. As a result, the desire for maximum income generation must be compromised with the desire for lower risk and volatility.

All fixed-income securities are subject to market price fluctuations, which are caused by two circumstances: (1) changing interest rates and (2) changing credit quality. Because a primary purpose of the fixed-income portion of the core portfolio is to reduce overall portfolio risk, a common strategy is to purchase only investment-grade short- and intermediate-term fixed-income securities. Even though these securities will never be the highest-yielding securities available, they will satisfy the objective of minimizing price volatility. In addition, this strategy naturally supports the other two goals of protecting principal and providing stable income because of the inherent nature of the securities themselves.

Another risk that must be controlled is reinvestment risk. Because it is impossible to predict future interest rates or lock in current high yields for long periods of time without incurring excessive market price risk, a short or intermediate laddering strategy is often employed within the core portion of the fixed-income portfolio.

This accomplishes the objective of providing relatively high income while also affording the opportunity to take advantage of future interest rate changes as additional liquidity is generated by both coupon payments and maturing bonds. By staying within the short or intermediate time frames, the portfolio is able to capitalize on opportunities presented by advantageous interest rate changes rapidly while also avoiding significant pitfalls from negative interest rate movements. With a laddered bond portfolio, it is also easy to match the risk profile of the portfolio with the risk tolerance of an investor merely by managing the average maturity of the portfolio.

Finally, acceptable liquidity parameters are required of the fixed-income portion of the core portfolio. In times of investor economic needs, the first source of liquidity is often the fixed-income securities because the chances of having to realize a loss are less. In addition, income payments may have been reinvested regularly, resulting in more availability of liquid funds. An investment's liquidity is directly related to the size of the market and the number of participants in that market. U.S. Treasury notes are very liquid, while below-investment-grade corporate bonds have much less liquidity. As a result, one of the attributes of the core fixed-income portfolio is that it comprises a collection of high-quality securities diversified across many industry sectors, maturity ranges, and coupon yields, all with high degrees of liquidity.

Summary

When attempting to create the core portfolio with separate account managers, the challenge is to select either individual managers who embody an investment style representative of core or a combination of managers whose portfolios collectively meet the objective of core. Of course, this is dependent upon the size of the overall portfolio—larger portfolios will permit multiple managers, and the smaller ones will require the identification of one or two managers who can satisfy the objective. The important point to remember is that whatever investment managers are selected, their investment style and discipline must be capable of instilling in both the investor and the financial advisor the confidence necessary to conclude that the assets placed in their hands are representative of a core portfolio.

If properly constructed, the core can form the foundation of the total investment portfolio and should meet your client's general investment objectives. It should be the first place an investor looks for comfort and security and the last place that causes an investor anxiety or panic. It will form the base from which all other more aggressive noncore investment strategies can be launched, and at the same time, serve as the safety net to which long-term investors can retreat in times of economic or financial turmoil.

In Chapter 10, you will learn how to write an investment policy statement that will do more to assure the success of your investment program than any other steps you take.

The Creative Process of Writing an Investment Policy Statement

T he creation of an investment policy statement is representative of a fundamental task that all investors should undertake. It should be an overriding objective of every financial advisor who is working in the separate account arena to have an investment policy statement for all of his/her clients.

A common mistake advisors make is that they simply don't take time to write an investment policy statement. Or they write vague investment policies that state the obvious without giving managers any genuine guidance. Statements such as "little or no risk," "maximize return," or "preserve capital" are virtually useless to a portfolio manager unless they are clearly defined and explained.

A written investment policy statement enables you to discover your client's long-term goals and objectives—plus, it will serve as a guideline for implementing the investment strategy. The written policy statement helps you maintain a sound long-term plan, when short-term market movements cause you to second-guess the actions you have previously taken.

All separate account investors should have an investment policy statement that outlines their goals and how their money will be invested to reach those goals. Here's why: People are human and can get caught up in the emotion of the day. It is only through long-term planning that your clients are going to be successful and not fall back into old habits. In the heat of a market downturn, it is critical to have thought out strategy ahead of time and to have it documented so that they will not deviate from its path.

Creating an investment policy statement embodies the essence of the financial planning process: assessing where you are now, where you want to go, and developing a strategy to get there. Having and using this policy statement compels you to become more disciplined and systematic, increasing the probability that your actions will be appropriate in times of economic or market distress, while also satisfying your investment goals.

There are six steps to establishing an investment policy:

1. *Set long-term goals and objectives clearly and concisely.* Long-term goals can be anything from early retirement to purchasing a new home. One of the most common goals we have found among our clients is to be financially independent. What that often means to our clients is that their investment portfolio will provide them with the income necessary to maintain their quality of life and that it will continue to increase at a pace greater than the cost of living.

2. *Define the level of risk your clients are willing to accept.* Along the road to reaching financial goals, there are going to be bumps caused by the downturn in various market cycles. It is important that your clients understand the amount of risk they're willing to tolerate during the investment period. In designing a portfolio, it must be determined what the absolute loss your client is willing to accept in any one-year period is without terminating his/her investment program. As we know, no one can predict market movements, and your clients have to be in a position to weather any storm.

One way to determine the level of risk in a portfolio is to look at its performance during 1973 and 1974. Investors should be honest with themselves. No one can predict the future. The years 2000–2002 might be similar to 1973 and 1974. It was during these years that we experienced the worst financial recession since World War II. There is a 5 percent probability that in the next 20 years we will experience a similar downturn. You probably remember waiting in line for gas. The Standard & Poor's 500 (S&P 500) lost 37.2 percent and small-company stocks lost 56.5 percent. Most investors would have a hard time maintaining a long-term perspective and staying with their investment program in markets like this.

If an investor is working with a financial advisor, he/she can request an analysis of how the portfolio mix would have performed during 1973 and 1974. The portfolio mix with which the investor would have been comfortable should be selected. If the account would have been closed because of that downturn, there was too much risk and a lower-risk model portfolio should be constructed. Investments tend to be cyclical, and no one can predict their performance in the short term. The best-performing year for both the S&P 500 and small-company stocks was 1975, when they earned 37.2 and 65.7 percent, respectively, which interestingly was right after the bear market of 1973 and 1974.

A more recent reference point is the bear market of 2000 through 2002, which, as of this writing, is continuing. This market has resulted in the Nasdaq index dropping more than 75 percent from its all-time high! And, the result could be that, for the first time in more than 50 years, the major market averages will end up down three years in a row. Consider the performance of various portfolios, various managers, various investment styles in this type of market and then determine with what portfolio structure your client is most comfortable.

3. *Establish the expected time horizon.* Investors have to determine the investment period in which their capital will be working for them to achieve the designated financial objective. For the equity portion of their portfolio, the minimum expected investment period should be at least five years. For any portfolio with less than a five-year time horizon, the portfolio should consist predominantly of fixed investments. This five-year minimum investment period is critical in analyzing and determining the level of risk the investor is willing to assume. For all investment endeavors, the investment process must be viewed as a long-term plan for achieving the desired results. One-year volatility can be significant for many equity asset classes but this surely is not representative of a long-term investment process as embodied in an investment policy statement. However, over a five-year period, the variability of returns is greatly reduced with more predictable results and identified risk parameters.

As the chart in Figure 10.1 indicates, if you're planning to invest for a lifetime, the range of returns of a diversified model portfolio (encompassing only equities) becomes minimal.

4. *Determine the rate-of-return objective.* Even sophisticated investors tend to focus on their rate-of-return objectives rather than risk. The rate of return is going to be a direct result of the willingness to take risk and the length of time the assets are invested. In getting started, your clients should write down a range of returns that would be acceptable.

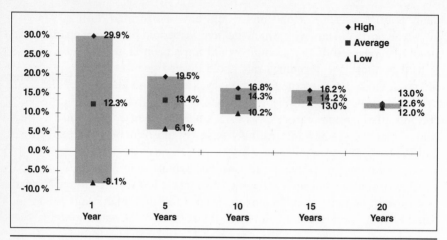

FIGURE 10.1   Conservative Model Returns, 1972 to 1993.

You should then conduct a study of modern portfolio theory investment results to determine what the optimal portfolio should look like given the amount of risk your clients are willing to assume. In this way, you will be focusing on actual historical results to determine the various asset class weightings that have the greatest potential of meeting their rate-of-return objective while maintaining the risk profile they are willing to assume.

5. *Select the asset classes to be used to build the core portfolio.* List all the different asset classes that you might want to consider in the portfolio. You may be surprised with the differences between what you've been using in the past and what you should be using. Once you've identified them, you need to determine how you're going to allocate capital to each asset class and what asset classes will represent the core portion of the portfolio (Table 10.1).

6. *Document the investment methodology to be used in managing your portfolio.* As we discussed in Chapter 3, there are three basic investment methodologies: (1) security selection, (2) market timing, and (3) core investing. The only proven methodology for the prudent investor is to use core investing strategies that, when implemented, result in a properly diversified portfolio with understandable levels of risk.

However, admittedly there are many investment methodologies to achieve the same objective. Some of these would include lump-sum investing, periodic investing over specified time frames, market weighting allocations, as well as style-specific versus a blended approach. Regardless of which

TABLE 10.1   Risk/Return Comparisons

Level of Decline (%)	Target Growth Rate (%)	Approximate Time Frame	Core Strategy	Riskometer
3	3–5	0–6 months	CDs, money markets	
6	5–6	3–12 months	Bond fund, money markets, CDs, cash	
8	6–8	6 months– 2 years	Conservative balanced portfolio, bonds: Portfolio 1	
10	8–9	18 months– 3 years	Balanced fund: Portfolio 2	
15	9–11	3–5 years	Conservative equity: Portfolio 3	
23	10–13	5–7 years	Equity fund: Portfolio 4	
35	11–14	5–10 years	Equities: Portfolio 4	
50	12–15	5–10 years	Equities: Portfolio 4	

Action: Write down a range of returns that would be acceptable. You can use this range of returns for each risk level as the framework to determine the return expectation for the portfolio, as well as for the component asset classes.

Target growth rate: _____

Make sure the target growth rate aligns with the time horizon.

Notes: Find the target rate-of-return percentage; be aware of the level of decline that may be experienced, and then look at the Riskometer to see what the level of risk is.

approach is undertaken, separate account managers and separate account programs are flexible enough to meet the demands of any investor or financial advisor.

The written policy statement will enable you to better define your client's investment expectations and put you in a position to decide how best to implement it.

Selecting Separate Account Managers

Many advisors have a stable of investment managers they like and have used for other clients. They prefer the approach of these managers, and probably have good contacts at the investment management firms, as well. Most brokerage firms have an approved list of managers, or allow only a preselected collection of managers to offer managed accounts through their brokers. This involves a *bottom-up* selection process.

Bottom-up means first selecting a handful of preferred managers, and then building client portfolios around them. The alternative to this is a *top-down* approach; that is, first determining which types/styles of managers are needed for an allocation, and then finding the best manager to fill each slot. Both approaches have their strengths and weaknesses (Table 11.1).

Either way, manager selection begins with the screening process (Figure 11.1). Most firms use in-house analysis to find and evaluate the managers that best fit their due-diligence criteria in each sector.

One of the first steps in the screening process is to visit investment managers and go through due-diligence checklists, as well as trying to identify the key factors that have made that manager particularly successful. The fact-finding team then comes back and presents its findings to the evaluation committee. The evaluation committee's job is to scour the findings for flaws. Things like, "Hey, let's go back and check this," or "I've heard of this firm

TABLE 11.1 Strengths and Weaknesses of Two Investing Approaches

	Strengths	**Weaknesses**
Bottom-up	■ Best managers used ■ Smaller stable of managers for the financial advisor to follow ■ Usually allows managers to go to where the performance is	■ Higher correlation among managers ■ Tendency to have few managers managing most of client assets
Top-down	■ Each style represented by best-in-class manager ■ Style box friendly ■ Lower correlation among managers	■ Managers constrained by style ■ Financial advisor has to do due diligence on many different managers

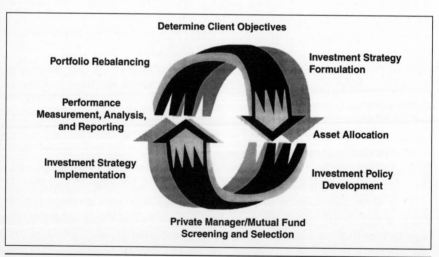

FIGURE 11.1 Selecting Suitable Separate Account Managers—Investment Consulting Process.

before," or "I had a bad experience ten years ago with this firm," or "so-and-so switched firms ten times," get pitched back to the fact-finding team, which then has to go back and justify its conclusions. Only after thorough reviews, extended discussions, and relevant analytical analysis is a final decision made (Figure 11.2).

Screening Process Criteria

The process of qualifying the manager is better known as *due diligence* by the investment industry. This simply means that care has been taken to substantiate the suitability of a manager. However carefully this process is implemented, the criteria in performing due diligence is subjective in nature, and the process is difficult to learn. Here's a basic outline of the steps involved.

Preliminary Screen

There are preliminary criteria that must be met before a manager can be considered. Criteria may vary depending on the asset class of the securities. The preliminary screening usually includes the following criteria:

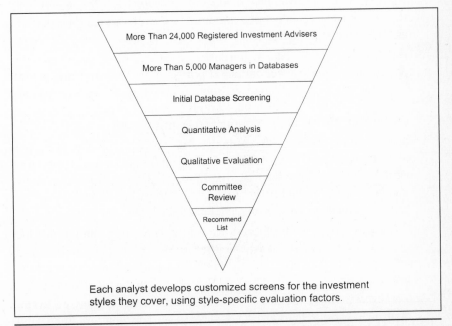

FIGURE 11.2 Separate Account Research—Manager Filtering Process.

- *Assets under management.*   At least $300 million under management.

- *Length and documentation of track record.*   A verifiable five-year track record, based on the Association for Investment/Management and Research (AIMR) standards. Personnel responsible for the track record should still be at the firm.

- *Consistency of personnel.*   Little or no turnover among the investment professionals.

- *Registration.*   Properly registered with the Securities and Exchange Commission (SEC).

- *Compliance.*   No involvement in any investigation or litigation that would be deemed material.

Quantitative Criteria

The next step is to evaluate the manager's investment style, behavior, consistency, added value, and performance in different market cycles. These criteria may change depending on the asset class under consideration (Figure 11.3).

Predictability of performance relative to benchmark.   R-squared and tracking errors are calculated and analyzed over various time periods against an appropriate benchmark.

Style analysis.   Firms take different approaches, which may include: return-based analysis, fundamental portfolio analysis, and investment philosophy and process analysis. Some firms use a variety of databases to analyze style by a return-based regression methodology. This analysis can also illustrate the amount of style drift over time.

Risk-adjusted performance.   An analysis of performance generated per unit of risk taken is performed by looking at the following factors over various time periods: alpha, Sharpe ratio, and Information ratio. These numbers are analyzed relative to the appropriate benchmark, as well as to other managers in the same asset class.

Consistency.   Along with other indicators, this measures the ratio of the quarters in which the manager outperforms to the quarters in which he/she underperforms, plus the manager's performance over rolling time periods.

Market cycle analysis.   The performance of the manager may be examined over various market cycles, such as up and down markets, and when the manager's style is in favor versus when it is out of favor.

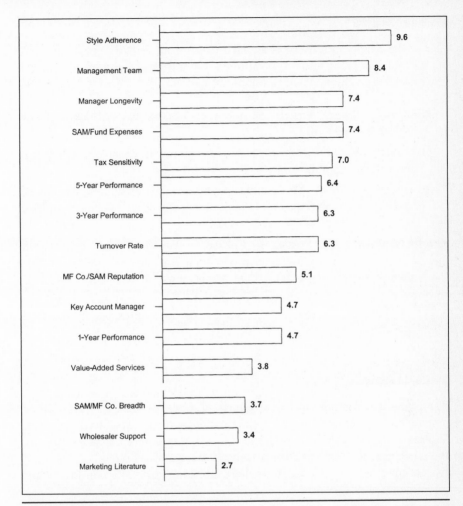

FIGURE 11.3 Rate Selection Criteria (1–10)—Style Adherence Was the Most Highly Rated Selection Criterion.

Source: 10/18/01 Asset/Mark Conversation (Cordes); 10/18/01 FundQuest Conversation (Clift); 10/17/01 Run Money Conversation (Kitchens); 10/17/01 Greenrock Conversation (Malone); 10/15/01 LPA Conversation (Zentner); 10/12/01 ADVISORport.Com Conversation (Collins); 10/15/01 Vista Analytics Conversation (Page); Tiburon Research & Analysis.

Qualitative Analysis

This analysis helps determine if the factors that contributed to past perform-ance are still in place and are positioned to contribute well into the future. The following components are evaluated:

Personnel. Tenure, experience, depth, continuity, and skill level of key investment personnel.

Investment philosophy and process. The portfolio construction process and underlying philosophy.

Investment research. The generation of earnings estimates, sources of credit research on bonds, and the number of industry specialists and the areas they cover.

Implementation of the investment process. The checks and balances in place at the money manager are examined to ensure that the invest-ment process is implemented uniformly across all accounts.

Business structure. The business plan and financial condition of the firm are analyzed, as well as the compliance procedures and back-office operations.

Investment Committee Review

The analyst conducting the due diligence on the investment firm compiles a summary report along with a recommendation, and presents it to the sponsor firm's investment committee. The investment committee discusses, probes, and challenges the report before arriving at a consensus opinion on the man-ager. Managers that survive all of these steps are generally considered for recommendation to clients.

Ongoing Monitoring Process

Once a manager is approved, it is the responsibility of the firm to monitor the following on a quarterly basis:

- Consistency of application of the stated investment discipline
- Dispersion of returns among accounts
- Reported aggregate performance versus performance in individual accounts

Managers can be removed from the recommended list once deterioration is noted in the qualitative factors mentioned previously, or if a manager consistently underperforms his/her benchmark over a market cycle. Some examples of deterioration are:

Personnel change.   The potential for disrupting the investment process increases dramatically whenever a key investment professional departs.

Investment process.   A manager will be terminated if the style and risk posture changes from the mandate for which the manager was hired.

Consistency.   If a money manager does not adhere to the stated investment style, he/she will not continue to be recommended as an approved manager for that style.

Inability to manage growth in assets.   If a money manager's corporate infrastructure is unable to provide good operational support, communication, and client service, the manager will be removed from the recommended list.

Unexplained poor performance.   Persistent, sustained underperformance relative to the money manager's peer group may trigger removal from the recommended list.

What about Performance Numbers?

We all have individual investment requirements. Individual investment needs often cause managers to handle portfolios in different ways. The way managers choose to report on these portfolios leads to different performance results. Consequently, performance numbers often tell less about a manager than the investor assumes.

In looking at money managers, what you really want is consistency of results. Don't just pick the managers who had the highest rate of performance over the last couple of years; invariably, they will underperform over the next couple of years.

What's ADV?

You do have other alternatives for gathering information about managers. Because the SEC regulates investment managers, you can gain access to additional information from the disclosure statements on file with the government.

The most important of these disclosure documents is the form ADV, which must be filed by all investment advisors seeking registration with the SEC, with annual updates thereafter. By law, the manager must provide Part II of the form (or equivalent disclosure) to prospective clients. While Part II is the only form legally required to be furnished to the public, it is a good idea to request both Parts I and II.

The form ADV provides basic background information on the manager's state registrations, disciplinary or legal problems, ownership, potential conflicts of interest with fees or commissions, financial condition, and the background of the firm's principals. Investors should keep in mind that the SEC never passes on the merits or accuracy of the information provided in the ADV. Its purpose is to place basic information about the manager on public record.

Having access to an ADV gives you the opportunity to do some basic background checking. Obvious areas of interest are prior employment of the firm's principals and the manager's educational background. When legal actions against the firm are discovered, investors should try to obtain copies of the court-filed complaints. By checking with the SEC's enforcement division, the investor may uncover actions taken by the SEC against the manager for regulatory violations.

The Form 13F Filing

If the manager manages $100 million or more in equities, then SEC regulations require that a quarterly 13F filing be made. This filing states the equity positions and the number of shares in those positions held by the manager. Because the manager submits his portfolio positions quarterly, these reports often accurately predict the manager's performance for the coming quarter.

Some managers may argue that, because portfolio adjustments often occur between filings, the 13F is an inaccurate performance measure. Most managers have portfolio turnovers of about 25 percent a year or higher. Even at a 40 percent–per year turnover rate, the average quarter has only a 10 percent change in portfolio positions—a relatively small amount. This gives you another way of comparing the manager's publicly reported performance with his/her SEC 13F filings.

What to Ask a Separate Account Manager

A manager's disclosure is, by nature, a one-sided viewpoint. There are numerous questions we could list here that would be prudent to ask the manager, but for the sake of brevity, let's address two of the most critical. First, what is the history of the management team? If managers have come and gone, then it is important to know who they were and why they left. As with any organization, a management team must work well together if it is going to succeed. If there is dissention among those making the decisions, portfolio consistency might suffer.

The second question, if truthfully answered, is one of the most telling pieces of information about any manager. Ask the manager to state the total asset value and the number of new accounts acquired and lost during the past five years. A good manager has little to fear from this question. On the basis of this one piece of evidence alone, most investors could save themselves much trouble.

Other factors investors might want to know are the size of the firm, how long the firm has been in business, its client list, and any referrals the principals might want to disclose. Common sense dictates that these basic questions need to be explored. Investors should be careful of firms that are growing so fast that service and performance could suffer. These managers must place additional time and attention on the administration of their business. This can sometimes be detrimental to securities research and portfolio performance.

In your own research, use some of the questions we use. If it's not practical for you to get to that level, you can go to major brokerage firms or similar services offered by independent advisors. We will now go through a checklist of criteria for performing manager due diligence. The key element is to discover if the research provided you is absolutely independent and conflict-free.

Once you're comfortable that the advice you're being given is conflict-free, then you can evaluate the manager's history and experience.

Conducting and Managing the Interviews

When it comes to interviewing managers, any question is fair game.

- Know who is responsible for key decisions such as establishing the level and timing of cash reserves; deciding the emphasis to be placed on themes, sectors, and industries; determining which stocks are to be purchased and sold; developing the actual portfolio; and reviewing portfolio results.

- Dig into the background of the staff. Newer firms might oversell the backgrounds of the key people and their accomplishments at other companies because the new firm does not yet have a track record.

- Quiz each candidate about his/her investment style. When does the firm do well in a market cycle? When doesn't it? You could take this approach one step further by asking the candidate about the actions he/she takes when the market moves against the firm's style.

Part of understanding the investment process requires an assessment of risk at the portfolio level. Among the considerations should be: How is diversification used? How often are strategic changes made?

Your client must understand the relationship between risk and return to make informed and prudent investment decisions in order to properly evaluate money managers you recommend.

Measuring Manager Performance against Inappropriate Benchmarks

Use the indexes, but blend them proportionately to match the composition of your portfolio. If you restrict your balanced manager to a specific asset allocation mix, measure the account against the indexes in the same proportions. That means for an account with a 40 percent allocation to bonds and a 60 percent allocation to stocks, the bond return should be measured against 40 percent of the return of the Shearson Lehman or Salomon bond indexes or other appropriate benchmark, and the stock return should be measured against 60 percent of the return of the S&P 500 or other appropriate index.

You must also measure returns against the indexes that match the asset class or substyle in which you are invested. How many times do clients use the S&P 500 to assess the performance (or lack) of their Nasdaq stock positions? And how many times do they measure the performance of their S&P 500 positions against the Dow? Maybe the Dow is up 12 percent, but their portfolio gained only 8 percent. The Dow is only 30 stocks. The S&P is 500. If their S&P portfolio didn't own all 30 Dow stocks, how can they expect it to have performed the same way? Or how can they expect their small-cap portfolio to measure up against the Nasdaq 100?

The Manager Profile

The manager profile, which explains the investment style, philosophy, and process of each money manager, also gives a snapshot of the manager's performance history and his/her largest current holdings.

Research Reports

Research reports or quality performance summaries review the current status of qualitative factors for each money manager. They also explain the market and business cycle factors that affected recent performance.

Sector Summaries

Sector summaries place the recent performance of each money manager within the context of the relevant investment style sector, and compare manager performance with a peer group. Once a money manager is placed on a firm's approved list, the research team continues to monitor the characteristics that indicate that manager's relative strength.

This ongoing oversight is designed to help you identify and evaluate changes in a manager's process or effectiveness, and to help you recommend changes to your clients when appropriate.

You really want to look for consistency in the manager's style and in performance comparisons with his/her peer group. This type of monitoring will help you assess the predictability of the manager's results—a key element of the benefit the manager will offer your clients. When presenting a separate account manager, you want to look like an expert.

What Can You Expect Administratively from a Managed Account?

There is generally more paperwork involved with a managed account, but the nice part is the ability to see the individual holdings that the manager picks. This allows you to be more involved with what's actually happening in the account. This is far better than waiting to see a proxy report showing the trades and the motivation behind them. The proxy report comes months after the fact. In a separate account, you see the trades when they happen.

Performance Reporting

The AIMR Board of Governors endorsed a set of performance presentation standards designed to raise the ethical and professional practices of the investment management industry. The performance standards provide investment managers with a standardized format for calculation and presentation of their performance results for clients.

In his book, *Investment Policy,* Charles Ellis cites commitment to client service and soundness of business strategy as important criteria for manager selection. He says you also must have a clear concept of how the firm will add value to your portfolio.

Manager selection involves planning, obtaining basic information, interviewing, selecting, and formalizing. The planning is done during the investment policy and asset allocation stages.

One big mistake is choosing the firm that made the best presentation. Don't turn the manager selection process into a beauty pageant, which is what happens if you base your decision mainly on the 30-minute or one-hour marketing pitch each firm gives. One of the key factors in choosing a manager is gaining a solid understanding of the firm's investment process. You won't always get that from a presentation.

Knowing When a Manager Is Heading for Trouble

These tips will serve as possible red flags when monitoring money managers:

- Your client's portfolio is reassigned to another staffer.
- The departure of one or more key investment people at the manager's firm or the promotion of the manager.
- Several major clients terminate their accounts with the manager.
- Assets under management decline.
- Assets under management increase dramatically.

Such information should be given to an advisor immediately. You can learn of any of these occurrences from competing money managers and from the trustees and executives of other funds. Once you learn of the defections, dig for the reasons for them, and determine the effect they may have on your client's portfolio.

Perhaps your client's investment policy statement calls for balanced management and the manager restructured the portfolio to emphasize or deemphasize either equities or fixed-income securities. This will upset your client's asset allocation strategy, and you may wish to fire this manager and choose another.

If a firm's assets have decreased, your job is to find out why. Maybe the firm has become too successful and is having difficulty digesting its rapid growth. Perhaps the key decision makers who built the portfolio's record are being forced to bring in second-stringers—younger, less experienced portfolio managers—to handle all the new accounts as well as some of the old ones.

What effect will this have on the portfolio's record going forward? Or maybe a firm has taken on too much money too fast and is, therefore, being forced to change its investment style.

Performance Slipped

Don't panic—a slippage in performance doesn't necessarily mean that the firm has lost its luster. If you hired the firm as a large-cap manager, and small-cap stocks suddenly are soaring, it makes sense that your manager's results will be less than stellar. Before firing the manager, reexamine your client's investment policy to determine if you want to stick with a large-cap strategy.

If communication with your manager breaks down, it could mean the principals of the firm know they are in trouble with their current client base. Perhaps they can't market their equity numbers because they are mediocre, so, in

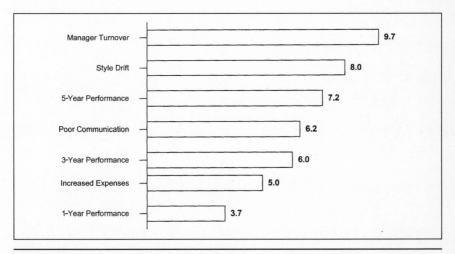

FIGURE 11.4 Rate Selection Criteria (1–10)—Manager Turnover and Style Drift Were the Two Factors Most Likely to Lead to Being Dropped as a Manager.

Source: 10/18/01 Asset/Mark Conversation (Cordes); 10/18/01 FundQuest Conversation (Clift); 10/17/01 Run Money Conversation (Kitchens); 10/17/01 Greenrock Conversation (Malone); 10/15/01 LPA Conversation (Zentner); 10/12/01 Thomas Weisel Partners Conversation (Braitberg); 10/15/01 Vista Analytics Conversation (Page); Tiburon Research & Analysis.

an effort to maintain revenue growth, they diversify their product line to hide the mediocrity and avoid discussing the problem areas.

Maybe ownership of the firm has changed. Firms can change hands or go public because the previous owners want to add some liquidity to their net worth (Figure 11.4).

After selecting the appropriate managers, it would be beneficial to revisit the investment policy statement to confirm that the investment parameters based on the client's goals and objectives have indeed been followed.

CHAPTER 12

The Control Account

I t is unrealistic to think that your affluent clients are going to liquidate everything and place it in a one-product solution such as a separate account. What they *will* do is use the separate account to consolidate their more liquid holdings, such as:

- Mutual funds
- Vested company stock
- Cash proceeds from the company
- Inheritance
- Individual stocks

The Control Account Sales Process

Using the separate account as a control account dramatically alters the separate account sales process. Asset allocation and picking the best manager take a back seat to customizing the separate account to fit neatly and efficiently into the investor's overall investment strategy. Creating the highest probability of meeting the investor's objectives on time with net dollars becomes the highest priority.

In this environment, the roles of the sponsor and money manager start to look very similar. If a sponsor is coordinating the control account, he or she is definitely taking on the fiduciary role and are controlling investment decisions. The money manager can very easily step up to provide these additional fiduciary services. As the competition heats up for this role, it will be difficult to distinguish a sponsor from a money manager.

If this control account theory is correct, then fewer stylized managers will be required in the separate account market. Instead, a smaller number, capable of providing a broader array of capital market expertise, will be desirable. Large firms that have expertise in the full array of investment styles, and can package those styles into one core offering, will be in high demand.

By the very nature of multiple-style investing, a large firm that offers this capability starts to look like a sponsor. Basically, the only piece that is missing is the front-end process of coordinating the product offerings with the investor's other long-term investments.

Out-of-date strategies may be appropriate for nontaxable institutions for which the investment time horizon is infinity and for which results must be reported quarterly, but they are not appropriate for high-net-worth individuals. The separate account's customization features are most advantageous for taxable investors. High-net-worth taxable investors are very different from institutions in that:

- They pay taxes, which is the single largest barrier to investment performance.

- They have a specific time horizon and a specific point at which they need liquidity.

- They know, or their advisor can help them determine, approximately how much money they will need.

These are all, at the end, tax-related issues. When managing money for high-net-worth investors, taxes have to be viewed as an investment expense.

The Best of All Worlds

Some separate accounts can be managed to take into consideration less liquid investments as well as tax-efficient investing. If an investor has a large position of restricted stock, the separate account can diversify around that position. The separate account is usually the only investment in which this high-net-worth investor can control the taxable outcome in lieu of selling his/her investments. Therefore, the separate account can be used to minimize the tax liability of the investor's overall investment strategy.

As taxable events occur in the less liquid investments, the results should be fed into the control separate account to allow the portfolio manager to either try to mollify realized gains or take advantage of realized losses to reposition or rebalance the separate account.

Theoretically, the most efficient separate account might have one core manager who diversifies over multiple capital markets, but some investors may be uncomfortable with only one manager.

Cerulli Associates' solution is the *unified managed account* (UMA). The idea is to place several different managed accounts run by different managers into one account.

The Unified Managed Account

This singular offering acts as an umbrella under which an investor may hold assets in different types of investment vehicles—including separate accounts and mutual funds. In this environment, investors will see a coordination of efforts and a focus on a comprehensive investment-planning approach in the advisor-client relationship. As such, the UMA is focused on client needs rather than the investment vehicle or the program. The asset allocation decisions are made by the manager of all the underlying managers. The idea is to make sure that the growth manager isn't selling Philip Morris while the value manager is buying it. But under this scenario, the broker-advisor merely becomes the manager of the manager of the manager—got that?

Jack Rabun of Cerulli explains that it would remove the advisor even further from the asset allocation process. For many this would be welcomed. But these advisors must also consider that their part of the fees can and should be lowered in this case, because they are giving up part of the service responsibilities of the account.

Divergent and expanding investor needs led to the birth of the UMA. Clients demand and desire financial advice, guidance, and appropriate portfolio diversification. The UMA is not only aligned with clients' interests, but is also in tune with the way advisors conduct their businesses using multiple investment vehicles to suit investor needs. Coordinating a complete investment plan for a client is exceedingly burdensome due to the fact that managed account programs are not synchronized with each other.

For example, a client may be invested in both a mutual fund advisory and a consultant program—each having its own set of paperwork, account statement, and performance report. The UMA ushers in a simplified and consistent advice delivery platform centralizing client profiling, performance reporting, investment vehicle selection, asset manager research, and a single asset-based fee (Figure 12.1).

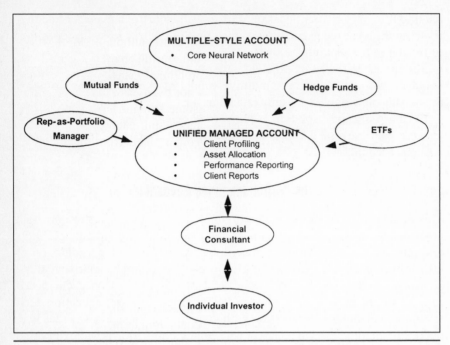

FIGURE 12.1 Unified Managed Accounts Platform.

It often makes more sense from the end-client perspective to collapse these programs into one integrated offering. For example, some portions of an investor's allocations may be large enough for a separate account, but other portions may be better suited to mutual funds. Collapsing the programs strips away the emphasis on product packaging and opens the door to expand managed account platforms to include alternative investment vehicles.

Brokerages continue to push up-market, attempting to service high-end clients who demand access to alternative investments such as hedge funds. Historically, the use of hedge funds in a managed account setting has been limited. Cerulli analysts believe that broader research access into the world of alternative vehicles is required prior to usage in a UMA. As access opens, brokerages will need to build the suitable research and monitoring capabilities.

To date, most brokerages have built their offerings distinctly, without anticipating future collaboration. However, broker-dealers are now looking to build scale, control costs, and meet the spectrum of advisors' and investors' complex needs. The UMA provides a centralized, consistent platform for brokerages to support and service their financial consultants' fee-based business.

Technology hurdles are the main constraint delaying advancement of the end-to-end UMA concept. The theory makes sense, although the question remains regarding how the account can be built. Cerulli analysts are tracking several large sponsor firms that are in the preliminary stages of mapping a UMA design. In practice, the transition has not been easy, especially when working with outdated legacy systems, and some systems have been at the drawing board for at least three years. System requirements are distinctly complex, leading sponsor firms to cobble together pieces from several technology providers.

Early strides toward UMA implementation have been made primarily by third-party vendors. For the most part, third-party vendors are building managed account platforms from the ground up, so outdated legacy systems are not an obstacle. As a result, both new managed account entrants and existing sponsors that are employing the services of a third-party vendor have been early adopters of the UMA.

Until now, these vendors have largely been engaged by independent broker-dealers, Registered Investment Advisors (RIAs), and banks due to the lack of appropriate in-house resources within these entities to fully support a managed account platform. However, the complex system requirements involved in building a UMA are opening more doors for third-party vendors. There are huge opportunities for this group to penetrate larger sponsor firms, such as regional brokerages, wirehouses, and holding companies.

Wells Fargo introduced its own version of the UMA in 2001. The program is not biased to mutual funds or separate accounts. The initial launch has been to the traditional bank brokerage channel, with around 1,000 advisors who market to clients in the firm's bank branches. Wells Fargo has segmented its customer base primarily by client asset level, and has plans to roll out a customized version of the platform to the distinct units that service the multiple segments.

Cerulli Associates believes that the UMA will develop into the standard broker-dealer-sponsored managed account platform. Client profiling and risk assessment in conjunction with a financial advisor will continue to be the most valuable attribute of the managed account experience.

An Argument against the Single Control Account

Many of the other programs that started in the early 1980s grew in large measure by taking money away from banks, which had been providing asset management and custody to large pools of institutional assets for years. They also served as a single-source provider of these and other financial services.

The advent of the investment management consulting industry (and the fiduciary responsibility defined by the Employee Retirement Income Security Act [ERISA]) resulted in a fundamental change in the way that institutions handled their qualified plan funds.

How were the new broker-consultants able to convince these clients to take their money out of the banks and give it to the new programs? There were two convincing arguments. The first sprang from academic research and was based on historical market behavior. It convincingly demonstrated that a tremendous share of portfolio performance was derived specifically from asset allocation.

The second was a less concrete concept, but one that resonated strongly with the sponsors of these huge retirement plans. It fit seamlessly with the management theories the sponsors were hearing. When the institutions' money was at the bank, they had only the bank's managers' expertise at their service, and the banks were not world-class money managers. The new broker-consultants offered them the best of breed, a multimanager scenario using large, household-name money managers.

Prompted by a desire for good returns and a fear of the liability suggested by the rather strict interpretation being put on that child of ERISA (i.e., the prudent investor), institutions reversed their generations-long practice of keeping all their financial dealings at one place (the bank) and poured money into investment management consulting programs. Because the clients were institutions, the consulting process that grew up around this phenomenon was heavily oriented toward *total return*. Taxes were, of course, largely irrelevant. And, because they had an essentially eternal time horizon, the only risk that concerned the client was short-term volatility.

As the institutional market matured, program sponsors turned their attention to wealthy individual investors. In creating individual programs, however, providers simply cloned their institutional process and lowered the minimum account size to put it within reach of the individual. What was good for the goose was good for the gander, right? In the exciting market environment of the late 1980s, these programs were very successful and highly productive for their sponsors and the consultants who built practices around serving individual clients.

Finally, in the late 1980s and early 1990s, mutual fund wrap programs took the process to an even lower minimum investment level. For the $100,000 needed to open one wrap account, the investor could get several mutual funds within a single account, with consultant oversight and periodic rebalancing for consistent asset allocation.

Through the 1990s, the market roared and sponsors of managed money programs, including mutual funds and separate accounts, provided access to significant wealth accumulation potential for virtually every level of investor. By the time the 18-year bull market softened and subsequently then corrected, there were many more affluent investors (and many more financial advisors) than the world had ever seen.

During the correction, the individuals who were investing taxable assets quickly developed an appreciation for the difference between total return and after-tax, or absolute, return. In this atmosphere, separate accounts gained ground swiftly, thanks to their greater flexibility, which enables easy rebalancing, and the potential for tax efficiency. In addition, new technologies enabled money managers to increasingly systematize sophisticated tax-efficient strategies like tax loss harvesting and tax lot optimization.

So, back to the present, we look at the UMA and see a curious thing: a tendency among consumers, rooted in their understanding of the importance of coordinating investment activity, to value the benefits of a single source provider.

Using a single source provider and, therefore, a single perspective on what's best for the investor, you can certainly argue that we have an evolved product, vastly improved technological support, and a far better informed consumer. The UMA is the product that best serves this new fact set.

Packaging Investment Styles

Let's look at various packaging investment styles, including multiple-discipline products, multiple-style accounts, single accounts, and turnkey asset management programs.

Multiple-Discipline Product

You may know it under different brand names, but the multiple-discipline account (MDA) has quickly captured an impressive amount of assets. It appears to be a neat solution to the problem of making separate accounts accessible to a broader universe of investors than ever before.

The concept is as follows. A professional money manager runs a separate account, managing it across a broad spectrum of the equity market, usually an entire capitalization range or style category. To do this, MDAs are divided into subportfolios, called *sleeves,* that are managed to a specific subsection of the MDA's announced discipline.

This structure enables one money manager to run a diversified portfolio, controlling rebalancing and managing for absolute return, rather than requiring, for instance, three managers to communicate and coordinate on these issues, all of which are extremely important to the individual investor. Furthermore, the MDA is being offered at investment minimums in the neighborhood of $150,000.

Now, most sponsors of separate account programs offer per-account minimums of $100,000 or even $50,000, but it takes at least $400,000 to $500,000 of investable assets to achieve good asset allocation and diversification in style-specific separate accounts. For investors in the $150,000 category, we generally recommend diversifying among a series of mutual funds.

The advantages of MDAs lie in the ability of a manager to achieve significant diversification within one portfolio, serve the client's needs, and make a profit on the product, all at the $150,000 level. If this holds true for the long term, program sponsors will be able to make these products available to a huge new market.

The Multiple-Style Account (MSA)

Historically, single styles managed by a single manager in separate accounts have been the focus of this industry. You now have multiple-style account (MSA) arrangements emerging that package together a variety of investment styles in predetermined percentages—often with lower investment minimums—in both single and multiple account arrangements.

The evolution of broker-dealer-sponsored separate accounts can be compared with that of mutual fund advisory programs, a marketplace that has captured $128 billion in assets in three types of programs. In the late 1980s, the nascent fund advisory industry began its run with structured preset packaged portfolios (in which investment committees dictated the portfolio mix), followed by the introduction of middle-ground hybrid programs. Finally, open programs developed, in which the broker-consultant, after going through a stringent training program, becomes the money manager with nearly unrestricted discretion. Consultant programs are following a similar path, but moving in the opposite direction—from open to packaged programs.

Until now, separate account consultant program sponsors—in an effort to strengthen their products and services—focused their efforts on refining the due-diligence process, upgrading underlying technologies, and improving marketing efforts to reach their advisors. Tremendous corporate resources were channeled into these programs.

At the end of the process, though, clients still relied heavily on the advisor's ability to assemble a portfolio of managers. This was not a huge problem in the past, as knowledgeable advisor-consultants were largely responsible for building the industry. However, with the brokerage industry spotlight now on separate accounts, lower-level advisors are becoming more active in the business and will interact increasingly with new asset manager entrants—some of whom have little separate account experience. Cerulli's research reveals that, more than half the time, advisors select fewer than three managers, and most select a single manager.

Single Accounts

Citigroup Asset Management has developed a multiple-discipline account (MDA). As you will recall, MDAs are single portfolios that provide access to multiple investment styles, but with a level of professional oversight and coordination across all securities. Citigroup's family of MDAs, which combine nine proprietary investment styles in varying combinations, now totals more than $10 billion in assets. They offer seven equity-oriented portfolios of between two and four styles each, with investment minimums between $100,000 and $300,000. They also offer seven balanced portfolios, each with an integrated fixed-income component, to provide greater asset diversification. These portfolios include three to four strategies and allow minimums of $200,000 to $500,000.

Citigroup's MDA is not made up of new styles, but rather a combination of existing separate account strategies with performance histories of 10 years or more. Another differentiator is that all securities in an MDA are housed in a single account, which means that there is one performance report and one portfolio manager contract. Dedicated professional investment personnel oversee the coordination of the portfolios with the primary responsibility of avoiding securities overlap, monitor weightings, and when appropriate, take gains and losses across portfolios to maximize tax efficiency. This sets MDAs apart from offerings that merely assemble a mix of unaffiliated managers, resulting in distinct separate accounts where the portfolio managers do not talk to each other.

Citigroup expanded the concept by introducing another version of MDAs through its Salomon Smith Barney Consulting Group unit, a longtime leader in the managed account industry. The new offering, called diversified strategic portfolios (DSPs), has five multistyle portfolios with the mixes determined by the Consulting Group's proprietary manager research program. These programs provide single-manager access to five unaffiliated third-party managers that run one of the diversified portfolios. Managers include Putnam Investments, Strong Capital Management, TCW Investment Management, Alliance Capital, and JP Morgan Fleming.

UBS's Brinson Advisors also entered the fray with its Private Wealth Solutions program, which offers a range of multiple-asset portfolios (MAPs). The program, which targets affluent high-net-worth individuals, is sold through the UBS PaineWebber network and was introduced in early 2002.

The offering is a range of blended portfolios drawn from six underlying strategies and sold in one account. The investment minimum to access the new products is $150,000.

This multimanager format brings together the capabilities of several different managers in a single account, requiring coordination among managers to ensure that the overall portfolio is run in a tax-efficient manner. In theory, because each of these distinctly branded managers sits under the control account umbrella, the structure facilitates a heightened level of cooperation among them, though as this publication went to press, the exact specifics of this interaction were not yet known.

Although it is possible that totally unaffiliated managers may someday seek out complementary competitors to create unique MSAs, Cerulli Associates believes that the likelihood is low, and will ultimately become a moot point once technological advancements provide this ability to program sponsors.

Single-account MSAs are not the only way in which sponsors are trying to simplify the consulting process to deliver diversified separate account solutions to a broader range of advisors and clients.

What Are the Turnkey Asset Management Programs (TAMPs) Doing?

Firms like Lockwood Financial, the largest third-party provider of separate account consultant programs, are targeting advisors interested in a more automated investing approach by combining unaffiliated managers in a portfolio of different weightings. Lockwood's multimanager program, launched in May 2001 and called Managed Account Xpress (MAX), offers three series of stylized portfolios using a subset of managers from its stable of 52 asset management firms. Investment minimums range from $50,000 to $100,000, and assets can be invested in equity, balanced, or sector portfolios. Pricing ranges from 0.95 to 1.10 percent for equity and 0.40 percent to 1.10 percent for balanced, excluding the advisory fee charged by the financial advisor.

Lockwood's program, and others that combine multiple unaffiliated managers, is different from a traditional MSA in that Lockwood does not automatically combine the separate accounts established by each manager into a single account. Rather, they maintain distinct portfolios. However, if requested by both the advisor and client, they will household the accounts using aggregation technology at the workstation level. It is here that issues such as wash sales and security overlap are monitored. The firm is also reported to be close to adding a series of single-manager MSAs to its platform (Figure 12.2).

SEI is another firm promoting the multimanager separate account concept, building on its position as the industry's largest mutual fund advisory program sponsor ($26 billion as of year-end 2001). In SEI's program—started in April 2001—the firm replicated its hallmark approach of constructing predetermined multimanager portfolios and targeted the independent broker-dealer (IBD) market, a fertile environment for separate account packaging.

Unlike Lockwood, where Registered Investment Advisors (RIAs) can assemble their own separate account portfolios in addition to MAX offerings, advisors using SEI may only use SEI's sanctioned portfolios. In the SEI program, client assets are invested in multiple accounts, as opposed to the single MSAs discussed earlier. There is currently no ongoing securities coordination across individual styles, although all styles are initially constructed to reflect a fit with each other. This program resembles Frank Russell's separate accounts-based managed portfolios program in which client assets are invested with multiple managers in multiple accounts. Like other programs of

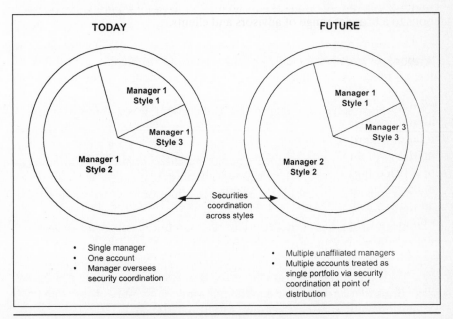

FIGURE 12.2 Multiple-Style Account.

this genre, the program currently lacks ongoing securities coordination across styles, although Russell does attempt to avoid securities overlap through a sophisticated front-end manager investment-style research method.

Cerulli Associates believes that the industry is just beginning a prolific separate account product development initiative. They expect more single-account MSAs, and they anticipate important advancements in technology and underlying securities coordination that will enable multiple accounts run by multiple unaffiliated managers to be managed as a single portfolio.

These products are poised to play an integral role in a client's total investment portfolio, where the separate account would serve as the neural network, or clearinghouse, for the client's full range of investments. Industry efforts are already under way to make this happen. As an example, Lockwood Financial, an early advocate of the control account concept, is restructuring its platform to incorporate the tax ramifications of investments outside of one's managed account portfolio. As this takes hold, it will further strengthen the power of the UMA and provide an additional boost to the popularity of managed accounts.

The Control Account Process

Using the separate account as a control account dramatically alters the consulting process. Asset allocation and picking the best manager takes a back seat to customizing the separate account to fit neatly and efficiently into the investor's overall investment strategy. Creating the highest probability of meeting the investor's objectives on time with net dollars becomes the highest priority.

If a sponsor is coordinating the control account, it is definitely taking on the fiduciary role and is controlling the investment decisions. The money manager, who is no longer perceived simply as one with a "hot" hand, can very easily step up to provide these additional fiduciary services. As the competition heats up for this role, it will be difficult to distinguish a sponsor from a money manager. Both sides should be looking for ways to provide these additional services.

If our control account theory is correct, then fewer stylized managers will be required in the separate account market. Instead, a smaller number, which can provide a broader array of capital market expertise, will be desirable. This would indicate further consolidation of the money management industry. Large firms that have expertise in the full array of investment styles and can package them into one core offering will be in demand.

By its nature, a large firm offering multiple investment styles will start to look like a sponsor. Basically, the only missing piece is the front-end process of coordinating the sponsor's internal offerings with the investor's other long-term holdings. We would not be surprised at all to see a large money management firm or mutual fund company purchase a smaller sponsor to acquire this front-end capability.

Large sponsors will realize that, with less perceived value in manager selection, they may want to internalize portfolio management. This would dramatically increase their margins and allow them to compete more aggressively with the new super–money managers.

The largest current sponsors (wirehouses) are already part of firms that have large proprietary asset management capabilities. You might see them start to feature those capabilities in their control account program rather than their external manager alternatives. You might also see sponsors start to acquire smaller money management firms to build a core offering. Once again, the distinction between sponsors and money managers will fade.

The large players will have tremendous economies of scale, making it very difficult for the smaller players to compete. As long as the separate account industry charges fees on assets, the large players will have a major advantage: They will have the ability to bring prices down to a level that makes entry into the business extremely difficult. This phenomenon has already begun. In the past three years, a number of smaller sponsors have either been squeezed out of business or into someone else's separate account space.

CHAPTER 13

What Does a Separate Account Cost?

Misunderstood pricing is probably the single greatest factor that has retarded the growth of separate accounts over the past 20 or more years. While the original 3 percent wrap fee was higher than the 1.5 percent generally associated with mutual funds or 1.0 percent for institutional money managers, the fee was actually a bargain because the execution costs involved with these other products often resulted in costs that were substantially higher than 3 percent.

Unfortunately, the fee became the defining element of the product—much like load, no-load, and 12-b mutual funds—and the separate account became known as the *wrap-fee* account. The financial press immediately latched onto the 3 percent fee and nicknamed the wrap fee account the "rip-off account." The attacks were unwarranted as it was an apples-to-oranges comparison, but the damage was devastating and sticks, to some degree, today.

What the press overlooked was that the fee included:

- The money manager
- The sponsor firm
- The custody and execution
- The advisor-consultant

Over the last 20 years, rapidly changing technology in the industry has challenged the very premise of the wrap-fee structure. The cost of monitoring accounts and of record keeping is dropping. From the manager's side, changes in technology have also led to decreased costs in executing transactions and portfolio management.

When someone wants to pull the comparison card, you can say: The separate account is one of the few financial products for which the entire fee is disclosed up front in a straightforward manner; furthermore, this fee is visibly highlighted each quarter.

Other products have hidden (or at least less visible) costs. Actually, pricing in the securities industry is a mess due to the never-ending quest by financial institutions to hide fees. Most investors are totally unaware that they're paying added-on expenses because the extra expenses are hidden in the net cost.

Many of the top separate account managers have minimum account sizes of $1 million or more. But under the wrap programs, they take lower minimums. According to Morningstar, the average expense ratio for a domestic equity mutual fund is 1.40 percent. This expense ratio does not include transaction (brokerage) costs. For the 10 largest domestic equity funds, the average brokerage charges are 0.13 percent, bringing the total costs to approximately 1.53 percent (an average-sized fund could have a much higher total cost, as the 10 largest funds enjoy economies of scale in their costs). For a $100,000 managed account, the management, brokerage, and program fees can total approximately 1.25 percent. (Neither of these total cost numbers include the financial advisor's fee, which is variable and controlled by the independent advisor.)

The media would never believe this, but it is entirely possible to buy a separate account investment for less money than its mutual fund alternative.

Due to the current complexity in pricing, in order to figure out the best way to purchase funds, consumers must rely on professionals with specialized software to process all the multiple variables. To add to the confusion, there are management fees, commissions, plus combinations of the two. Some brokerage firms offer the choice of either commission or one fee that includes a certain number of trades. The problem is that each fee structure is designed in a vacuum. The end results are client confusion and skepticism.

The solution is clear: All fees should be spelled out, broken down, and listed in their component parts. Bare-bones management and administrative costs should be detailed. Supermarket charges and markups should be highlighted as additional, as should any distribution charges paid to a financial intermediary. The same applies to wrap fees. The financial intermediary fee should be established and declared, with custody fees stated. The money manager's fee should also be disclosed. Each component should be broken out so clients can make a determination of where the costs are incurred and where the value is received.

The consultant can then charge a fee for advice, whether the client invests in separately managed accounts, mutual funds, variable annuities, or other packaged products. This eliminates the consultant's incentive to sell one product over another, and the client is assured that what's recommended is in his/her best interest. Disclosing the component parts of the fee to the client will have the effect of driving costs down as individual managers compete for the business on the basis of fees. Finally, fees for each of the components will fall as the accounts increase in value.

Unbundling the Fee

There are four possible components of the separate account: (1) money manager; (2) sponsor; (3) custody, clearing, and execution; and (4) advisor-consultant. Most separate accounts have subcategories that can be broken down even further. The first step in understanding separate account pricing is to unbundle its components. This is something the largest separate account manufacturers have thus far been reluctant to do. But this is now changing, as newer entrants into the field have had to unbundle their programs because they do not have all the manufacturing components available in-house.

The typical separately managed account manager has total costs that can range from around 1.25 to 2.5 percent.

Unwrapped Pricing for a $100,000 Account

Assuming the total fee to client is	2.50%
Separate account management fee	0.45%
Sponsor advisory fee	0.40%
Clearing/execution fee	0.25%
Consultant gross fee	1.40%

1. *The separate account manager.* This is the simplest component, its core function being portfolio management. Historically, separate account managers may have been excellent portfolio managers, but have not been very good business managers. When asked if they can functionalize the manufacturing expenses, their answer is usually a blank stare. They need to create pricing matrices from 1 percent, where they provide all services, to 30 basis points (bps), where they provide only portfolio management services in a sponsor's program. They will be required to price-differentiate their various investment offerings. Tax-advantaged management should cost more than total-return management due to its additional complexity.

Separate account managers who do not go through a sponsor can typically charge 1.0 percent. Managers who participate in a sponsor program are typically paid (for equity and balanced accounts) a high of 65 bps, scaling down to 30 bps. The larger sponsor programs are at the bottom of the scale. The large program sponsors also pay the manager a de-escalating fee based on the total assets the manager receives. For instance, on the first $250 million the manager receives 50 bps, on the next $250 million 45 bps, and so forth.

The starting point for the fee will vary from sponsor to sponsor based on the services the sponsor provides to the manager. There are dramatic differences among sponsor services provided to the money manager. For instance, does the sponsor pay for, provide, and reconcile a portfolio management record-keeping system or just provide a data dump? Many money managers today overlook these differences because gaining entrance into major sponsor programs is extremely competitive. However, as more separate account distribution channels become available, this shortsighted approach should cease. If it doesn't, the managers will find themselves in the position of a favored-nations-clause nightmare, being forced to accept rock-bottom prices even when the sponsor provides little service.

2. *The sponsor.*   Sponsor services vary both to the advisor and the investor, as well as to the money managers whose services they distribute. The most common services provided by the sponsor are:

- Research on money managers
- Asset allocation
- Separate account generation
- Client reporting (statement/performance)
- Account administration
- Billing
- Consultant interface
- Account set-up

Optional sponsor services are:

- Fiduciary responsibility
- Portfolio design teams
- Trust services
- Consultant training
- Portfolio record keeping

- Reconciliation
- Regulatory compliance
- Internet access to account data

Due to the various services, the fees vary but are quoted on an account or household level, not on total assets. Typically, on a $500,000 household, fees will range from 25 to 65 bps. As account size increases, the fee drops substantially.

Sponsors can be eliminated, but the core services must still be delivered. A money manager working directly with the investor or advisor-consultant has to perform the majority of the core services, making them a de facto sponsor, or supermanager. Fees for this type of relationship are higher.

The traditional sponsor will have to go through the most changes to the separate account components over the next decade. The large sponsor will be forced to move from what has been a very closed process to an open-architecture platform. Along with an open-architecture platform will come unbundled pricing of services. As this pricing evolves, true value comparisons can be made. Similar to the money managers, sponsors are currently pricing to what the market will bear, not on services provided. This has forced many of the traditional smaller sponsors out of business. They have not been able to demonstrate superior services that would justify a premium price.

3. *Custody, clearing, and execution.* Until recently, these services were bundled into the overall sponsor fee, making the actual costs almost impossible to determine. Due to sponsor entrants who do not self-clear, these costs are now being identified. In most cases, they are quoted in basis points (bps) on an assets-per-account basis rather than on total assets (money manager) or household (sponsor). For a typical $250,000 account, clearing, custody, and execution come bundled at between 20 and 40 bps.

These services are, in most cases, considered a pure commodity:

- *Custody.* The actual separate account securities storage and official record keeper. Traditionally, this has been the role of the bank.
- *Execution.* Execution of buy and sell orders from the money manager, which has generally been the role of the stockbroker.
- *Clearing.* When the manager executes a block trade of stock for multiple accounts, it must be delivered to the custodian and placed in the proper account, which is the clearing function.

Clearing, custody, and execution are performed by the separate account sponsor. This means that for a money manager in 20 sponsor programs who wants to buy a stock across all accounts, they must place 20 orders of the stock at the same time, one at each sponsor/custodian. This practice is ripe for change as it is simply not efficient; investors who have the same separate account manager, but different sponsor custodians, will get different execution prices. As of this writing, the Securities and Exchange Commission (SEC) plans to review these trading practices.

In the future, execution will be separated from custody and clearing. The manager will place one block order at the institution that has the best execution and the 20 smaller blocks will be cleared to each sponsor/custodian. This will ensure the best execution.

As separate accounts revamp their trading procedures to this new standard, you will see commissions on stock trades reappear. The separate account will have come full circle in 25 years. Once execution is unbundled, the market for best execution will take off. This market will be trade-by-trade, depending on difficulty, making bps pricing for execution impossible.

This may seem like a step backward, but it is not. Executions will be better for the investor. The cost of execution is close to zero on big block trades anyway. Also, as execution is stripped from the custodian, the bundled fee will decrease dramatically. One major clearing firm is already doing business with a 5-bps custody charge and competing for executions at $5 per trade.

Unbundling of the separate account pricing will continue. Even the large wirehouse sponsors will have to unbundle the manufacturing expense from the advisor fee so they can accomplish their consulting umbrella strategy. Unbundling within the four major categories will also begin so that an apples-to-apples comparison can be made. Due to regulatory pressure, this will probably begin with the area of custody, clearing, and execution. As the lines between money managers and sponsors blur, it will force the other categories to unbundle.

Unbundled execution will also solve another problem. Currently, sponsor/custodians lose money on some very active managers, but make enough on the lower-turnover managers to make the total business profitable. This means that investors with low-turnover managers are subsidizing investors with high-turnover managers. This is not only unfair to the investor, it creates artificial businesses. There are extremely high-turnover managers in the industry that would not survive competitively if the actual trading costs were factored into their performance. Unbundling execution will solve these inequities and be a major benefit to the investor.

4. *The advisor-consultant.* This group is relatively straightforward. The fee received for servicing the account in the traditional large sponsor is wrapped into the bundled fee. In the independent advisor world, the fees are

distinct. The typical advisor charges between 40 and 100 bps, based on household size. The average fee on a $1 million household is 68 bps.

This fee tends to differ by professional evolution. That is, an advisor who grew up in the brokerage business is on the high end. Advisors who came out of the accounting world are on the low end. If the advisor's core business is investment consulting, he/she tends to charge more than if it is a secondary business to the core business.

Pricing Summary

Let's look at how all the pieces add up in a traditional financial product structure—manufacturing expenses versus distribution (Table 13.1). Looking at these fees, it is apparent that separate accounts, or wrap-fee accounts, are not rip-offs at all. Their total manufacturing expenses fall right in line with no-load mutual funds. In fact, mutual fund expense ratios do not include execution figures, which the separate account figures in Table 13.1 do.

There is an industry trend toward an unconflicted, fee-based consulting process, rather than a transactional commission-based process. This trend is most evident in the financial planning business with the enormous success of Schwab's One Source program, where investors agree to pay a flat fee on top of varying mutual fund expenses.

During flat trading periods, a customer might be better off investing on a commission basis. However, in periods of heavy trading activity, the investor should save money using a wrap-fee arrangement. Because no one knows when such periods will occur, it might be wise to look past the economics

TABLE 13.1   Equity and Balanced Separate Account Component Pricing

	$100,000 Account	$1 Million Household	$10 Million Household
1. Money manager	50 bps	45 bps	40 bps
2. Sponsor	50	40	30
3. Custody, clearing, and Execution	30	20	10
Total Manufacturing Expenses	130	105	80
4. Advisor-consultant	100	70	40
Total cost to investor	230 bps	175 bps	120 bps

TABLE 13.2 Typical Break Points in Consultant Fees

Consultant Fees

Asset Level Breakpoints (5)	Consultant Fees (%)
0	1.00
$100,000.00	0.90
$2,000,000.00	0.85
$5,000,000.00	0.80
$10,000,000.00	0.75
$20,000,000.00	0.70
$100,000,000.00	0.65

Standard Program Fees

Asset Breakpoint Levels	Fixed-Income Equity Advisory Fees (%)	Advisory Fees (%)	Administration Fees (%)
First $500,000	0.40	0.25	0.10
Next $500,000	0.36	0.225	0.09
Next $4,000,000	0.32	0.20	0.08
Over $5,000,000	0.28	0.175	0.07

Standard Clearing Fees (FCC)

Asset Breakpoint Levels	Fees (%)	Minimum Clearing Fees
First $250,000	0.25	Managed account—$300
Next $500,000	0.10	Mutual fund—$100
Next $1,000,000	0.08	
Next $5,000,000	0.07	
Next $10,000,000	0.06	

and judge wrap-fee programs on more compelling issues—trust, integrity, and your client's individual needs. The customer needn't fear that his/her wrap-fee broker will do any excessive trades, because all trading is paid for in advance.

Will prices continue to decrease? Probably not! As the numbers illustrate, the manufacturing expense already mirrors mutual funds. As the big mutual fund complexes enter this market, they will not want to cannibalize their businesses, so they will not underprice them. In fact, you may see fees inch back up. As the fund complexes treat the separate account as a premium service to their mutual funds, they may also charge a premium price, using the logic: Why should a custom suit cost less than one off the rack?

Also, as the mutual fund complexes invade the separate account industry, they will adopt the policies that worked successfully in funds. This will lead to the inclusion of distribution fees in the manufacturing fee. This fee will be used in much the same way as 12-bs are in the mutual fund industry: to pay for distribution to the advisor or to the advisor's employer, the broker dealer, bank, insurance company, and so on.

The bottom line: expenses are becoming unbundled. You can buy funds any way you want, fee-wise. But if you look at the core elements, they break down this way: The fees are composed of four components, which are listed in Table 13.2. Similarly, fees for separate accounts are broken down, with the end result being that the fees for both types of money management services are about equal.

CHAPTER 14

Tax Management in the Separate Account

The erosion of returns from taxes happens so gradually over the years, that it escapes the notice of many investors. Nevertheless, the impact is there all the same, and it can be significant—even for those investors who are not in the top tax bracket.

Tax Efficiency

The average domestic equity mutual fund had a 23 percent unrealized capital gain at the end of 2000. This 23 percent unrealized capital gain means that an investor investing new money in a fund owes tax on a 23 percent capital gain when it is ultimately distributed. If it was realized prior to the actual losses that have been experienced in the last couple of years, the investor may find that he/she is paying a capital gains tax on an asset that has depreciated significantly in market value.

In many cases this is an unnecessary tax burden. Alternatively, the separately managed account investor does not buy into any unwarranted or unrealized tax liability, because the individual managed account investor establishes his/her own cost basis at the time the securities inside the account are purchased. As noted in Table 14.1, the tax attributes are compared between mutual funds and separately managed accounts.

TABLE 14.1　Tax-Related Features

Tax-Related Features	Mutual Funds	Separately Managed Account—Direct Ownership
Separately held securities	No—investor holds one security, the fund, which in turn owns a diversified portfolio of stocks.	Yes—investor holds securities in an account purchased by the portfolio manager.
Unrealized capital gains	Yes—average U.S. mutual fund has a 20 percent unrealized capital gain.	No—at the time of purchase the investor establishes his/her own cost basis for each security in the portfolio
Customized to control taxes	1. No—most fund managers manage for pretax return without regard for the tax liability they may create for investors. 2. All investors pay their proportionate share of taxes.	Yes—investors can instruct their portfolio manager to take gains or losses as available to manage their tax liability. Some managers will explicitly manage to control the tax consequences.
Gain/loss distribution policies	All gains distributed, losses cannot be distributed but can be carried forward inside the fund to offset future gains.	All gains and losses are reported on the investor's annual tax return.

As you are aware, mutual funds distribute their dividends and their realized capital gains to all shareholders on a pro rata basis. Dividends and short-term capital gains are taxed as ordinary income; the current federal rates for income tax range from 15 to 37.6 percent, depending on income level. (Note: ordinary tax rates are scheduled to decrease to a rate of 35.6 percent over the next several years.) A mutual fund's distribution of long-term capital gains is currently taxed at 20 percent for most investors, or 18 percent for assets acquired after or owned on January 1, 2001, and held for a minimum of five years.

For fund investors, the tax status of a fund's realized gains depends on how long the fund held the asset on which it realized the gain (not on how long the investor receiving the distribution has owned shares of the fund). Gains from assets that the fund owned for at least 12 months are distributed as long-term gains; gains from assets sold less than 12 months after the fund bought them are distributed as short-term gains.

Because the classification of distributions is a result of the fund's, not the investor's actions, it can be controlled to some extent by the fund's managers, if they so choose. By the same token, investors can be hurt by a fund's lack of attention to tax issues. In addition, new investors in funds with holdings that the fund bought many years earlier at low prices may inherit substantial gains that may be distributed in the future as taxable distributions.

For tax-deferred investors, comparing mutual funds is fairly simple, as tax effects don't have to be considered. Net total return (gross total return minus expenses) is the operative basis for comparison. For the taxable investor, however, the size and composition of fund distributions make a big difference. After-tax returns are the critical basis for comparing fund performance in any taxable investment situation.

Real Gains Are Reflected in After-Tax Returns

One of the tasks of a financial advisor is to communicate the impact of an unmanaged tax liability on investment total returns. The tax liabilities inccured, along with expenses and transaction costs, can significantly reduce returns.

Table 14.2 compares the benefits of tax management techniques applied to a hypothetical $1 million investment in an S&P 500–based index portfolio (1987–1996).

More for Taxes Means Less for Compounding

Income taxes can kill wealth accumulation. Every dollar paid in taxes today is a dollar that is lost to future compounding. A 1995 study based on the

TABLE 14.2   Analysis of Tax Management Potential*

Initial Investment: $1 Million	Without Tax Management Techniques	With Loss Matching, Loss Harvesting, and Managed Tracking
After-tax ending value	$3,551,000	$3,756,000
After-tax return	13.5%	14.2%

*Figures shown are not reflective of any particular parametric strategy or portfolio, either actual or modeled.

well-known data of Ibbotson and Sinquefield estimated that $1.00 invested in stocks on December 31, 1925, would have ballooned to $800.08 by December 31, 1993, if allowed to grow untaxed. Allow for taxes and annual transaction costs and the same $1.00 investment would have grown only to $157.72. Taxes and expenses reduced the annual pretax return by more than 25 percent, but because this money was not available for compounding, the net effect on the accumulated value was a reduction of more than 80 percent.

What Can a Separate Account Manager Do to Help?

- *Ability to accept low-cost-basis stock.*   The majority of separate account managers accept only cash. This is currently changing, and more investment managers are willing to accept securities, with specific instructions as to how to handle them. For example, most high-net-worth investors have low-cost-basis stock, and they're beginning to understand the inherent risk in holding the stock and the tax implications of selling it to diversify. These investors are looking for managers who can propose solutions for the investor ranging from a total sale, to partial sale, to holding the stock and diversifying around it using other money. The manager should develop a working knowledge of collars and put and call strategies to hedge positions. Accepting low-cost-basis stock is one of the basic tenets of true separate account management.
- *Tax-lot accounting.*   The fundamental technique to gain tax efficiency is to employ tax lot accounting. Among other things, this allows the

manager to respond to withdrawals and required turnover by selling higher-cost-basis stock first.

- *Tax loss matching and harvesting.*   This strategy seeks to realize losses within a portfolio to enhance after-tax returns through (1) matching gains with losses when the realization of gains is either desirable or unavoidable, and (2) creating an inventory of losses to offset gains elsewhere in an investor's portfolio. The extent to which tax loss harvesting can be exploited is partly determined by overall market returns and individual stock volatility. In periods of lower market returns and with asset classes of greater stock volatility, the after-tax value of this technique increases.

- *Tax-lot optimization.*   Most money managers use some form of portfolio or security optimization—that is, calculating how to mix your holdings to get maximum return for varying levels of risk. The roots of optimization lie in modern portfolio theory. The simplest models look at historical price volatility versus future projections. To manage after-tax money effectively, you have to add another variable, the tax lot cost of the securities purchased.

    This makes the optimization process far more complex. Not only will different clients have different cost bases, making optimization necessary on an account basis rather than on a firm portfolio basis, but individual clients will have different tax lots of the same securities. Adding to an already complex process, clients will be at varying tax levels. Sales and replacement purchases that make sense for one client may not make sense for another. Again, dispersion among clients should be expected and accepted.

    This process sounds daunting, but new technology, available now and around the corner, makes this level of management possible even today.

- *Year-End Loss/Gain Request.*   Besides harvesting losses to reposition the portfolio internally, the money manager should entertain requests from the investor to offset realized gains and losses outside his/her portfolio. For example, assume an investor realizes a $50,000 gain from the sale of a condo. The manager should attempt to harvest losses to offset the gain as far as possible. This is an incredible value-added service, especially in poor-equity markets. Rather than being admonished for poor performance, the manager is congratulated for saving the investor from writing a $10,000 check to the IRS. That is tangible value added and could contribute to an extended contractual arrangement with the manager even in performance downturns.

An extension of this service is to work with the other money managers in a multimanager household, creating communication links with the other managers to make the overall account more tax-efficient. The instigation of this type of communication usually falls to the program sponsor or advisor, but the money manager should be responsive.

- *Efficient trading strategies.* Most separate account managers suffer from the *defined benefit syndrome* in trading as well as portfolio management. In their attempt to keep accounts looking similar, they buy and sell in proportions. For instance, if the investor wants to withdraw $50,000 from a $500,000 account, the manager sells 10 percent of all 35 positions in the account. They do the reverse on a $50,000 contribution to the account. This is not what the high-net-worth investor expects. In fact, they view that type of management as the cookie-cutter approach, which can have negative indications for tax management efforts.

- *Managed portfolio tracking.* Over time, a portfolio built to mirror an index will develop return differences (tracking) as the index constituents change. For many investors, taxes incurred by a portfolio manager attempting to fully replicate all index changes represent unnecessary costs.

  By accepting a small degree of tracking difference (i.e., portfolios may replicate the benchmark closely but not exactly), investors can improve their after-tax performance but at the same time incur a risk of underperforming the index.

  Using tax loss matching and harvesting can enhance after-tax return by matching gains with losses when turnover is necessary—and create opportunities to offset gains elsewhere in an investor's portfolio.

  Following are some common misconceptions.

Misconception 1: Only Wealthy People Need to Be Concerned with Tax Efficiency

Many people associate tax-managed investments with tax-exempt investments, whose lower yields are favorable only for people in the highest income brackets. It's obvious that high-income investors are going to get the greatest benefit from tax management strategies: The difference

TABLE 14.3   After-Tax Yield Equivalents*

If You File Singly and Earn ...	or File Jointly and Earn ...	You Would Need Pretax Returns of (in %) ...	To Match a Tax-Free Yield of (in %) ...
$0–$25,750	$0–$43,050	4.71	4
		5.88	5
		7.06	6
$25,751–$62,450	$43,051–$104,050	5.56	4
		6.94	5
		8.33	6
$62,451–$130,250	$104,051–$158,550	5.80	4
		7.25	5
		8.70	6
$130,251–$283,150	$158,551–$283,150	6.25	4
		7.81	5
		9.38	6
$283,151+	$283,151+	6.62	4
		8.28	5
		9.93	6

*Calculations are based on federal tax rates for year 2002. State taxes would increase the pretax returns required.

between their income tax rates (as high as 37.6 percent at the federal level) and the long-term capital gains rate (20 percent) is greater. But even investors in the 28 percent federal income tax bracket can gain from tax management strategies—particularly if the effects of state taxes are included (Table 14.3).

Misconception 2: Portfolio Turnover Is the Key Indicator of Tax Efficiency

Turnover is certainly easy to measure, but some studies suggest that it's not always the most reliable measure of tax efficiency.

Dickson and Shoven (1993) found the statistical correlation between portfolio turnover and tax efficiency to be quite weak. They gave their results on a scale where:

1 = higher turnover always leads to higher tax efficiency.

−1 = higher turnover always leads to lower tax efficiency.

0 = no correlation at all.

If low turnover did correlate to tax efficiency, we would expect to see numbers close to −1. Instead, the correlations for investors in the highest tax bracket (assuming no portfolio liquidation) ranged from −0.11 for growth managers to −0.22 for growth and income managers. For investors in the lowest tax bracket with portfolio liquidation assumed, some correlations were positive, suggesting that higher turnover actually improved tax efficiency. While the study did show that there is a correlation, it was not the strong correlation that the simple equation of turnover with tax efficiency would suggest.

Misconception 3: Indexing Is the Best Approach to Tax-Managed Investing

It's true that index mutual funds have a number of innate characteristics that have tended to foster strong pretax performance along with high tax efficiency. For one thing, index funds have exceptionally low turnover rates, which means that their transaction expenses are generally lower. They are also likely to have more long-term capital gains and fewer short-term gains compared with actively managed funds.

But even with these features, index funds are not the ultimate tax-managed investments, for several reasons:

- *Stocks within an index fund change periodically.*   Companies may be added or deleted by the firm that maintains the index, in response to changing market realities or events such as corporate mergers. Strict indexing requires portfolio managers to buy or sell whenever stocks are added or deleted from the index. It means they also have to own all companies, even Enron, Global Crossing, and Lucent. This type of trading activity may not lead to a great deal of turnover, but it can lead to considerable recognition of gains.

- *Timing of sales may be inefficient.*   For example, in the course of following its passive strategy, an index fund might end up selling a stock just days before it would qualify for tax treatment as long-term capital gains.

- *The fund may have to invest in high-dividend stocks.* An index fund cannot limit holdings of a stock just because it pays high dividends. With the most popular index funds investing heavily in blue-chip stocks, index funds can generate substantial dividend income, which is taxed at the higher rate for ordinary income.

- *Rebalancing can generate capital gains.* An index fund's portfolio must be rebalanced periodically, and the manager may need to recognize capital gains to do so.

- *The fund cannot be managed for tax efficiency when it comes to share-holder redemptions.* Because it must maintain its similarity to an index in the proportions of each stock it owns, an index fund can't choose which stocks to sell when handling redemptions. Chances are good that it will end up having to sell many holdings that will generate short-term gains, which will affect the fund's tax efficiency for all shareholders remaining in the fund. In addition, most index funds are carrying sizable unrealized gains. This could lead to considerable realized gains if a large number of redemptions take place.

Misconception 4: Any Investment Style Can Be Tax-Efficient

Certainly any investment style can be modified to improve tax efficiency. But some styles lend themselves to tax-efficient techniques far better than others. For example, growth-oriented investment strategies seem to be more appropriate for tax-managed investing than value-oriented strategies. This is in part because a growth approach is oriented toward capital appreciation, while a value approach will tend to lead a portfolio manager to select a portfolio that produces comparatively higher rates of income.

Peters and Miller (1998) bear this out. Their study of fund groups for the 10- and 20-year periods ending in 1996 found that growth managers provided higher average pretax returns, higher after-tax returns, and greater tax efficiency than growth and income managers or equity income managers. (See Table 14.4.)

Managers that focus on large-company stocks are also better candidates for tax-managed investing than small-cap managers. One reason is that small-company stock managers have a built-in reason to sell; those that are most successful eventually outgrow the small-cap category, and must be

TABLE 14.4   Average Return Rankings for Asset Classes (1976–1996)*

Pretax (in %)		After-Tax (in %)	
Growth	15.36	Growth	11.92
Growth and income	13.75	Growth and income	9.89
Equity income	13.71	Equity income	9.31

Source: Donald J. Peters and Mary J. Miller, "Taxable Investors Need Different Strategies," *The Journal of Investing,* Fall 1998, p. 38.
*Assumes the maximum income and capital gains tax rates in effect for each year.

sold. This can lead to a high level of realized capital gains. In addition, small companies are often bought out, leading once again to excessive realization of capital gains.

Misconception 5: All Tax-Sensitive Investors Have the Same Needs

While generalizations can be comforting, it's essential to consider each investor's particular situation. Federal and state marginal rates vary from individual to individual. Some taxpayers—a growing percentage each year—are subject to the federal alternative minimum tax (AMT). This separate tax computation is applied to individuals whose deductions under the regular tax rules might otherwise eliminate their tax liability. Some investors may have other holdings or personal businesses that can provide some offsetting losses. And, as always, it's essential to keep in mind the individual's ultimate investment goal and time horizon.

A separate account portfolio manager can tie purchase-and-sale decisions to the individual's specific tax situation. For smaller investors, though, the costs of managing a separate account generally make mutual funds more appropriate.

Considering the use of securities that have appreciated significantly rather than cash when making charitable gifts is a technique that can improve tax efficiency. This gives away the capital gain.

Investors who are planning to leave a taxable portfolio as part of their estate are a special case, thanks to the current tax code provision for a step-up in basis upon an investor's death. This essentially means that when heirs withdraw money from the account, capital gains will be calculated from the fair market value of the security at the time of death. This effectively resets the clock on basis calculations, and means that heirs need not pay taxes on the portfolio's unrealized capital gains prior to the death of the owner.

Conclusion

Managing taxes is an important attribute of a good separate account manager. The basic structure of a separate account permits great flexibility and opportunity for customization of the account based on an investor's tax requirements. The process itself is not simple, and must be managed, but nevertheless, it represents an advantage of separately managed accounts.

PART

III

THE DELIVERY SYSTEM

Selling separate accounts is difficult. When you first begin selling separate accounts, it can be frustrating and confusing. There is a lot to know. You may feel anxiety or fear that someone is going to discover that you don't really know what the heck you are doing. But, if selling separate accounts were easy, everyone would be doing it—and your uncomfortable feelings can actually be one of the best indications that you are on the right course.

Operating Stages of Marketing

The separate account is a complex investment product with many customizable features. Each feature requires education, discussion, and consideration in the context of the investor's particular overall strategy for financial gain.

Very few investment advisors know, much less plan, their sales efforts. Recent studies by Russ Prince have shown that their marketing style is reactive. First, learn the product inside and out, understand its application, then combine your knowledge with a practical marketing program, and you will soon be among an exceptional few investment advisors.

If you have been trading every day and decide to switch to fee-based separate account management, you must spend time convincing clients to convert. While you are educating, you are not selling. You can't do both at the same time, so your transaction business drops simply because you are not spending as many hours selling. This is where most advisors stop.

Do an honest evaluation of your client base. It is easier to sell current clients on additional services than it is to create new client relationships. A separate account client investing $1 million with you can generate $10,000 annually. You need to set a goal for the number of clients you want to convert. Assign a value to each separate account client. Develop a conceptual understanding of sales efforts and trade-offs.

By understanding what it takes to bring in and maintain assets under management, you are better able to determine where you should be focusing your sales efforts. Is meeting with affluent clients once a year enough? Or would it be better to select 10 top clients and meet with them once each quarter? If you track your sales efforts, you will know. Planning your sales efforts in this way will allow you to begin to estimate the value of a separate account client.

A qualified individual will usually allocate 50 percent or more of their investable assets to separate accounts. Most investors do not have a working knowledge of the separate account product, and it is unlikely that any investor will commit that level of assets without extensive counseling. Historically, the selling cycle can range from one to six months, requiring at least one in-person presentation by a consultant as well as one to two months of a phone-and-literature education process.

It's a Process, Not a Product

The investment process is the key to sales success and should be the focal point of your communications. Marketing material for separate accounts should highlight your investment process and convey how you are unique or differentiated from other advisors. You have an opportunity to brand your message. A highly recognizable theme can reinforce a positive image of the separate account in the minds of clients and prospects alike. This section will help show you:

- What to do next
- How to replicate your business
- How to convert your existing clients to separate accounts
- How to transform your practice into a separate account fee business
- How to sell new prospects
- How to market your service to high-net-worth individuals and to institutions
- How to conduct separate account seminars and one-on-one presentations
- How to use credibility marketing to build pathways back to your business

Chapter 15—Converting Existing Clients

You must decide which of your clients will receive the greatest benefits from fee-based conversion. By using the Fee-Based Conversion Worksheet, you can identify which clients make solid candidates for conversion and prioritize those who should be targeted first.

Chapter 16—Prospecting for High-Net-Worth Investors

How to run a successful marketing campaign, market your credibility, and position yourself as the expert. This chapter will walk you through each step.

Chapter 17—Compliance

Giving advice is seen as carrying a liability and you need to understand ways to minimize that liability—therein lies a real opportunity.

Chapter 18—Leveraging Your Operations

These are simple strategies that can help build your separate account business. Operations is often overlooked, but when combined with the investment process, it can help in making a successful transition to separate accounts.

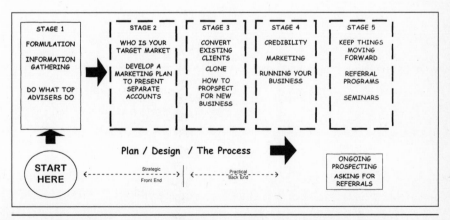

FIGURE III.1   Operating Stages of Marketing Separate Accounts.

Chapter 19—Understand the Employee Retirement Income Security Act (ERISA) and Separate Accounts

These rules, governed by the Department of Labor (DOL), impose heavy responsibilities on any persons involved in the management of employee benefit plans. Unfortunately, many advisors are not aware of the responsibilities, liabilities, and penalties under ERISA until they find themselves in violation of the Act. Financial advisors will find it particularly useful in establishing compliance procedures within their practices.

Chapter 20—Look into the Future

We're going to take a look into the future of separate account management: the problems and obstacles as well as the changes that are needed for the industry to be successful in the coming years.

Converting Existing Clients

We start this chapter by examining the fastest way to build a separate account business—converting your existing client base. You learn how to clone your top clients and build a model separate account business. Next, we explore a method of building the marketing arm of your business by creating a marketing board from within your client base. You learn what to say and how to explain the changes in your practice to your clients so that they understand why the addition of separate account management is the best solution for them.

We've provided a 22-question survey form that can help you uncover valuable information about your clients. Midway through the chapter, we examine ways you can best leverage your time—through seminars and by forming strategic alliances with outside financial professionals.

Directions for Completing the Conversion Worksheet

Using the template in Figure 15.1, for each client, score each of the categories and then add the values together to come up with a total score. When values are summed for each client, the clients with the highest scores represent the best clients for conversion.

Client name. For your entire list of existing clients, list each client's name in the first column.

Client Type	Score
A list	14+ points
B list	10–13 points
C list	5–9 points

Name	Investor Profile	Investable Assets	% under Your Control	Tax Consequences	Liquidity	Total Points	Grade
1.							
2.							
3.							
4.							
5.							

Name	Investor Profile	Investable Assets	% under Your Control	Tax Consequences	Liquidity	Total Points	Grade
6.							
7.							
8.							
9.							
10.							

FIGURE 15.1 Fee-Based Conversion Worksheet

Investor profile.   Identify whether the client is passive or active. Active investors who like to constantly be involved in the investment process (i.e., more do-it-yourself types) are not good candidates for fee-based conversion. For a passive client, score 4 points; for an active client, score 1 point.

Investable assets—$200,000+.   Clients should have investable assets of at least $200,000 to be eligible for conversion. For assets of $1 million, score 3 points; $500,000+, score 2 points; for assets of $200,000 to 500,000, score 1 point. Assets under $50,000 will not be eligible at this time for separate account conversion.

Percentage estimate of client's total assets under your control.   Complete this column for each client based on your estimate of the percentage of assets you control relative to the client's overall investable assets. If you control 50 percent or more, score 3 points; 26 to 49 percent, score 2 points; 25 percent or below, score 1 point.

Tax consequences—capital gains exposure.   Tax consequences play an important role in the conversion process. You must identify the severity of the tax consequences associated with selling the investment(s) that will be converted to separate account management. Each client will have different tax avoidance priorities. *The process of evaluating the impact of taxes is subjective.* In the case of clients with capital gains, the fewer concerns about taxes, the higher the score. If there are no tax implications, score 3 points; if there is some concern about taxes, score 2 points; if avoiding tax liability is a high priority, score 1 point. For clients with overall tax losses, score just the opposite—those with tax avoidance as a priority should be given the higher score.

Liquidity.   It is important to identify the holding period/liquidity of the existing investment. If the assets are not subject to holding period/liquidity restrictions, score 3 points; if the assets are subject to some holding period/liquidity constraints, score 2 points; if the assets are subject to substantial holding period/liquidity constraints, score 1 point.

Prioritize qualified clients.   Based on the Conversion Worksheet, add up the points in each category to arrive at a final score for each client. Use this score to determine each client's potential for converting to fee-based business.

Once you have given each client a score, go to the last column in the worksheet and give each client a grade. This grading system makes it easy to prioritize each client's conversion potential. As you'll see, the highest total scores represent the most promising prospects for fee-based conversion.

Work your A-list clients first, and so on. You've got the names. Now, what's the best way to convert them over?

Systematize Your Sales Process

Table 15.1 provides you with the keys to building your separate account–based business.

The Quick-Start Method to Conversion

Step one is to identify existing clients who could benefit from your new asset management services. Sort your clients into three groups. The first group includes those with a minimum of $250,000 in liquid assets, such as individual stocks, bonds, mutual funds, and money market funds. The second group is made up of clients with assets in semiliquid form, such as annuities, CDs, or mutual funds with large redemption fees. The third group includes clients with illiquid investments, such as limited partnerships and real estate. Know when these various illiquid investments might be sold or otherwise liquidated.

Set up one-on-one presentations and fact-finding meetings with your clients. These are the first two steps of the investment management process. Typically, you will want to combine these meetings for existing clients. You have already established a relationship, and they will be more open to discuss your new business.

TABLE 15.1 Building Your Separate Account Business

Separate Account Conversion Steps	Tools
Step 1: Identify and evaluate clients.	Fee-Based Conversion Worksheet
Step 2: Prioritize qualified clients.	Separate Account Rating Scale
Step 3: Introduce the concept.	Direct-mail letter
	Seminar invitation
	Sample client statement
	Sample tax reporting package
	Risk profile questionnaire
Step 4: Client solutions/closing meeting.	Risk profile questionnaire
	Allocation strategies and presentations

You may be uncomfortable telling clients that you're now doing things differently, and you will be inclined instead to test it out with new prospects—but that's a big mistake on two fronts. First, you really don't know the story well enough to tell it to new prospects. The second reason is more important as it focuses on the benefit to the client. You have chosen to build this asset management business because of huge potential benefits to your clients. You should not penalize them for being existing clients.

Call your clients and tell them that you are changing the way you are doing business in order to give them the highest level of value-added service and that you now have the ability to offer separate account management to them. Tell them this is an opportunity usually only available to multimillion-dollar pension plans. Explain that you'd like to update your clients' investment plans to see if they would personally benefit from this new approach.

Tell each client that you plan to review his/her values, goals, and current financial picture, in order to prepare a personal investment policy statement. You will find out exactly where your client is now and where he/she wants to go, and how—if you were in his/her shoes—you would optimally modify the existing investment program, if needed.

Do not make it too hard on yourself. It's really not that complicated. You first need to update where your clients are. You should be doing that anyway, and they expect it. Then you need to find out where they want to go. By telling them that you're changing the way you're doing business in order to give them the most value and that you'd like their input, they'll be even more excited about meeting with you.

Advisors who are good public speakers can leverage their time very effectively in the conversion process. Instead of time-consuming individual meetings, public speakers can meet with many clients at the same time through workshops. Invite clients who have already converted to separate account management to the meetings. Often, they will share their perspective unsolicited and will be outspoken, presold advocates who can increase your success dramatically.

Some clients feel less pressured in a group seminar than at a one-on-one meeting. Many feel they get more out of a seminar because they hear answers to questions asked by other people that they might not think to ask. Close the seminar by offering to do individual investment policy statements for each client. Schedule individual meetings at the end of the workshop, or call attendees the next day to do so. Because your client base is qualified, you have the framework to make this happen. Start your meeting off by explaining, "Many people don't realize that the most expensive and time-consuming aspect of being a financial professional is finding new clients. We often spend a substantial part of our time and efforts prospecting and marketing. This takes away from the time we can devote to the activities that make us better resources for our clients. You should ask, 'As one of my best clients, how would you prefer that I spend my time—looking for new clients or thinking about your money and keeping an eye on issues that could affect your personal financial health?' "

Cloning Your Top Clients

This is a simple system that will allow you to stay focused and expand vertically within your target markets. Identify your top 10 clients. These are not necessarily the top 10 by revenue alone, but also the ones you most enjoy working with. Quality of life is critical, and you need to enjoy the people with whom you work. By cloning your favorite clients, you have more favorite clients, and you can build the ideal business.

Often, these 10 people are the ones who have made the biggest financial impact on your business and whom you most appreciate. They are likely to already be giving you unsolicited referrals. Gaining an understanding of why these clients choose to work with you will help you understand what future clients will be looking for. If you can uncover your unique abilities through these relationships, you are on your way to developing a profitable and enjoyable business.

Let's say you are working well with a few key physicians and have an understanding of their unique needs. When one of their financial parameters changes, it is easy for you to emerge at the right place at the right time with the right solution. You are uniquely positioned to solve a particular market need or problem. These physicians will be pleased to refer you to other physicians like themselves.

Marketing research shows that, in most cases, 80 percent of an advisor's revenue is generated from the top 20 percent of his/her clients. Find out everything you can about the top 20 percent who generate this revenue for you. These top clients will each provide you with two or three qualified referrals each quarter, if you make it easy for them to do so. The top 20 percent of your clients will be replicated, and you will be working with high-quality people with whom you most enjoy working.

Position yourself as a trusted ally of this market niche, not as someone on the outside. Your job is to gain a reputation as an industry insider, not as a salesperson. It is better to position yourself early in the game. Your clients can also help you uncover an effective delivery system into their marketing niche.

Create a Client Marketing Board

Invite favorite clients to participate on your advisory board. All you need is one contact. Ask him/her to be on your marketing team, and get that person started working on your behalf. It often only takes one call to set up a meeting to get this going. A marketing board of your clients takes you into their worlds. Explain to your best clients that you like their advice, that you are calling your group a client marketing board. You'd like to run ideas past them to help you market yourself.

We almost always meet with people who are referred to us by someone we know. This type of referral and networking alliance is a powerful technique.

Colleagues and associates will invariably be willing to help you out, give you names, and offer suggestions on how to build your strategic network. Call your favorite clients and tell them, "I need your help. I am developing a more focused approach to my marketing. I have created a profile of my favorite clients and you are one of them. I really respect your opinion. Would you let me take you out to lunch? I would like to get your ideas and opinions about marketing to people like you in your field."

This works. We have never had a client say no to this. When you tell somebody he/she is one of your favorite and respected clients, and that person has already entrusted you with his/her own life savings, you're going to get a positive response. At the luncheon meeting, we take out a worksheet that's made up of 22 questions and we walk the client through it, question by question, taking notes. You'll be surprised by the answers you get when you do this.

One of our advisors felt that this really wasn't a valuable exercise when she first undertook it. On her first client interview, however, she found out she was not assured of getting the million-dollar rollover that her corporate client was going to soon be receiving. Even though she had been his financial advisor and tax preparer for many years, he didn't see her as an asset manager. Questions 11 through 13 bring up competitors. In this client interview, the advisor found out that the client had a friend who was also a financial advisor, and this was the person the client was considering to manage his assets. Had she not conducted the interview, she would have surely lost this million-dollar sale. Instead, she found out what she was up against; she presented her story, and made the sale. She's now convinced.

Questions to Ask

1. What are your lifetime financial goals?
2. What have been your greatest personal financial frustrations?

3. What are the major financial challenges that people in your situation (industry, etc.) face today?

4. What else could I do to help you solve your problems or achieve your goals?

5. To what business organizations do you belong?

6. To what social organizations do you belong?

7. What sports or other activities do you enjoy?

8. What publications do you like to read?

9. How did you first hear about me?

10. What originally prompted you to do business with me?

11. With whom else did you consider working?

12. Who do you feel are my competitors?

13. How do I compare with my competitors?

14. What is important to you in your relationship with a financial advisor?

15. What are the major benefits you have enjoyed by working with me?

16. If they asked, what would you tell your friends about me?

17. What is the most compelling thing I could say to someone in your situation that would interest him/her in doing business with me?

18. Knowing what you know, if you were me, how would you market to people like yourself?

19. Do you have any friends or associates who might benefit from meeting me or attending one of our workshops?

20. Do you know of anyone who works for a company that is about to downsize its workforce?

21. Do any of your friends own their own businesses?

22. Do you know of anyone who would like to sell his/her highly appreciated house or business?

Once you've gone through the questions, thank your clients for their help. If they've done a good job and you'd like to continue the conversation over the years, tell them that you're creating an informal board of advisors for your business, and ask them if you can call them occasionally to get their opinion and ideas on your marketing plan. Almost always, they will say yes.

Here are a few examples of situations uncovered during client interviews by advisors who work with us.

- A good friend of a client has just inherited a large amount of money and needs the help of a financial professional to preserve it.

- A friend of a client is just about to retire and will receive a $500,000 lump-sum distribution from his retirement plan. He needs a money manager for the first time in his life.

- A local corporation, where a client was previously the CEO, is down-sizing. He identifies 1,200 people who will soon receive over $200,000 each in lump-sum distributions.

- A friend of a client has just taken his company public, thereby increasing his net worth. This friend wants to prudently diversify his wealth and needs an advisor to help him do it.

- A client's colleague is selling his $2 million house and wants to be shown how to avoid capital gains tax by using a charitable remainder trust.

- A client's relative is a wealthy small-business owner who wants to transfer his business to other family members without the government taking a huge chunk out for taxes. He wants to find out how a family partnership might solve this problem and how to get the rest of his financial house in order.

This system of cloning your best clients will allow you to easily double the total number of clients in your business, thereby doubling your income. And you can continue this process as long as you'd like. If you don't have existing clients or your favorite clients are not in the marketing niche that you want, then call on certified public accountants (CPAs) or other centers of influence who are in that target market and do the same exercise.

Introducing the Concept of Separate Account Management

Approach A—Conduct the Seminar (Figure 15.2)

The object of the seminar is to acquaint your current clients with the separate account offerings of your firm. You want to build enough enthusiasm for them to request a follow-up one-on-one meeting. This follow-up meeting is designed to collect the specific profile information necessary to provide them with an eventual fee-based recommendation.

Here is a typical example of beginning-with-the-end-in-mind planning. Chart out a time plan for follow-up meetings. Decide on the number of work-shops you will be doing and an approximate number of prospects that will be attending. This will give you an idea of the amount of follow-up you will need

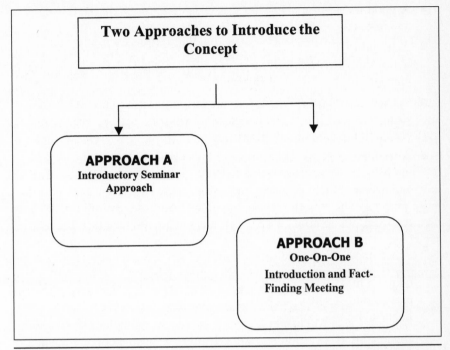

FIGURE 15.2 Introducing the Concept of Separate Account Management.

to do. If you do not have a client base from which you can clone your desired target market, or if you are new to the business, we recommend that you hold small workshops on a monthly basis. This should be the same basic workshop each month, allowing for constant improvement as you move ahead.

Phone Call Follow-Up Stage

If your workshop is on a Thursday, don't wait until Monday to begin making your follow-up calls. Start the day after or, better yet, the day of the event. Make contact with everyone within three days. Before calling a prospect, be sure to go over his/her response sheet so that you have a good idea of the type of person with whom you are talking. When you make your first follow-up call, make it clear that the meeting you hope to set up is part of the investment consulting process—and, as you promised in the workshop, you are willing to put together an investment policy statement customized to this person's situation.

The Workshop

Built into each workshop is a call to action that creates excitement and motivates participants to want to personally meet with you after the workshop. We offer participants something that usually only the largest pension plans provide—an investment policy statement that addresses each person's own unique objectives and spells out exactly what we would do if we were in his/her shoes. Our strategy is to create a win-win situation. We do this by teaming up with a good speaker who has the same target market and who will share expenses as well as help promote the workshop.

Depending on your target market, the ideal time for workshops will differ. For retired individuals, days are best; for executives, evenings or Saturdays work better. We have been very successful with Saturday morning workshops that run from 9:00 to noon. We have greeters hand out nametags and address cards for each attendee. We have the attendees check the registration material for accuracy. Having the wrong address for a prospect at this stage is not a major disaster, because he/she will correct the mistake, but letting the wrong address go uncorrected can be as bad as having no address at all. The registration personnel also hand out seminar workbooks.

It is a good idea to have at least two people speaking and to schedule a refreshment break between speakers. The break gives people a chance to approach and talk with the presenters. In fact, presenters often find themselves surrounded by people with questions. It is a golden opportunity to make personal contact with those attending the seminar. Obviously, it is important for the presenters to be relaxed, friendly, and sincere.

Explaining the Separate Account Management Process

The last part of the seminar process involves getting those in attendance to want to have an investment policy statement or statement of objectives written for them. You can have participants complete a response sheet. The aim of the response sheet is not to grade how well you did, but to determine what participants liked, what they didn't like, and most important, to find those who desire a complimentary follow-up meeting that will result in an investment policy statement. Prioritize the follow-up request forms. We give the participants the opportunity to mark *yes, maybe,* and *no.* If they mark *no,* we don't call them.

The Presentation

In the workshop, your presentation should start with addressing the audience's values. Start by telling participants that the four most powerful words in the English language are *I need your help*. Then ask, "How many of you are confused about investing?" (Show of hands.) Pause and tell everyone to look around; almost everyone in the audience should have raised a hand. Make sure that you give them time to respond, and then acknowledge them. Then say, "If you're not confused about investing, you're not paying attention." That should get a chuckle and help them begin to see what is in it for them; you are going to help them through all the confusion in the investment arena.

Next, try to determine the level of sophistication in the audience. Ask how many in the audience consider themselves to be sophisticated investors. (Show of hands.) Typically in groups of 30, we have one fellow in the back of the room raising his hand defiantly. That person is likely to be your biggest challenge. Then say, "Let me share with you our definition of a sophisticated investor: someone who has lost money at least once and did not enjoy the experience. Now, how many of you are sophisticated investors?" (Everyone raises a hand.) It's a very powerful method to get people involved in the process.

Outline the key concepts of separate accounts, and illustrate the building-block approach. This is a very powerful way of introducing separate account investing. Throughout the presentation, mention the various steps of the investment management consulting process, and reiterate the importance of the investment policy statement. By the time we're ready to close the workshop, attendees are extremely comfortable with the thoughtful discipline of not only our investment approach, but also the process we use in working with new clients. Ask the audience to check off on a response sheet whether they would like a complimentary personal investment policy statement prepared individually for them.

Don't judge success by the number of people in the workshop. Don't judge success by the number of people who check off that they want to meet with you. Judge success by the real results you achieve—new assets under management. In most cases, groups numbering between 10 and 30 have been the most successful.

Promotion

Promotion basically consists of both relationship marketing and direct marketing. Let your clients know that you are holding monthly workshops and that their colleagues and friends are invited to attend. If your clients perceive that the process you use to work with new investors is consistent and high in quality, they'll be comfortable giving you the referrals for which you ask at each quarterly meeting.

In addition, when you are getting started, it can be advantageous to conduct a very targeted direct-mail campaign. You might be tempted to simply run a newspaper ad, but you may find that doing so does a better job of having competitors attend your workshops than qualified prospects. Teaming up with a radio personality who runs the top local financial show can be successful. If you are just getting started and don't have existing relationships, this might be something to consider. Think about how you prefer to be contacted and you will begin to understand why teaming up with a CPA or other financial professional can greatly enhance your success.

The most successful workshops that we've done were sponsored workshops, rather than public workshops. We enlist another organization to cosponsor the workshop, such as a charitable organization or professional association. This not only reduces costs dramatically, it provides a foot in the door to their specialized donor or client lists. Choose the association or professional organization wisely, however, to make sure that it is consistent with your ideal client profile.

Approach B—One-on-One

By choosing the one-on-one approach as your introductory method, you will need to cover the benefits of your broker-dealer and conduct the fact-finding process all in the same meeting. This meeting should run about one hour. You may need one or two subsequent meetings to cover all the ground necessary to discover the clients' attitudes about money, their expectations of you and what their money can realistically do for them, and for you to establish the kind of trust that will allow the client to open up about fears or concerns they may not readily talk about.

These hidden feelings can have an important bearing on the investment plan you set up for the client, so it's important to take the time necessary to establish this trust. The quality of the relationship you establish on the front end can mean the difference in a long-term relationship that can lead you to become the family advisor and negate the perception that you are still just selling a product, packaged as a separate account.

Preliminary Steps to the Meeting

- Send direct-mail letter in advance.
- Call client to establish the first one-hour meeting.

Conducting the Meeting

- Thirty minutes for presentation.
- Walk through your presentation with your client.
- Offer a free follow-up fact-finding meeting.

Schedule a Follow-Up Solutions Meeting (Refer to Step 4 for Details)

Let your client know that you need to set up a follow-up meeting to discuss the results of his/her profile and your recommendations. By making the recommendation at a later date, the client perceives that the investment program is going to be completed objectively—in their best interest and tailored to their specific needs.

Tips: Conducting an introductory one-on-one meeting should be done in the following environments:

- On your quietest days (i.e., typically Thursday and Friday afternoons)
- After you have built a solid partnership of trust and loyalty with the client
- When you have at least 40 percent of the client's total assets under your control

Follow-Up Solutions Meeting

Preliminary steps.   Evaluate the results of the client profile. Contact the client to arrange an appointment date and time. After setting the appointment, you should contact your client approximately 48 hours in advance to reconfirm your meeting.

Coordinate appropriate client materials.   Package appropriate investment-specific marketing materials needed to describe and support the client's specific strategy(ies).

Review the results of the profile with the client (approximately 15 minutes).   Share with your clients what the profile has revealed about their risk tolerance, preferences, and the direction in which they need to be moving to reach their goals.

Thirty-minute recommendation/solution (30 to 45 minutes).   Describe the overall recommended plan: how it relates to the client's profile and

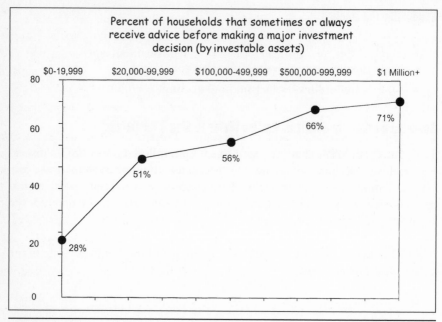

Percent of households that sometimes or always receive advice before making a major investment decision (by investable assets)

FIGURE 15.3 As Assets Grow, Investors Are More Likely to Seek Advice.
Source: 1999 SRI MacroMonitor.

what it will do for him/her. Based on the investment strategy(ies) recommended for each client, you will have a variety of support materials that can assist you in walking through the appropriate tools and strategies with the client (Figure 15.3).

Creating Strategic Alliances with Other Financial Advisors!

Strategic alliances work well with anyone who shares a similar target market with you. By creating a strategic alliance, you can open doors, build trust, and create new business opportunities for both organizations. A strategic alliance is a synergistic and mutually beneficial partnership that results in a win-win arrangement. In the past, financial advisors would call other professionals and invite them to lunch with the misplaced hope of getting referrals.

We'd spend most of the lunch meeting attempting to differentiate ourselves from other financial advisors so that the accountant would be comfortable sending their clients to us. The fact is, however, that financial advisors look pretty much the same to CPAs, much as all CPAs look pretty much the same to financial advisors. To build a strategic alliance, you need to focus on being perceived as an ally, helping the CPA firm to be hugely successful. By focusing on this, not on how you differ in investment approach, you will become successful at partnering with CPAs.

We have found that there are five steps to developing a successful strategic alliance:

Step 1: Formulation and preparation. Prepare a list of the local and regional CPA firms in your area. Identify the senior partners. For most financial advisors, it doesn't make sense to go after the Big Six firms. You'll end up frustrated at their inability to move quickly due to large bureaucracies. Local and regional firms are under tremendous pressure to develop marketing strategies. They need your help. Identify firms that are in your existing target market. You're likely to have access to a local business journal that publishes a list of the top firms. Use this as a resource and aim high. Look for top firms that share your targeted market and are regional or local.

Step 2: Make the call. Call the targeted CPA partners and set up an appointment to discuss joint marketing opportunities. Be bold. The purpose is to explore ideas of how strategic alliances might be mutually beneficial. Our experience has been that every time we've called a targeted CPA firm, they've wanted to get together. Why? They need help with business development. When they hear that you are in the process of exploring strategic alliances with CPA firms and you're interviewing three or four to identify which would be the best partner, they are going to want to meet with you. On the first call, explain that you're not looking for referrals, but a true strategic alliance-marketing partner. That will differentiate you from almost all the competition.

Step 3: The first meeting. Take a few moments to introduce yourself— but no more than three minutes. Remember, CPAs can't tell the difference between investment advisors. Immediately shift the conversation to their concerns and how an alliance might address those concerns. Even if you see opportunities, don't move on them immediately. Go slow and create a larger opportunity. Take notes. Share with them what marketing research suggests are their challenges. Ask how the firm is currently addressing each of the challenges that CPAs face.

1. *Dealing with the liability of working with any marketing partner.* CPAs are concerned with liability. Most CPA firms have been sued, and certainly the Big Six have had high-profile lawsuits. Share with them up front that you are also concerned with liability, and would

like to discuss this issue with them in more detail. Also mention that you are convinced that because you use an asset class investing approach (since reading this book), they will have minimal liability exposure in working with you.

2. *Developing new business clients.*   Ask them what they're doing currently to develop new business. Have they worked in the past with a financial advisor? Has it been successful? What are some of the most successful marketing projects that they've undertaken in the past? Don't be surprised if they haven't done anything. Most firms are just beginning to be proactive in marketing.

3. *Acquiring new revenue from existing clients.*   Explain that you understand many CPAs are losing revenue from existing clients because of other readily available tax services, such as the computerized software programs. What are they currently doing to generate new revenue? Would they be interested in exploring other avenues with you? Ask what they're doing to retain their existing client base, and tell them you have some ideas.

4. *Maximizing client benefits.*   Tell them about the benefits of working with you. Ask if they have ever thought about increasing the benefits that they offer clients by developing a strategic alliance with a high-quality investment advisor.

Tell them that you want to share any information they've given you with your marketing people. Hopefully, you have some marketing people, or at least an informal marketing advisory board you can bounce things off. (If you have followed the steps properly, you do have an informal marketing advisory board.) Tell the CPA partner that you'd like to set up a second meeting for brainstorming and kicking around possibilities of how you might work together. If working with this CPA firm looks like an exciting opportunity, discuss looking at the next two years. If it doesn't, thank them for their time, ask for some of their business cards, and move on.

Step 4: The second meeting/market exploration.   The purpose of the second meeting is to discover shared opportunities, goals, and expectations for the future. This should not be done over a meal. You should allocate at least an hour to explore shared expectations from having a strategic alliance over an initial time period of 12 months. Compare their vision and yours of how you might jointly accomplish your mutual expectations. You want to have a series of questions prepared that will be stimulating and open-ended—and listen. Take detailed notes of the points discussed. If the meeting is successful and you want to work with this person further, set up a third meeting where you will present a draft of a plan to maximize the opportunity to work together.

Step 5: The third meeting/planning. Prior to this third meeting, you've reviewed all the notes from the previous meetings and have written up a marketing action plan, which delineates ideal goals and minimum goals of this strategic alliance. Typically, goals are expressed for the CPA firm in revenue and for your asset management business by the amount of assets you acquire under management. The ideal goal is what it takes to make a very successful program over the next 12 months. The minimum goal is what is necessary to achieve in order to continue. By having goals, you will get much more focused on working together. Then, write up the strategy.

We have found that setting up systematic workshops together serves a number of purposes. One, by having workshops, not only do you get exposure to the other firm's client base, but you also develop consistent markets together. Most important, your strategic alliance partners finally get to hear your story in a very professional manner when they sit in on the meeting. That alone is worth conducting the workshop.

Write out specific tactics and outline each of your responsibilities in developing workshops or other events and strategies together. Once you have this strategic plan in writing, you are ready for the third meeting.

This meeting is simply about getting agreement on the structure of fulfilling your initial project together. Review the overall plan, the strategy, the goals, and the targeted action steps to reach your mutually agreed-upon market. Discuss both short- and long-term expectations. Review the budget of expenses and how they will be shared. Typically, expenses are shared 50/50. Look for points of leverage and opportunities that weren't explored in the initial written plan. For each step, reach an agreement as to whom, what, when, and how each step will be accomplished.

Developing an ongoing series of workshops for your mutual clients and prospects is a great starting point and a very powerful one. It will consistently reinforce the relationship and allow you to learn more.

Using the relationship-selling strategies we have just discussed will all but ensure the success of your asset management business. You must stay focused and go through each of the five steps in order to achieve the highest level of success of which you are capable. If you work the plan, you will realize your goals.

Now you're going to set up systems.

Systems Make the Difference

It's time to turn your financial sales job into a successful separate account management advisory business. The difference between your firm and others is that you will be able to produce substantially greater results with significantly less effort. Now you're going to set up the right systems to document and replicate your separate account business.

What is the most successful type of business today? The franchise. And what's the most successful franchise? McDonald's. By creating a reproducible system that consistently delivered results, Ray Kroc was not only able to sell hamburgers, he was able to sell the business itself over and over again. The business became the product. A turnkey operation was created that almost anyone could run.

You must build a turnkey business, even if you never open any more offices. Why? It's the only way to ensure consistent experiences for clients, whether you're there or not. That's extremely important.

Design systems to create a meaningful advantage by differentiating yourself from competitors in your clients' eyes. In his book *The E Myth,* Michael Gerber writes, "It's the systems that can give the consumers the perception of controlling their own experience." He goes on to say that every great business sells control—control over customers' experiences. Control is the ability to give customers what they want the first time, and to faithfully replicate what they have received from that point on.

What is the difference between systems and replicating? A system consists of integrated components that work in an absolutely predictable fashion. Replicating is the documentation of those systems. Once you have replicated your business, the experiences you provide to clients can be repeated time and time again.

Prospecting for High-Net-Worth Investors

When the elite Army Rangers or Navy Seals prepare to conduct a military action, everything from guns to training manuals is laid out on long tables for physical review. Everything is coordinated with the mission; if it doesn't fit, it's eliminated. Likewise, everything you present should look as if it were put together with one purpose, using one language. If done correctly, the outcome suggests that there is someone in charge (you!), organizing chaos into a purposeful whole.

Many of us hurry to print up a glossy corporate brochure, as if that's the magic silver bullet. Yet, one of my clients—who has a $2 billion management company—still doesn't have a formal corporate brochure. In fact, this client never mails out any marketing or sales material—especially anything that's glossy and looks like mass marketing—because that's sure to turn off his affluent prospects. Instead, he uses third-party material, such as an article reprint, to showcase his investment beliefs and philosophy.

Examine your information delivery system. Does your positioning statement resonate in everything you do and stand for—from your partners to trainees, the person answering the phone, in sales presentations, interviews with media, phone scripts, direct-mail pieces and all marketing materials? Identify key influences and build a buzz that will communicate your message to many others. Build a battery of support material. Accumulate newspaper and magazine articles—whether written by yourself or by others—that explain, echo, or applaud your position.

It is critical to understand your audience so that you can deliver your message in the way your audience finds relevant. For instance, consumers and stockholders each want to hear a different story. The stockholder wants to hear about the latest earnings; the consumer is interested in price. The underlying theme, however, is going to be the same.

Pretend you are a prospect and look at your materials as if seeing them for the first time. Is your message clear? Can you improve on it? Is it compelling?

Seek feedback from anyone who can affect sales or perceptions—the media, the industry, your clients, consumers, and staff—through written surveys, phone calls, and e-mail. Feedback can help consolidate the story and hone the separate account message.

Writing a custom positioning statement can be a powerful experience, which helps you discover and clarify what you stand for, and/or enables you to redirect your attention. This process will help you remember that while a customer may be buying a separate account, what they are really buying is confidence in you.

One of the most effective ways of positioning yourself is to network. *Get the word out.* Let people know what you are doing. Send notices to trade associations that you might want to become involved in. If you join an association, don't fade into the woodwork; become an active member.

As an active participant in an association or industry, sponsor awards, contests, or scholarships that give others recognition and help them grow in their professions. Or simply work with the association sponsoring an award or scholarship. Such activities might not immediately show on your balance sheet, but they will help you gain recognition as a leader in the industry—an image you definitely want to project.

Always give your clients more than they expect. *Keep in touch:* Keep in touch with key clients. Send them advance notices of seminars. Frequently send out reprints and sales literature, with a personal note attached. A newsletter can keep your customers up-to-date. Whatever you do, don't give established customers a chance to forget or replace you.

Prospecting

High-net-worth investors are predisposed to separate account programs. This group needs professional money management and customized investments that address their individual financial goals and tax situation. This should be your target market group.

Most define wealthy as someone who displays an abundance of material possessions. In today's world, however, that's not a very accurate definition. We define wealthy investors as someone with a net worth of $1 million or more, excluding their personal residence. How you reach this group is the purpose of this discussion.

After you've spent time converting your existing clients to your separate account program and cloning your best clients, you may feel satisfaction to the point of complacency. Be careful—you've just started. You want to keep your momentum going by initiating a separate account marketing plan directed to the wealthy.

This is generally a group that does not want you to contact them directly. They want to be the ones doing the contacting. This puts you squarely on the horns of a dilemma. If you contact a prospect directly, they'll think of you as a salesperson. If you don't contact, you could go out of business. Your job is to market yourself in such a manner as to attract them to you (Figure 16.1).

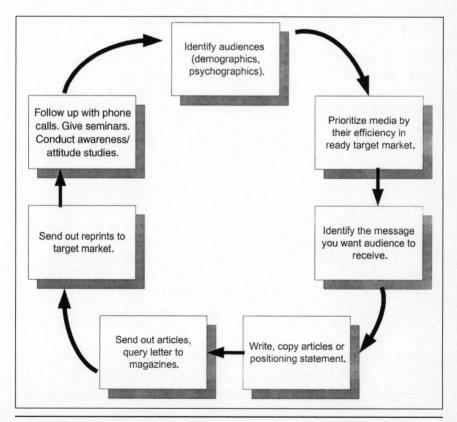

FIGURE 16.1   Integrating Credibility Marketing and Publicity.

It is crucial to consider carefully which specific market to target because your problem-solving skills must match up with the needs of this market (Figure 16.2). Your chance of succeeding in developing a wealthy market will also largely depend upon your ability to communicate and effectively provide world-class service.

Because your revenue will be augmented substantially by penetrating this new market, it follows that your quality of life will also be dramatically improved.

The Step-by-Step Process

Step 1: Market viability—identify and find your opportunities.

- *Is this market exciting?*   How many wealthy people does it have? If they are a part of a larger market group, can they be segmented and reached directly? Concentrate on the niches within the market that can give you the greatest results. Can this market be reached profitably? Do you enjoy being with the people in this market? Do you have a natural interest in what they do?

- *Examples of primary markets.*   These markets are broad—composed of thousands: self-employed professionals, small-business owners, retirees, preretirees, key executives, sales and marketing professionals, inheritors, widows, sports athletes and/or their executive agents, divorcees, farmers/ranchers, qualified plans, and so forth.

The Wealthy Have Strong Views of What They Deem Important:

84% of delegators prefer to deal with a single individual.	63% prefer to invest through a large nationally known firm.
73% want to consult with an expert.	63% prefer to spend as little time on their investments as possible.
72% like to plan ahead 5 to 10 years.	53% need help preparing a plan.
70% would like to become more knowledgeable.	53% do not trust stockbrokers.
70% want to deal with people who know them by name.	52% are not sure if their own financial decisions are right.

Figure 16.2   Your Target Is Affluent.

- *Examples of niche markets.*   These markets are small and generally contained within the larger preceding markets and consist of a hundred people or so: a single company that is downsizing (lump-sum distributions), a hospital and all of its doctors, the key executives of a corporation, the real estate agents of a realty company (for charitable remainder unit trust referrals), alumni associations, the Automobile Dealers' Association, the California Dental Association, and so on. There are 122,000 trade associations—many are composed of nothing but millionaires. Frequently, small companies that have just gone public have a number of instant multimillionaires. Many companies are downsizing, with employees receiving lump-sum distributions of anywhere between one-quarter to one and one-half million dollars. Some country clubs have such high fees that only millionaires can belong. Millionaires do flock together. You need to find out where they flock.

  - ***The smaller the niche market, the better.***   This seems contrary to logic, but it's not. If a niche market only has a hundred millionaires in it, it is very probable they will know each other and be a better source of referrals to you. In larger markets, no one knows anyone and cannot help you much. Smaller markets are much easier to penetrate fully for that reason. It is also easier to identify the common needs, wants, desires, and frustrations of people in a small market that you can address. Most financial advisors don't need more than a hundred millionaires at any given time, anyway.

  - ***The best way to find the best niche market.***   Niche markets are worthless unless you have found someone that is influential and willing to be a delivery system into that market. Therefore, the best way is to find the person that will be your delivery system first—then pick that market as the one that has the best potential. This influential person can be found through either the questioning process of cloning or one of your own established contacts that either has direct access to a niche market or has control or influence over someone who does. Either way, you need to ask the right questions to be aware of who has access to these kinds of exciting and profitable markets.

Step 2: Identify the typical financial problems of the people in this market.
The following are some typical financial problems experienced by high-net-worth investors.

- *What can I do with my low-cost-basis stock?* Most HNW investors have low-cost-basis stock, and they're beginning to understand the inherent risk in holding it and the tax implications of selling it to diversify. They're looking for separate account managers who can propose solutions, from total sale to partial sale to holding the stock and diversifying around it using other money. Accepting low-cost-basis stock is one of the basic tenets of true separate account management.

- *Tax loss harvesting.* A good after-tax separate account manager will employ tax-loss harvesting to raise the cost on the investor's portfolio gradually. A buy-and-hold strategy, although tax-efficient short-term, can create long-term tax issues because it creates an inflexible portfolio.

- *Tax-lot optimization.* Factoring the tax-lot cost into traditional portfolio optimization protocols makes an already complex process even more complicated, but current technology and the new tech tools that are just around the corner make it possible, even today. Tomorrow, investors will be demanding it before they give you their taxable assets to manage.

- *Year-end loss/gain requests.* Besides harvesting losses to reposition the portfolio internally, winning separate account managers will entertain requests to offset realized gains and losses outside the portfolio. If you can offset, say, a $50,000 gain from a condo sale by realizing $50,000 in losses in the portfolio, you've positioned yourself as the guy who made it unnecessary for the client to write a $10,000 check to Uncle Sam. Talk about relationship cement!

- *Fulfillment capability.* Moving away from tax-oriented management, the ability to service client needs includes the willingness to manage a portfolio around a large central holding. A highly compensated executive may have stock, option, and job exposure to a single stock. Winning money managers will be able to avoid not just that stock, but the entire industry or sector, if necessary.

- *Security blocks.* A relatively simple function that should be on every money manager's service offering today is stock blocking. For example, if the model portfolio holds chemical stock A, and the client doesn't like their environmental policies, the winning manager will be able to block Company A and replace it with another, acceptable stock from that sector or industry.

These are some typical financial problems facing high-net-worth investors. Solving problems and tailoring the portfolio to the needs of the individual is still virgin territory in separate accounts.

Step 3: Identify your solutions to those problems.   List their problems and the specific solutions you can offer. Be complete. Also list all of the best people (specialists) that could be used (through a strategic alliance) to implement the solutions. List 1, 2, 3, and so on.

Step 4: What is your desired position as a problem solver?   How can you position yourself as the problem solver for the problems in your specific market? How can you stand out in an overcrowded, competitive marketplace? Without positioning yourself as a problem solver, no one will come to you to solve their problems. It's that simple. And it's also that important if you want to expand your practice.

Your desired position is dependent upon your problem-solving skills and whether they match the problems of your targeted market. You can't fake it. To serve a market successfully, you have to develop a specialty. Therefore, either match your skills to the market or match the market to your skills—there's no in-between!

One huge advantage of specializing in a targeted market is that you can specialize in solving that market's problems better than anyone else. Being a person with many skills, but a master of none, gains you the reputation and credibility of a master of none. So position yourself as a specialist and a professional expert in solving the problems of a targeted market; then prove it with your solutions. See Step 9: Unique selling proposition (USP), for ways to communicate your problem-solving capabilities.

Step 5: Organizations—identify.   Is there a key organization(s) that represents this market segment (e.g., a trade association, a club, a civic group)? Do the associations or organizations have an information package that you could get from the director?

Step 6: Centers of influence and strategic alliances—identify.   Who are the centers of influence for this targeted market? Is there someone who could help you identify the qualified prospects and perhaps even introduce you to them?

There are many people who can help identify qualified prospects. Studies show that the wealthy hold their highest trust for their accountants and attorneys. Centers of influence can be directors of trade associations, presidents of social clubs, or community leaders. Many others become influential by either occupation, personal trust, or popularity.

The best way to find centers of influence to work with you is to solve problems for them. Sell the one with influence first, and by doing so, it is easier for all the rest to follow. This is a good way to position yourself and communicate your expertise all in one effort. Centers of influence can have a dramatic influence on mass decisions. The center of influence could be a church pastor or rabbi, a well-known athlete, a public official, or a local individual who, because of his/her service, has earned many people's trust. A center of influence might even be one of your own top clients. If you don't know who the center of influence is for a given market, just ask. Get many opinions, because there may be more than one person.

Wealthy people place the most trust in their accountants and attorneys. Insurance agents are frequently high on the list, too. Therefore, a strategic alliance with someone already trusted in your selected market could bring rapid success as soon as you can develop the trust of that strategic ally. By establishing strategic alliances with centers of influence you can cut through the defenses surrounding wealthy prospects. The sound you want to hear is "My CPA recommended I call you. He (She) said you could help me."

The wealthy rely on accountants and attorneys, because they don't see them as salespeople, they see them as unbiased. Frequently, though, accountants and attorneys are ill-equipped to furnish investment advice. It is a specialized field, and just as in their own professions, investment methodology has changed continually.

- *Separate account fee-only alliances.* Fee-only financial advisors are now being accepted by fee-only accountants and attorneys as a source of specialized and professional talent for helping their clients with investments. This has opened the door to fee-only financial advisors to form strategic alliances with them. They often need to be called in anyway to implement many financial strategies like family partnerships and living trusts. By combining the skills of accountants, attorneys, and insurance agents in strategic alliances, you can offer more to the client and, as a result, rise above the competition.

  The way to develop a strategic alliance with a center of influence is to help him/her solve his/her problems and meet his/her objectives and goals. If you can gain the trust of centers of influence, you can get what you want and need: prequalified referrals with an endorsement from someone whom the wealthy trust.

Step 7: Publications—identify. Does this market have its own newsletter or publication? Would the director of that publication print an article from you if it addressed the needs of the people in the association and was not a sales pitch? Call the director of the association and get the criteria or rules for outside authors.

Step 8: Most compelling sales message—identify.   What is the most compelling sales message to your specified market? What can you say that will exactly identify the problems or needs they have, and how will you solve them? This should be written and should be no more than just a few paragraphs.

Step 9: Unique selling proposition (USP)—identify.   What do you offer that is unique as compared with other money management or portfolio management services? It must be something unique, something that people want, and something that your competition doesn't offer. What else differentiates you from the competition?

If asked what you do for a living, what could you say that best positions you (by virtue of what you do) that would create interest in the listener? It should be a verbal benefit statement. Your USP should be a verbal calling card—not longer than one sentence. USP examples include:

- "I'm in the business of helping wealthy people manage their assets."

- "I specialize in making work optional for small-business owners."

   If you say, "I am a financial planner," or "I am an advisor," you position yourself as a product pusher and not a problem solver.

   Of course, you will need to make your verbal benefit statement or unique selling proposition compatible with the solution or benefit needed by your targeted market. Try out your positioning statement on a few prospects to see if they will come back and ask you "How do you do that?" Your goal is to be known as a problem solver to the market in which you work.

Step 10: Communicate your benefits to your market.   One of the benefits of targeting is that you can communicate directly to qualified prospects without having to go to the masses to find your perfect, qualified prospect through sheer luck and expense. The problem with mass mailings and other mass-advertising efforts is that unqualified people also respond to you en masse, thus causing you to waste time sorting them out. To go directly to your wealthy targeted market is cheaper, and it is a more efficient use of your time. Less time, less cost, richer clients—all equal higher profitability and a whole lot less frustration.

However, you still need to find the most efficient way to communicate your unique problem-solving capabilities. Generally, the best way to do this is through an organization or a center of influence that represents that market. Either of these two could also provide a list of that market's constituents.

Studies have shown that it generally takes five to eight communication impressions over time to turn prospects into clients. It takes this time to gain their trust when major decisions are at stake. Unfortunately, most salespeople only make about three efforts at communicating and then quit. Instead of having to make multiple impressions on 1,000 unqualified prospects in a random market (e.g., radio, mass geographic mailing), you could make 10 impressions on 100 qualified prospects in a specified niche market. It's a lot more efficient in terms of cost, time, and results when you are communicating directly with your desired, qualified prospects who need you (and it's a lot more fun, too!).

For optimal results, combine as many different types of communications as possible for each prospect. You can use any number of the following types of communications: targeted mailings, trade association speeches or news articles, endorsements from centers of influence, workshops, notifications, telephone follow-ups, and more.

The primary goal of all professional services marketing people is to get face to face with prequalified clients (preferably preendorsed, too). To do this requires you to communicate your unique skills to your market in such a manner that will make them want to see you and that will gain their trust. Again, this requires five to eight communication contacts in various forms.

Following are six different detailed options of how to communicate your unique skills. Consider using as many of these options as possible with each of your targeted prospects.

Option A: Be a speaker at their organization.   The fastest and most efficient way to communicate to your market is to speak to an association, club, or organization that represents that market segment (and be introduced by someone whom they already trust). It takes the same amount of time to speak to 100 people that it does to speak to one, so you might as well save 99 hours. It's a way to leverage your time, if you're a good public speaker. If you're not, either develop the skill required or find a strategic ally with whom you can share the podium. Speaking helps to rapidly elevate your credibility as a problem solver. Caution: Do not use this speaking opportunity to sell your product! This is not generally allowed by associations, and it would not be appropriate anyway, because you want to position yourself as a problem solver, not a product pusher!

Option B: Write an article and publish it in their newsletter. Write an article about one of their wants, needs, or problems, and position yourself as an expert in solving those problems. This article, by the way, can be used for the rest of your life to build credibility with all your current and future clients. If it truly addresses a need of the group without selling them a product, it will be readily accepted. It's easier to get in a newsletter or trade publication than you think. Try it.

Option C: Give workshops or seminars to a select segment of your market. For this to be successful, you need to find a key contact to give you a list of prequalified people to invite. Huge numbers are not necessary. Don't forget that if you are working with very wealthy prospects, you no longer have to use expensive mass-media campaigns to communicate to a bunch of unqualified, disinterested prospects in the vain hope that a few of them are wealthy. You should be targeting, not randomly shotgunning. Ten very wealthy clients could make your year. So a meeting with 5 to 10 highly qualified people would be very desirable. However, 100 very wealthy clients in one room does elevate your chance of great success!

Option D: Social farming. Put yourself in places where there are high concentrations of people in your targeted market. If you look like them, talk like them, and do the same things they do, they will get to know you very quickly.

Option E: Target a mailing with a telephone follow-up. Use your key contacts to help you define a list of qualified prospects within the market segment. Mail a personalized letter to them addressing a problem they have that you can solve. Always make it a call for action by inviting them to a workshop or offering them a free half hour of consultation time. Follow-up by telephone no later than three or four days after the letter has been mailed.

Option F: Follow-up educational articles. Send third-party articles that prove your knowledge of investment methodology and problem-solving capabilities. Consider sending your prospects a book like *Investment Policy* by Charles Ellis or anything that provides education and trust in modern portfolio theory. These should be sent on an automated schedule.

Using Your Database

A database is required to keep track of each client's progress through the various steps of initial communication, follow-ups, and final sale. If you're going to make five to eight separate communication impressions on a prospect (possibly by combining all the aforementioned options), you have to keep track so that no prospect is lost through the cracks of your memory.

To do timely, sequential impressions with each client requires a scheduled follow-up system with an automatic reminder alarm for each subsequent step of your tactical sales plan. To miss an appropriately timed follow-up could waste all that's gone before.

Review and Monitoring/Tracking Program

Where have you been? Where are you going? How are you doing right now?

Review Your Marketing Strategy

Set up simple tracking systems to review your marketing strategies. Conduct a major review of your progress every six months. This will create momentum, strengthen your vision, emphasize successes and achieved goals, and help you to stay on your marketing track. Ask yourself these questions:

- Is my marketing program strong enough?
- Is my approach achieving the results I want?
- What parts of my business do I need to strengthen?
- Do I need to create more demand for my services and products?
- Am I reaching the clients I really want?
- Am I providing what these preferred clients really want?
- Am I addressing their key current financial concerns?

Getting Too Close?

The key to building a successful separate account business is to develop intimate relationships with your clients. This can give you a significant competitive advantage. This is not to imply that all of your clients need to be your best friends.

Financial advisors whom we have asked to describe their relationship with their clients have responded, "Great." Most mean they have a great rapport. They are often close friends with their clients. While this generally makes business more enjoyable, it can also backfire and blur the lines between your business and your personal life.

Friendship is not the highest value that affluent clients look for in an advisor. Clients want professionals whom they can trust and who truly impress them. You have to build trust and systematically impress your clients in every moment of truth you have with them. A moment of truth is any contact you have with your clients when you have the opportunity to delight them.

Referrals

If you have been in separate account management for any length of time, you are sitting on a marketing goldmine. Most successful financial advisors have an almost unlimited resource of free prospects. While most other businesses have to spend between 15 and 25 percent of revenue and half their time in acquiring new customers, all you have to do is ask your existing satisfied clients for referrals and you will have more prequalified prospects than you can handle.

According to Institutional Investor, Inc., 60.5 percent of wealthy investors feel they are influential in referring advisors to others. In a large demographic group survey, it was found that satisfied clients want to give referrals. When you understand a target market's business concerns, and prospects perceive you as one of them, your audience is especially receptive to your message (Figure 16.3).

If clients don't give you referrals, ask them why not. That may sound blunt, but if you want to continue to spend 80 to 90 percent of your time working with your existing client base rather than prospecting, you need their referrals. Marketing through referrals is a more cost-effective method of obtaining prequalified prospects and doesn't dilute energy from servicing existing clientele.

Invite new clients to be on your marketing advisory team. Don't work with just anyone. Each client must be a good fit for a separate account. Your sales process allows you to determine in the first meeting (a) if you can provide measurable benefits; (b) if the prospect's financial profile meets your target marketing plan; and (c) if the prospect's goals and attitudes fit, allowing the development of a lasting advisory relationship.

If you are going to give advice, be prepared to back up your recommendations with evidence or proof. Most likely, it will be the first time that your client has worked with somebody who actually believes in what he/she is recommending and can prove it. Clients will respect you tremendously for following your knowledge and convictions.

Always Communicate the Benefits of Owning a Separate Account

How are you going to communicate this message? One of the benefits of targeting your market first is that you can communicate directly to existing

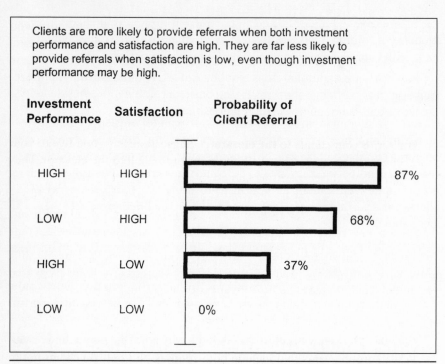

Clients are more likely to provide referrals when both investment performance and satisfaction are high. They are far less likely to provide referrals when satisfaction is low, even though investment performance may be high.

Investment Performance	Satisfaction	Probability of Client Referral
HIGH	HIGH	87%
LOW	HIGH	68%
HIGH	LOW	37%
LOW	LOW	0%

FIGURE 16.3 Probability of Referrals by Investment Performance and Client Satisfaction.

Source: Prince & Associates, 1997.

clients—instead of randomly contacting the masses to find a few qualified prospects. So, what is the most effective way to communicate your unique problem-solving capabilities? Most traditional marketing programs are out of alignment with how the wealthy actually select their investments. The common theme that runs through all selection criteria is *established relationships.* Any intelligent investor considering entrusting you with his/her life savings will first check to see if you are competent, trustworthy, and have done a good job for respected associates. This method of finding an advisor through referral is familiar, reliable, and the preferred way we all like to find, for instance, a doctor or dentist. The secret to a successful marketing program is aligning your approach with the way your clients *want* to be sold. After communications, now measure results.

Your marketing theme of problem solver should become automatic and resonate in everything you do, from contacting a prospect to addressing a seminar. Commit your marketing plan to writing and do something to move your plan ahead every day. Do not fall into the trap of getting lost in the running of your business without taking a step back to build the business you really want.

Following are additional steps that you can use to build and maintain your relationships. Although some may seem basic, in combination, they do help to generate and maintain powerful relationships.

Walk with your clients to the elevator. Suggestion: Say good-bye to your client at the front door; walk them down the hall to the elevator. They appreciate the extra effort and attention.

Use personal note cards. Hardly anyone today takes the time to write personal notes, even though people really appreciate them and it sets you apart from everyone else. The cards look like invitations when they are opened, and, in effect, they are—they are invitations to do business and refer business to a thoughtful financial advisor.

Recognize birthdays. The contact is probably more important than the sentiment. Over the years we have used personal letters, cards, certificates, and other forms of recognition.

Sponsor client-appreciation events. Our biggest successes have been with group events that include both spouses. Not only do clients get to meet each other; there is a group dynamic, which creates increased prestige and referability for the advisor/planner.

Offer specialized resources. Each year, send your clients a letter containing a checklist of reports they can order from your office.

Send newsletters. You can write your own newsletters or use a professional service that publishes financial newsletters. The important thing is to have your name in front of clients regularly, with information that reinforces the image you wish to project to your target audience.

Send holiday greetings. Thanksgiving, Christmas, or other holiday cards are well received, especially if you do something different. For example, use these cards to inform your clients of the charitable contributions you have made during the past year.

Make good use of your website. Our website is designed with one purpose in mind: We want to be the financial gatekeeper to the World Wide Web for current and prospective clients. It includes information about our company, links to over 20 other financial websites, various financial calculators, newsletters, articles, market quotes, portfolio tracking, and other information.

Use distinguished service awards.   A bouquet of flowers and a certificate of appreciation can be sent to an employee who has provided outstanding service.

Create a scholastic gift.   Gift a $1000 merit scholarship to an outstanding local high school student who is majoring in business.

The follow is a list of resource books to help you with marketing.

Bibliography

Chambers, Larry. *Credibility Marketing.* Dearborn, 2001.

Chambers, Larry. *The Guide to Financial Public Relations: How You Can Stand Out in the Midst of Competitive Clutter.* St. Lucie Press. Catalog JM121.

Gladwell, Malcolm. *The Tipping Point: How Little Things Can Make a Big Difference.* Little, Brown & Company, 2001.

Godin, Seth. *Permission Marketing: Turning Strangers into Friends and Friends into Customers.* Simon & Schuster, 1999.

Sacharin, Ken. *Attention: How to Interrupt, Yell, Whisper and Touch Consumers,* 2000.

Best Resources for Publishing Contacts

The Writer Magazine. Cincinnati, OH.

Writer's Market (annual). Cincinnati, OH: Writer's Digest Books, 2001.

Gage, Diane, and Marcia Coppess. *Get Published: 100 Top Magazine Editors Tell You How.* Henry Holt.

Cool, Lisa Collier. *How to Write Irresistible Query Letters.* Writer's Digest Books.

Herman, Jeff, and Deborah M. Adams. *Write the Perfect Book Proposal: 10 Proposals That Sold and Why.* New York: Wiley, 1993.

Lyon, Elizabeth. *Nonfiction Book Proposals Anybody Can Write.* Hillsboro, OR: Blue Heron, 1995.

Holmes, Marjorie. *How to Write and Sell Your Life Experiences.* Writer's Digest Books, 1993.

All-In-One Media Directory. (Lists all American TV, radio stations, daily and weekly newspapers.) Gebbie Press, www.gebbieinc.com.

Magazines on the Internet—browse by category. Then visit the magazine website.

Bacon's Media Directories, 800-621-0561. Includes most media outlets in the country and is available in libraries and on CD-ROM.

Burrelle's Media Directories, 212-279-4270. Individual directories for print, radio, television, and cable.

Hudson's Subscription Newsletter Directory, 800-572-3451. Sorts out the growing number of professional newsletters worldwide.

How To Get on Radio Talk Shows, 303-722-7200. Lists 700 radio talk show producers in need of expert guests for telephone interviews.

Who's Who in Association Management, 202-626-2723. Published by the American Society of Association Executives. Industry or professional organizations are likely members, and are listed by subject and region.

CHAPTER

17

Compliance

Giving advice is perceived as carrying liability, and firms are seeking ways to minimize liability—therein exists a real opportunity.

Clients are seeking expert advice and are willing to pay for it. Everyone is trying to transfer the advice-giving responsibility to someone else—but that's the only part of the investment process that cannot be commoditized, and therefore it's extremely valuable.

Personalized advice is the one piece of the investment process that can't be standardized. The broker-consultant who personalizes an investment program and deals directly with the client is not easy to replace or duplicate. When such a broker switches to another firm, most clients move with the broker. Any firm is just another commodity of similar products, services, and pricing, but a financial advisor who gives personalized advice is not.

Financial planning is more complex than it's ever been, due to new tax law changes. If you're simply offering products to clients and letting them select their investments, you're in jeopardy of losing your accounts to someone who is willing to give advice. You shouldn't be backing away from your clients' need for advice; you should be charging headlong into fulfilling that need. After all, that's what investors are looking for.

Your Best Approach

It's best to present an environment where advice is readily available because that's what ties a client's loyalty to you. However, in the area of giving advice within the financial services industry, there are no rules that enable the financial services professional to come to terms with liability. There are definite prudent standards in investing, but no rules about giving advice.

We believe that if you want to give advice and minimize your liability in giving that advice, managed money should be a key component of your business. Managed money has the closest thing to a set of standards to be followed that exists in our industry today. The best defense against liability is to act in a prudent fashion and to document each step you take when giving advice. The process of offering managed money services requires you to leave an audit trail of prudence when making decisions for a client.

Let's face it, these days lawsuits are a common curse of doing business, but you should never let that be the deciding factor in whether you should give advice. When you do give advice, make sure it's sound. Back it up with data. If you let the fear of potential lawsuits stop you from giving advice, you'll become a commodity (and easily replaceable) like all the other components of the financial services business, and eventually you'll likely lose your clients.

Most of us think of regulatory agencies as antisales groups that set up roadblocks without understanding the business, certainly not with an interest toward helping sales. The reality, however, is that the compliance department of your organization can provide a competitive advantage, especially when the time comes to sell your practice. By doing business by the book, and incorporating the key addresses and disclosures necessary to appease the regulatory groups, you are creating a very powerful presentation.

Make sure you get everything approved by the appropriate parties before you use the documents or concepts. Be aware, however, that the rules governing registered representatives and registered investment advisors are not the same. The National Association of Securities Dealers (NASD), for instance, considers communication to 10 or more persons to be advertising. On the other hand, to registered investment advisors, advertising means communication to more than one person. You and/or your compliance officer need to understand many sets of rules.

Compliance procedures should include monitoring incoming and outgoing correspondence, but when Internet e-mail is used, that's difficult to do. Most companies now are putting in spot-check mechanisms, as opposed to checking every piece of correspondence. The NASD and the Securities and Exchange Commission (SEC) have new directives and have funded monitoring of the Internet. They now search the Internet to find potential violations. The biggest risk, however, comes from competitors who disapprove of what you're doing, because they're likely to report any unusual or suspect activities.

Financial services professionals acting as investment advisors must register with the SEC as well as state regulators—and it's natural to feel a sense of victory when the regulatory authorities approve your registration. In reality, however, your regulatory obligations as a Registered Investment Advisor (RIA) have just begun.

Your Record-Keeping Responsibilities

One of the easiest ways to successfully survive an SEC examination is to set up separate files corresponding to each of the major record-keeping responsibilities imposed by the Investment Advisors Act of 1940 (the "Advisors Act"). Set up these files, even if a few are empty or merely contain a single sheet of paper indicating that the rule is not applicable. This approach will show the SEC examiner that you are familiar with all of your record-keeping responsibilities; and even though a specific rule may not apply to your particular operation, you are cognizant of the rule.

Fifteen of the 16 record-keeping rules come directly from Sections 275.204-2(a)(1) through 9(a)(15) of the Advisors Act. The 16th rule comes from the Insider Trading and Securities Fraud Enforcement Act of 1988. Your firm should keep the following 16 files:

1. *Journal.*   Keep a journal in accordance with generally accepted accounting principles.

2. *Ledger.*   Maintain a ledger in accordance with generally accepted accounting principles.

3. *Securities purchases.*   Keep a complete record of all securities you have purchased or recommended.

4. *Canceled checks.*   Save all of your canceled checks and bank statements for a five-year period. (Caution: The five-year period is a federal standard, but some states, such as Pennsylvania and Wisconsin, require retention for a six-year period.)

5. *Paid and unpaid bills.*   Assemble and save all documentation of paid and unpaid bills.

6. *Trial balances and financial statements.*   Retain all trial balances and financial statements of the firm for a five-year period (or longer, depending on state requirements). The trial balances *must* be run on a quarterly basis. The SEC will not be pleased if you are unable to provide these trial balances on a quarterly basis for the past five years.

7. *Written communications.*   Keep records of all written communication between you and your advisory clients.

8. *Discretionary accounts.*   Maintain a list of all accounts in which you have been granted discretionary authority.

9. *Evidence of discretionary authority.*   Retain all documents that grant you discretionary authority.

10. *Written agreements.*   Save all written agreements executed between you and the advisory client.

11. *Communications recommending specific securities.*   Keep a copy of all advertisements, notices, or circulars that recommend specific securities to clients.

12. *Securities transactions where the RIA has direct or indirect ownership.* Maintain a separate record of all recommendations of a specific security in which you or your principals have direct or indirect ownership. This is the most difficult step to follow. It means that you must maintain an independent log documenting whenever you—or any associated person of your RIA entity—recommend to a client a specific security in which you, your spouse, your children—or any other entity which you control—also has a position.

13. *Securities transactions where the RIA has direct or indirect ownership, but is primarily engaged in business other than advisory activities.* Comply with the requirements of the previous item even if you are not primarily involved in the investment advisory activities.

14. *Brochure retention.*   Keep copies of brochures (copies of your Form ADV—Part II or substitute disclosure brochure) given to clients. Keep a signed receipt from all advisory clients. Also, don't forget that at the end of each year, in accordance with the Brochure Rule, you must offer to deliver an updated version of ADV—Part II or your substitute brochure, even if it has not changed, to all advisory clients of the prior year.

15. *Solicitors' documents.*   Retain copies of all disclosures signed by paid solicitors who refer advisory business to you and with whom you share advisory fees.

16. *Insider trading compliance.*   The Insider Trading and Securities Fraud Enforcement Act of 1988 amended Sections 204A and 214A of the Advisors Act to require all RIAs to adopt a written Firm-Wide Policy Statement and a Written Procedures to Implement statement. The Firm-Wide Policy Statement sets forth the specific steps that the RIA is taking to police the dissemination of material, nonpublic information.

The Written Procedures to Implement statement sets forth how the principals of the advisory firm are making sure that the firm-wide policy is observed. Federal securities laws require even small shops to adopt these two written statements. All officers, shareholders, directors, associated persons, and clerical personnel must receive each of these two statements. They should sign them as well.

What to Do When the SEC Visits

Some people don't call before they visit. Among them are industry examiners. Knowing that, it behooves each of us to be ready to welcome examiners at any time. Being prepared means that you have preassigned responsibility for representing the firm during the audit process, for having systems in order, and for knowing the kinds of documentation that are likely to be requested and having them readily available.

When auditors first show up, they will want to speak with the company's control people, generally the officers of the firm. Usually they'll tell you the audit is for cause or is a routine audit. This meeting sets the tone of the audit. Essentially, it's the place for setting the ground rules. You'll have a designated person (generally your firm's compliance officer) to handle requests from the auditors and to answer questions. Employees should not talk with auditors unless the compliance point person is present. Ask the auditors to respect that request. (Even a casual conversation in the hallway could lead to unwanted inquiries.) We want to ensure that one person hears all that is said and is available to clarify any misunderstandings.

You want to make auditors comfortable, and want the visit to provide as little disruption to your normal business activities as possible. To that end, provide them with workspace including tables/desks, phone, and access to a copy machine.

It's important that you know what's been provided to the auditors in case of any necessary follow-up. Do not provide any more than is asked for. Ask for all requests in writing.

Auditors can ask for any of your records. Generally, they start with accounting and then review client files. They are looking for evidence of the firm's attention to details—to receipts matching bills, to focus reports matching internal reports, to signed account agreements in every investor file, to the documentation of proper licensing of representatives. They will ask for a compliance manual and compare the firm's written procedures with actual procedures. They'll ask to see the correspondence files and look for the appropriate sign-offs. There is a good chance that, if you've done some advertising, the auditors have seen it and will be looking for a copy in the advertising files. If you've provided performance numbers, they'll want to check the calculations, so back-up information is crucial.

When all is said and done, an audit is an educational experience. Viewed positively, it forces us to review our business practices periodically, and it points us to those areas that need improvement.

Effective Marketing Materials

In public relations, you're building the firm and, by definition, your name is attached to all marketing materials. Everything you say via advertising must be carefully considered and balanced. If you're extolling the advantages of a product, you must also reveal the disadvantages. You're required by law to give balanced presentations.

One of the requirements of the regulatory agencies is that registered representatives with outside business activities inform their compliance departments, in writing, of those outside activities. The compliance department must be aware, for instance, if you are selling real estate. In addition to the notification requirements of the representative, there is a requirement for the written acknowledgment by the supervising firm.

Reprints are not preapproved advertising material. If you plan to send reprints out to investors or potential investors, you must first receive reprint permission. Then you are required to file the material with the NASD (if you're in an NASD firm) and receive approval for its use as marketing material.

In 1994, the NASD came out with a ruling that broker-dealers must oversee the activities of investment advisors. Broker-dealers are still adjusting to this ruling because many had an attitude of, "I don't want to know about or participate in any advisory activity." Now there is a responsibility to know and to oversee, which, if you are a registered representative, you must honor.

The SEC doesn't like the use of hypothetical performance numbers, but they're allowed when actual numbers aren't available. When actual numbers are available, the SEC requires the presentation of those numbers. An advisor must disclose, if applicable, that his/her clients had investments materially different from the model. The advisor must disclose prominently that the results do not represent actual trading, and must describe the effect of material market or economic conditions on the results.

The rule in compliance is not to take anything for granted. You can't stick your head in the sand in this area. Set up your files as suggested. Keep accurate records; it will pay off. Someday you may want to sell your firm, and one of the first things they will ask for is to see your compliance files. The best way to prevent any roadblocks is to stay ahead of any compliance issues. Have a system in place, follow the system, and document in writing your process. It will pay huge dividends when and if you decide to sell your business.

Further Reading

Schreiber, Don. *Strategic Business Planning: How to Convert Your Practice into a Business.* Dearborn, Chicago, Ill., 2001.
Bowen, John. *Creating Equity.* Securities Data Publishing, New York City, NY, 1996.

Leveraging Your Operations

These are simple strategies that can help build your separate account business. Operations are often overlooked, but when combined with the investment process, it can help in making a successful transition to separate accounts.

Operations are a critical defensive strategy that many advisors ignore. With operations, if you make a mistake, you no longer impress your clients, and ultimately you're likely to break their trust. A simple mistake such as sending out a report only a few cents off raises questions about your credibility and ability to conduct business. After all, if you can't get reports right to the penny, what kind of job are you doing with your investment management? What other mistakes are you making? By turning this equation around, you can delight and hugely impress your clients. Operations could become your biggest profit center because highly satisfied clients will share their experiences with their associates. This is the great leveraging effect of having delighted clients.

One of the easiest ways of being derailed is to ignore compliance. Advisors often view the compliance department as the antisales group. But you can turn this around, too, and use it to your competitive advantage. By footnoting everything you do, disclosing any potential conflict, and going way overboard to meet your clients' needs and treat them fairly, you've created a huge advantage. Investors can see that you're on their side.

Your Back Office

The key to a successful separate account business is having clients who trust you and who are impressed with what you do. Most financial advisors focus on marketing and sales to accomplish this. Unfortunately, it is difficult to measure how effective you are beyond the number of new accounts you obtain. Most prospects who decide not to work with you tend not to provide you with any quality information regarding why they did not choose you as their advisor. If you are reasonably successful in marketing, you may fool yourself into believing you are doing well even if you are making many mistakes. With operations, your clients will not let you fool yourself.

Focus on the details. Unfortunately, most firms fail because of enormous growth-strained operations, which ultimately leads clients losing confidence in your ability to manage the day-to-day details. To manage the day-to-day details, you need to look at operations proactively and as a true profit center.

The first step in building an operations center is to focus on results that you want—no errors. Write down your procedures. Starting with the new account process and continuing through every time you touch your client, you have an opportunity to impress your client and continue to earn the confidence with which they entrusted you.

Clients trust you with their life savings. If you can't even provide an acceptable statement, it raises serious questions about your competency in their minds. As well it should. Your clients are constantly making judgments about you. They compare you subconsciously with your competitors and with their friends' financial advisors constantly, no matter how good your relationship is with them. They may forgive an error the first time, but it puts them on guard. The second time, they're not as forgiving. And the third time, they're probably gone. It's the three-strike rule! Self-checking mechanisms save you from the embarrassment of showing a client a report that's wrong. Great systems ensure the success of your back office.

In designing your system, you must address each of these processes and make separate account management appear effortless to your clients. The best analogy is that your operational systems should appear to your clients as a swan on a beautifully sunny day effortlessly gliding across a tranquil lake. That is what your clients should see, even if the true picture is the view of the webbed feet scrambling madly underneath the surface of the water.

Opening New Accounts

Common embarrassing mistakes are signatures that are missing and blanks that aren't filled in. Much of whether the paperwork goes smoothly or not depends on the custodian, but it also depends on your thorough understanding of the paperwork requirements. Always take the time to adequately prepare for meeting with a client. Use a highlighter to mark all the areas you need to fill in with information so you don't pass something by. Don't go into the meeting, full steam ahead, everything's on, and then later bother the client with some detail you should have taken care of up front. It's better to be prepared than to be embarrassed later. Many separate account managers have additional paperwork.

Start by opening your own account, and go through the steps of opening an account with each new custodian with whom you'll begin working. Practice the following three steps:

Step 1: Walk through the process from *A* to *Z*.

Step 2: Money doesn't have to be deposited; just open the account.

Step 3: Fill out all the paperwork; make all the mistakes.

Managing Distributions

One area where we have seen custodians make mistakes is distributions. A client may require monthly income to be paid out of his/her separate account on a certain day. Many times when you first start with a new custodian, there can be a disconnect surrounding who is responsible for the distribution. Of course, you'd think it was the custodian's fault. They thought it was your fault. The client did not care; he/she wanted his/her check. In your clients' minds, you are responsible for any mistakes the custodian makes; you selected the custodian.

To correct any chance of error, you should have a process that records when a custodian should pay a distribution. Our office compares what they expected to be distributed with what actually was withdrawn from the account using the download they received the business day following the expected distribution date. Then they track if the correct amount went out from the proper account at the right point in time. Don't guess. You want to know right then if the custodian has executed all instructions properly. More important, you want to solve the problem before it can be affected or noticed by the client.

Make sure you've got the right system for tracking every distribution, including a list of incidents that have happened and the details surrounding them. If a distribution is not received by the client, you can readily create a running chronology. Alert the custodian to the specifics of the incident and get an explanation back. That way you are immediately on top of it. As a business grows, the tracking of all transactions becomes increasingly important.

Make a complete record of each error, noting all the details and the contact person's name at the custodian's office who dealt with the matter. Analyze how you could have improved results and note that on the record. Your goal should be to be able to pull these records up from your database at any time.

Ensuring Data Integrity

Another concern is data integrity. With massive data coming in, you have to ensure that all that information is streaming correctly. Every time a transaction occurs, the computer must record and reconcile it—whether it's a deposit, a distribution, a trade, a name change, an address change, whatever the details—no matter how large or how small. Data integrity helps in figuring out what to do in specific situations that arise and in establishing procedures. For example:

- What if a transaction hits an account and you don't recognize it?
- What if there is a split on a stock?
- What if there is a merger?
- What if a stock is coming in at a zero basis? How do you report this to your client?
- More important, how does your portfolio accounting software track these anomalies? How does your portfolio accounting system handle these and other types of transactions?
- How do you ensure that the stock doesn't drop into your system at a zero basis, which generates an incorrect tax report?

You want to have a data integrity system in which people are in charge of looking at all the information on a specific transaction and coming up with an analysis and solution. A person isolates the situation, learns and understands it thoroughly, and determines how it should be handled by the firm's portfolio management accounting system, and ultimately how it is reported correctly to the client.

Your goal is to work with the custodian to ensure that a particular transaction is not going to contaminate your database, but rather will ultimately improve the database by being handled well. Repeatable procedures can develop out of individualized solutions that work. You may have clients with multiple accounts making up one larger portfolio. In calculating internal rates of return within that portfolio, it is important to determine a starting date of management. Rather than using the date money is received, use the date that trading and billing actually began. Set it up so that each individual account can be reviewed, or that the portfolio as a whole can be reviewed. It's important to be consistent in the way an internal rate of return is calculated. Always keep the same pattern, never deviating, and you'll avoid one way of getting into trouble in an audit.

If your custodian makes a mistake or takes forever to get money into an account, the advisor is blamed. Advisors are thought of in the same light as the custodians they use. The company you keep, good or bad, is often how your clients judge you. Only work with the best. It is too costly not to.

As an advisor, cross-checking on your client's behalf is a large part of compliance and one more part of your fiduciary responsibility. As the quantity of clients and the dollar magnitude of your business grow, your systems become even more crucial to the protection of not only your clients but also your professional standing. You need to build in systems that will ensure you won't get blindsided by a bad trade that the custodian puts through or an incorrect commission charged.

Facilitating Transfers

Transfers of money from one financial institution to another (contrabroker), say from Franklin/Templeton Funds to Charles Schwab, must go smoothly and quickly. Clients are rightfully concerned when their money is in transition for any period of time.

At our firm, Thornburg, we've created a transfer process that ensures double-checks of every transfer and watches all transactions to make sure they happen correctly. We establish a close relationship with the custodian's transfer specialist and develop a tag-team spirit with the custodian to ensure expediency and to trap any errors or blowups that may have occurred.

There is an established system for assisting you in properly executing a transfer efficiently between broker-dealer firms. One is the Automated Customer Account Transfer (ACAT) system that allows three to five days for execution of a transfer—or at the very least, to have it online.

Handle transfers carefully; track every step of the way. You need to know when each transfer was initiated, exactly what point in the process it's in, and when the last follow-up occurred with the broker-dealer or contrafirm. If something unforeseen occurs, you should know within the week. If the money is to go straight to the custodian, an advisor may not find out about a problem for two or three weeks. Use the intranet to track the status of all accounts. Today you have the ability to see everything your firm does. It's important to have state-of-the-art systems in place so that anyone looking at your firm perceives quality, even if you're a very small firm.

There are many nuances and details with respect to transfers. For instance, if the transfer involves a partial account transfer or a proprietary fund, the ACAT system cannot be used. If there's a limited partnership or an asset that the custodian can't handle, the ACAT will reject the transfer. Then you've got to go back to your client with your tail between your legs. You need to let your client know up front what can and what cannot be transferred on a timely basis. Remember to manage their expectations before you manage their money. Transfer errors typically happen within 7 to 10 days of their initiation with the custodian, so a week has been lost in the process. The client is not going to be happy, and you'll be back at square one.

You need to work with a custodian closely to make sure that your transfers are clean and that all of the dollars you're asking for can come over within your custodian's parameters. Can the custodian handle X-Y-Z managed account? Can the custodian handle X-Y-Z limited partnership? Or does the client need to sell those holdings at the broker where his/her funds are currently residing? On an ACAT transfer, if everything is clean, you're done within 7 business days, whereas in a non-ACAT transfer, the process normally takes 20 to 30 business days. If you must step out of the automated transfer process, make sure your client understands how long the transaction might take. With a normal brokerage account transfer, the process normally takes 20 to 30 days.

Transfers—Key Points

Make sure the client's assets are where you think they are and in a form that can be transferred from the existing financial institution to the target one. Send the transfer by certified mail, if it's going direct.

Make sure your custodian sends the assets to the proper person at the contrabroker. For direct rollovers from a client's 401(k) into an IRA account, make sure the client received and completed all forms received by his/her employer to transfer his/her 401(k). Explain the process in its entirety to the client. Keep copies of everything.

Liquidating Assets as an Alternative

Often, the quickest way to transfer your client's total position at the brokerage house is to liquidate it. The transaction cost will most likely be higher than it would be if the new custodian handled it—but your client may have saved many days. Another big advantage with liquidating at the original brokerage house is that if the market runs up or runs down, you have access to the client's funds immediately. With an ACAT transfer, the funds are frozen until the process is complete. You can't start entering orders within that account, and the broker's liability is potentially open. The client may be stuck in the middle, watching the market sink as his/her funds are in transition. This is not the way to begin a new relationship.

After tracking any problem, close the loop by giving feedback to the client on the solution arrived at.

Summary

Accurate tracking of separate accounts is one of the biggest challenges in our industry. This is largely because most of the operations for separate accounts are still done manually. Although technology that can automate systems is available, companies are too entrenched in their existing systems to be able to change easily.

The reason for this is the sheer volume of new accounts already in place. There's too much at stake to change. Most of the large wirehouses still use an antiquated system that runs on an old DOS infrastructure.

Realistically, it will be years before there is a sea change in operations. It is up to you, the advisor, to understand the existing system and to keep your clients informed. For example, your clients may not know it, but when they transfer 50 securities to a separate account, many times those positions must be input manually.

The chances for error are huge. You also need to let your clients know what time frame to expect. From the time a client signs the contract to the time the account is traded with the money manager, the process can take up to several months. You may want to invest clients in short-term exchange-traded funds or another appropriate product during the waiting period.

What can you do? Explain your firm's timetable for paperwork, compliance, and money manager review. Interview your operations people to determine the path the paperwork needs to take, and then write up a step-by-step guide that you can give to your clients.

The money manager has to ensure that everything is in place: that all signatures are completed and investment objectives are clear and doable. If something goes awry, the money manager can be held liable. As the money managers have fiduciary responsibility to meet your clients' goals, they need to understand what your clients' expectations are. They need to see the investment guidelines to make sure that the suitability is met before they accept an account.

It's not only the advisor's responsibility to educate clients on what a separate account is, but to manage client expectations as well. Advisors shouldn't have to worry about the systems. That's the responsibility of the investment manager and the advisor's firm.

Cash is by far the quickest and easiest method of transfer. Stocks can take weeks, sometimes months, to process. Sometimes there are proprietary products and funds that need to be sold before being transferred. It's not like wiring cash.

Keep in mind the amount of time it may take to get invested once the account is funded and the money manager has accepted the account. Typically, it takes at least two weeks to build a fixed-income separate account, but investing an equity account can take as little as one day. Most fixed-income money managers seldom buy straight off the offer; the likelihood is that they'll be outbid for a position. If that's the case, the money manager may have the intent to invest the account quickly, but it may take a few weeks.

Bond managers are not just looking at the inventory out there—they need to be putting their professional judgment to work, providing a spread that is valuable to your clients' overall return. One case where this becomes tricky is when a client requests a withdrawal. Advisors should explain to clients that they could hinder the performance of their account by forcing a manager to sell quickly to meet short-term cash needs. If the managers are allowed sufficient time, they can better choose the appropriate securities to sell and potentially receive a better price.

You should also explain to your clients the tax consequences; if it's an equity portfolio, they could have 40 trades. If it's in a taxable account, that's 40 taxable events that their tax accountant needs to figure out at the end of the year. For instance, if a client wanted a fixed income portfolio liquidated immediately, the price would be whatever the market was that day. Advisors should explain to clients that they could probably get a lot more money if the money manager is allowed more time.

There's a lot of value added from a separate account. It's up to you to help manage clients through that process. The more you can educate yourself, the more benefit you are to your clients.

Understand the Employee Retirement Income Security Act (ERISA) and Separate Accounts

This information can give you an edge. It is important that you understand how and why the Employee Retirement and Income Security Act (ERISA) works. You will also see how ERISA applies to separate accounts. You'll be able to talk intelligently with trustees, plan sponsors, or anyone involved in the management of employee benefit plans.

Compliance with the ERISA rules has been a major concern of trustees and plan sponsors since this landmark legislation was passed in 1974. The scope and complexity of ERISA has led to a widespread lack of understanding of its basic principles and a commensurate lack of understanding of liabilities to which trustees and fiduciaries may be subjected.

These rules, governed by the Department of Labor (DOL), impose heavy responsibilities on any persons involved in the management of employee benefit plans. Unfortunately, many trustees and advisors are not aware of the responsibilities, liabilities, and penalties under ERISA until they find themselves in violation of the Act.

This chapter has been prepared to provide advisors and fiduciaries charged with the responsibility of managing pension plan assets with guidelines for compliance with the complex maze of ERISA rules. Most important, it offers a framework for assisting in the development of a system of conformity, which will fulfill their fiduciary obligations. Establishing compliance procedures is a necessary part of dealing with assets that are subject to the rules of ERISA.

ERISA was enacted to protect the interests of participants in employee benefit plans from abuses and discriminatory practices. ERISA was also adopted to tie together both trust law principles and the special nature and purpose of employee benefit plans.[1] It had, as one of its central purposes, a public policy of ensuring the adequate investment returns necessary to provide secure retirements for defined benefit plan participants.

While based in large part on traditional principles of trust law, ERISA recognized the limitations of these principles in portfolio management. Departing somewhat from the Prudent Man Rule, ERISA set a standard of prudence to govern pension investments that is more attuned with economic reality and important academic developments in investment theory. The Act fundamentally changed trust investment law from procedural to more process-oriented.

The American Law Institute's 1992 Restatement (Third) of Trusts restated the legal principles that should govern trust investments with the purpose of reconciling trust investment law with changes in investment practices. The Restatement (Third)'s revised standard of prudent investment is known as the Prudent Investor Rule and follows the innovations of ERISA. This will be presented, along with the effects of the Uniform Prudent Investor Act of 1994.

These rules apply to all qualified plans, including defined benefit, defined contribution plans, 401(k) plans, 403(b) plans, individual retirement accounts (IRAs), and others. What these laws and rules really tell you is how lawyers can build a lawsuit where there is a failure to follow ERISA's rules. Once you have got a reasonable understanding of both separate account processes and ERISA and see the connection, you can show your fiduciary clients how to protect their personal liability. And they will listen to you about that topic.

History

Prior to ERISA, a company could have a pension fund that wasn't really backed by anything. If the company wasn't profitable or went out of business, the pension evaporated and participants suffered. In those days, there were no 401(k)s, and IRAs hadn't been invented. For retirement, most people relied on a pension plan, even though few truly understood how the plans worked or where the money was coming from. They just assumed their company was going to pay them a certain amount of money per year after they retired.

Because there was no oversight of pension plans, there were abuses. The system was out of control, so in 1974, the federal government enacted the Employee Retirement and Income Security Act (ERISA). The Act mandated that it was unfair for employees to work at a company for 20 or 30 years and then lose their retirement benefits in the event the company experienced financial problems. Employers were required to fund their retirement plans, putting money aside so that if the company went bankrupt, employees were still guaranteed pensions.

The Act outlined rules and determined how much money must be allocated for pension funds based on how many employees a corporation had. It further stipulated that anything done with this pool of money must be for the benefit of the employees. As that was the only consideration, it eliminated the inherent conflict of interest that results when a company tries to serve itself and its retirees at the same time.

Standard employee retirement plans now include profit sharing, pension, and 401(k)s. However, any plan that is maintained by an employer for the benefit of employees is covered by ERISA, including stock bonus plans, insurance plans (life, health, and disability), and vacation and scholarship funds.

ERISA also provided a federal standard of conduct to be followed and observed concerning the management of retirement fund assets:

> Anyone who is a trustee, sponsor, or otherwise exercises any authority or control over any type of employee benefit plan is a fiduciary. The fiduciary should act with the "care, skill, prudence, and diligence under the circumstances then prevailing that a prudent man acting in a like capacity and familiar with such matters would use in the conduct of an enterprise of like character and with like aims." (ERISA Sec. 404(a)(1)(B))

A fiduciary would not only have a duty to become familiar with ERISA and to follow its standards, but also to seek outside assistance when appropriate. It became extremely important for all plan fiduciaries to understand the scope of their responsibilities and the potential penalties for shirking their responsibilities under ERISA. A fiduciary can be held personally liable for breach or violation of these responsibilities, even to the extent of having to restore lost profits to the plan.[2]

An important point that must be understood is that the scope of the fiduciary responsibility is much wider than generally recognized because the ERISA definition of fiduciary is so broad. To be considered a fiduciary, one must only have an element of authority or control over the plan, including plan management, administration, or disposition of assets. The definition also includes any person who renders investment advice to a plan for a fee.

Named fiduciaries are those listed in the plan documents as having responsibility for plan management. Persons who are delegated duties by named fiduciaries are also considered to be named fiduciaries.

To the extent that plan sponsors influence or maintain discretionary authority over the plan management or its investments, they are also considered to be fiduciaries. Corporate officers, directors, and some shareholders often exert enough control to also be deemed fiduciaries. Investment consultants and advisors are fiduciaries if they provide advice on the value and advisability of owning investments, and/or if they have the discretionary authority to purchase or sell investments with plan assets. It is important to note, however, that if trustees or named fiduciaries properly select and appoint a qualified money manager, they will not have a cofiduciary responsibility for acts and omissions of the advisor, unless they knowingly participate in or try to conceal any such acts or omissions.

The key to understanding this legislation is to realize the government's interest is in protecting the participant, not the fiduciary or plan sponsor. Virtually every time a conflict arises between the interests of the participant and those of the sponsor, legislation favors the participant.

Liabilities and Penalties

Any fiduciary that breaches ERISA's fiduciary obligations can be held personally liable for losses caused by the breach of duty. As discussed earlier, the definition of a fiduciary is broad and the responsibilities are not mitigated by simply delegating fiduciary duties.[3]

Moreover, fiduciaries may be personally liable if they know or should have known of a breach by another fiduciary. Pleading ignorance, bad communications, or inexperience will not be adequate legal defenses. Delegation to prudent experts and the proper overseeing of them are the only defenses upon which a fiduciary can rely.

ERISA makes no provision for punitive damages, but it does provide for the assessment of a penalty against a fiduciary of 20 percent for any amount recovered as a result of an ERISA violation.[4]

> Any person who is a fiduciary with respect to a plan who breaches any of the responsibilities, obligations, or duties imposed upon fiduciaries by this title shall be personally liable to make good to such plan any profits of such fiduciary which have been made through use of assets of

the plan by the fiduciary, and shall be subject to such other equitable or remedial relief as the court may deem appropriate, including removal of such fiduciary. (ERISA Sec. 409(a))

Penalties may be imposed for up to six years after the fiduciary violation, or three years after the party bringing suit had knowledge of the breach. A willful violation carries personal criminal penalties of up to $5,000 ($100,000 for corporations) and up to one year in prison.

Losses to the plan, as well as profits made from the improper use of plan assets, must be restored to the plan. Failure to disclose information to plan participants can result in daily monetary penalties. The DOL can also remove the fiduciary and take control over plan assets.

Civil actions can be initiated by plan participants, beneficiaries, other fiduciaries, and/or the DOL. As participants become more knowledgeable about their rights (and sophisticated about investment alternatives), lawsuits will undoubtedly increase. You're seeing that today with Enron, Worldcom, and Global Crossing.

Governmental Agencies

Three governmental agencies—the DOL, Internal Revenue Service (IRS), and Pension Benefit Guaranty Corporation (PBGC)—oversee retirement plan compliance with various rules and regulations. The DOL has the primary responsibility for promulgating and enforcing fiduciary compliance. Because of the tax-deferred status of qualified plans and IRAs and their interplay with general tax compliance, the IRS oversees participation, vesting, and funding standards. The PBGC ensures that *defined benefit plans* (future retirement benefit is fixed, current contribution by sponsor is not) are properly funded to meet current and future obligations.[5]

This is how you can tie into the separate account process in your market.

Prudent Investment Procedures

The General Standard of Prudent Investment Procedures was originally formulated as a general statement that would allow fiduciaries the flexibility appropriate to particular circumstances. This standard requires that reasonable care, skill, and caution be applied to investments, not in isolation, but as an overall investment strategy, which should incorporate risk and return objectives reasonably suitable to the trust.

Here is where you can show the value of separate accounts as a solution.

You start by raising your client's fear level: Did you know, Mr. Client, that there are only a few types of civil lawsuits that can be filed against that would cause you to lose your house? The area of fiduciary responsibility is one of them. You've got to protect your personal liability, and separate account management can help. Let me show you how. Then explain to your client that a fiduciary is held to a standard of competence and level of skill equal to that of a professional money manager in making investment decisions.

Mr. Client, not knowing your responsibilities is no defense, and the cost of your defense will probably be yours personally and will not be paid by either the plan or your company. However, this liability can be relatively easy to avoid by following these steps.

Step 1. ERISA requires that qualified plans have a written investment policy statement, and 401(k) plan fiduciaries should write the policy statement. You can help them do this; that should be part of your services.

Proof statement. A qualified plan must establish a *written investment policy,* and the policy must be followed. ERISA Sections 402(b)(1) and 404(A)(1)(D).

Step 2. A fiduciary must diversify the investments of a plan to minimize the risk of large losses. That is also one of the features of your firm's separate account program.

Proof statement. A qualified plan's assets must be diversified. ERISA Section 404(a)(1)(C).

Step 3. Fiduciaries can hire an outside separate account manager to manage plan assets. This fulfills two important concerns; first, it fulfills the obligation under the Prudent Expert Rule. Second, the trustee is not liable as a cofiduciary for any acts of omission by the investment manager.

Proof statement. Qualified plan investments must be made according to ERISA Prudent Man requirements. ERISA Section 404(a)(1)(B).

Step 4. The fiduciary (trustee) must maintain an oversight obligation; therefore, adequate monitoring, evaluating, and reporting procedures must be in place to fulfill this responsibility. And this is exactly what you can provide with your firm's separate account program.

Proof statement. The performance of qualified plan investments must be monitored and reviewed. ERISA Section 405(a) provides that a fiduciary may be held personally liable to the plan for all losses. Arguably, the review should be more frequent than once in every three- to five-year market cycle.

Each fiduciary must assume that his or her investment decisions will be examined in detail in the future.[6] Documentation is critical and spans a wide array of both internal and external reporting requirements. Internal record-keeping functions require building an audit file that can be quickly produced and reviewed to verify compliance. External reports are required to satisfy plan participants and regulatory authorities.

You can be the messenger to your ERISA clients: The message is that fiduciary liability can be avoided if you have a written statement of investment policy, a professional manager is appointed, and the plan has a system of monitoring and reporting in place.

Written Investment Policy

The written investment policy statement is a critical first step in building a structure for ERISA conformity. A written investment policy statement enables you to clearly define your preferred investment methodology and communicate long-term goals and objectives. It serves as a framework for allocating the assets among various investment classes, hiring investment managers, and monitoring performance. Help them write one!

Investment Management Procedures

ERISA does *not* differentiate between large and small plans when mandating investment management procedures. (There is no industry standard for defining small and large plans.) Studies have found that more than 80 percent of the smaller pension plans are not in full compliance with the prudent procedures previously outlined.[7]

There is a wide disparity in the expertise of persons holding themselves out as counselors and the quality (and cost) of services they provide. One of the most important qualities an investment counselor must prove is independent advocacy for the interests of the plan.

If an investment counselor can represent only a small handful of money managers, it is difficult to believe that the counselor can reach an unbiased decision about which managers are the most appropriate for the plan. To ensure that the interests of the counselor and the plan remain aligned, the separate account manager (investment counselor) should be compensated only by the plan based on the services provided.

ERISA does not differentiate between those plans that can afford expertise and those that cannot. ERISA holds all plans to the same level of fiduciary responsibility.

Diversification of Plan Assets

It is an investment axiom that diversification is the key to reaching long-term goals, yet this area is one often violated by pension plans. While ERISA does not specify recommended percentages among asset classes, diversification is the only prudent action a fiduciary can take to protect the long-term health of the plan.

Prudent diversification requirements
(...A fiduciary shall discharge his duties with respect to a plan solely in the interest of the participants and beneficiaries...): (C) by diversifying the investments of the plan so as to minimize the risk of large losses, unless under the circumstances it is clearly prudent not to do so. (ERISA Sec. 404(a)(1)(C))

Lack of diversification has been an easy target for litigation since (1) it is easier to prove than specific imprudence,[8] and (2) once a plaintiff proves lack of diversification, the burden shifts to the fiduciary (defendant) to demonstrate that nondiversification was prudent under the circumstances.[9]

The DOL regulations define diversification as a mechanism for reducing the risk of large losses. No further definition is provided. Diversification is a separate and distinct legal obligation from prudence. In an action for plan losses based on an alleged breach of the diversification requirements, the burden of proof is on the claimant to demonstrate that there has been a failure to diversify.

Satisfaction of the diversification requirement is usually determined based on all the facts and circumstances. If diversification is found not to exist, then the burden of justifying failure to follow this general policy is on the fiduciary. Congressional intent behind the diversification requirement is to protect a plan from serious loss due to economic hardship or natural catastrophe (i.e., fire, storm, earthquake). Of course, failure to diversify (e.g., a large cash-equivalent position) may be prudent in the face of a declining or unstable market.

Example

GIW Industries allowed plan participants to allocate their account between one of three investment options. One option, selected by most participants nearing retirement, invested 70 percent of assets in long-term government bonds. The court determined that this violated the diversification requirements of ERISA since investment losses were not recovered by the time participant withdrawals began to take place. In this case, the court scrutinized the fiduciary's failure to investigate the plan's disbursement history and future funding obligations and the risk/return characteristics of long-term bond securities, subjecting the plan to significant imprudent cash flow risks. *(Burton & Jacobsen, Inc.)*[10]

The following should be considered when evaluating diversification of the plan's portfolio:

- The amount of plan assets
- Type of investments (stocks, bonds, real estate, etc.)
- Projected portfolio returns versus funding objectives
- Volatility of investment returns
- Liquidity and future cash flows
- Maturity dates and retirees' pension distributions
- Economic conditions affecting the company and plan investments
- Company and industry conditions
- Geographic distribution of assets

There is not a specific minimum or maximum for each asset class. ERISA states that a fiduciary should not invest an unreasonably large part of the funding in any one investment type. Interestingly, ERISA explicitly states that a plan invested solely in bank CDs meets the diversification requirements. However, court cases seem to refute ERISA on this point (for example, *Blankenship v. Boyle*).

A corollary to this is whether the fiduciary has considered enough comparable investments to ensure that the best alternative was chosen for the plan. This may involve a formal search for a separate account manager or a schedule of bond maturities at various qualities that correspond to future benefit payments. The fiduciary should be confident that enough alternatives have been reviewed to make the most suitable choice for the plan, given inflation, comparable yields, risk versus return, and other factors. Choosing a local money manager merely for convenience will not suffice. A broad menu of choices that fit the plan's goals should be reviewed and a rationale given for choosing (or not choosing) certain investments.

Significant diversification advantages can be achieved with a small number of well-selected securities representing different industries and having other differences in their qualities. Broadened diversification may lead to additional transaction costs, at least initially, but the constraining effect of these costs can generally be dealt with quite effectively through pooled investing. Since optimal diversification may require participation in large portfolios, a professional trustee may be required to use pooled investments in certain circumstances.

Asset Allocation

Diversification has evolved to include asset allocation. Today every plan sponsor knows about the studies that show how the asset allocation decisions have the greatest impact on the overall long-term performance of a portfolio. You need to know that they know.

Risk Management

The duty of a fiduciary does not call for the avoidance of risk, but rather for the prudent management of risk. This requires that careful attention be given to a particular trust's risk tolerance, that is, to its susceptibility to volatility.

The degree of risk permitted for a particular trust is ultimately a matter for interpretation and judgment. It is important that fiduciaries make a reasonable effort to understand the levels of risk and the types of investments suitable to the fund.

Assumed Risk Tolerance or Variability of Return

For investment purposes, risk is defined as the probability or likelihood of not attaining one's investment objectives within a given time period. Equities have a historical compounded return of 10.3 percent (geometric mean), but are considered risky because the return the investor may actually receive in any given year can vary significantly from this mean.

Expected Rate of Return

Once each asset class is selected (stock, bond, etc.), the fiduciary is required to determine the expected rate of return of that market, given the appropriate levels of risk. In other words, the choice must be made in the context of overall risk; and the investment choice should represent the *fair* return, not necessarily the *highest*.

The fiduciary should set a realistic expected return that, at the very least, will ensure growth of assets over inflation. A fiduciary faced with investments of equal risk should not choose the one with the lower returns, if a higher return is available.

A common mistake fiduciaries make is to assume that the best way to avoid risk is to seek the safety of cash and/or fixed-income securities. Over extended periods of time (e.g., 10 years), inflation can deteriorate the real return of a fixed-income portfolio.

Prohibited Investment Transactions

The fiduciary cannot derive a current benefit from the use or management of retirement plan assets.

> A fiduciary with respect to a plan shall not cause the plan to engage in a transaction, if he knows or should know that such transaction constitutes a direct or indirect:
>
> (a) Sale or exchange, or leasing, of any property between the plan and a party in interest
>
> (b) Lending money or other extension of credit between the plan and a party in interest
>
> (c) Furnishing goods, services, or facilities between the plan and a party in interest
>
> (d) Transfer to, or use by or for the benefit of, a party in interest
>
> (e) Cause a plan to acquire and to retain employer securities or employer real property in violation of Section 407(a). (ERISA Sec. 406(a)(1)(A)-(E))

Monitoring and Evaluation

The delegation of plan asset management provides two specific benefits to the plan and its fiduciaries. First, it fulfills the obligation for exercising prudence as defined within the Prudent Expert Rule. Second, the fiduciary is not liable as a cofiduciary for any acts or omissions of the investment manager *as long as the fiduciary maintains adequate oversight of the manager.*

It is critical to bear in mind that the fiduciary's responsibilities are ongoing and liability exists even when professionals (e.g., money managers) are hired and subsequently breach their fiduciary duties or fail to meet plan goals. In other words, delegation alone will not protect a fiduciary; a system of delegation and oversight will. This oversight obligation consists of regular monitoring and evaluating, which are facilitated via a systematic reporting procedure. These systems must be in place if a fiduciary is to fulfill his/her responsibility.

The process of monitoring should mirror the plan's funding and investment objectives. Being able to evaluate past performance, service, and plan policies is as important as the ability to facilitate future changes.

The following minimum standards should be considered when designing a monitoring process:

1. Establish the benchmarks or indices against which the manager will be judged.

2. Determine the appropriate time frame and frequency of review.

3. Compare real versus nominal return.

4. Measure return benchmarks in relation to risk benchmarks. (What if the manager's returns are slightly subpar, but risk elements are superior?)

5. Analyze manager performance relative to peers.

Define the degree of personal attention desired.

ERISA hasn't changed a lot since 1974, although there have been some exemptive orders (class exemptions) and court cases that clarified the Act.

The protection of employee benefit plan participants under ERISA is forthright, but the DOL has realized that rules without compliance are meaningless. Increasing surveillance and audits of small- and medium-sized plans are inevitable. It has been estimated that approximately 80 percent of small plans (those with assets under $3 million) are currently in violation of ERISA regulations. The role of the plan sponsor will intensify in the near future and an extensive understanding of ERISA is going to be key to long-term success in this area.

We do not hold ourselves out to be specialists in pension legislation, nor are we attempting to offer any legal advice. We do advise employers to deal with their retirement plan consultants, attorneys, or CPAs if they have specific questions regarding their retirement funds.

Financial advisors and intermediaries would be well served to follow the guidelines in this book and reduce the number of plans that are in noncompliance. This is a good business practice, an opportunity for the financial intermediaries to add value, and a good public service to protect members of the public.

Following is a sample of an agreement that financial advisors can use with their clients to help them comply with the mandates of ERISA. This document assures that the separate account manager is made aware that the investor and the fiduciaries are subject to the requirements of ERISA.

Supplement to a Management Agreement

This supplement applies only to clients for which XYZ Co. has been appointed as an investment manager of any portion of the assets of a plan and related trust governed by ERISA (collectively, the Plan) by the Trustees of the Plan (the Trustees).

The term *Client* in this Supplement shall include the Trustees. If the *named fiduciary* (as defined in ERISA) of the Plan who is authorized to appoint a Money Manager as investment manager is defined by a term other than *Trustees*, then all references to *Trustee* and *Client* herein shall include such fiduciary. In the event of any inconsistency or conflict between this Supplement and any other terms or provisions of the Agreement, then this Supplement shall control.

1. The Client and/or their Investment Professional are responsible for notifying Money Manager that the Client is subject to ERISA.
2. The Client hereby represents to have full power, authority, and capacity to execute the Money Manager Investment Management Agreement (the *Agreement*). If the Agreement is entered into by a Trustee or other fiduciary, including but not limited to someone meeting the definition of *fiduciary* under ERISA or an employee benefit plan subject to ERISA, such Trustee or other fiduciary represents and warrants that the Client's participation in XYZ Co.'s program is permitted by the relevant governing instrument of such plan, and that the Client is duly authorized to enter into this Agreement. The Client agrees to furnish such documents to the Money Manager as required under ERISA or as the Money Manager reasonably requests. The Client further agrees to advise the Money Manager of any event or circumstance which might affect this authority or the validity of this Agreement. The Client additionally represents and warrants that (i) its governing instrument provides that an *investment manager* as defined in Section 3(38) of ERISA may be appointed and (ii) the person executing and delivering this Agreement on behalf of the Client is a *named fiduciary* as defined under ERISA who has the power under the Plan to appoint an investment manager.
3. The Money Manager further acknowledges that, in regard to those clients for which it serves as an *investment manager,* it shall be a *fiduciary*

as defined in Section 3(21)(A) of ERISA for that portion of the Plan's assets it is managing.

4. The Client agrees to obtain and maintain, for the period of this Agreement, the bond required for fiduciaries by Section 412 under ERISA and to include the Money Manager among those covered by such bond.

5. The Client has read, fully understands, and agrees to be bound by the terms and conditions of the Agreement currently in effect, and as may be amended from time to time.

6. The Trustees acknowledge that they are responsible for the diversification of the Plan's investments and the Money Manager does not have any such responsibility.

Risk Disclosure Statement

XYZ Co. provides investment services to meet varying investment needs and risk tolerance. Clients should carefully consider whether such an investment is suitable in light of their financial condition. Prior to authorizing the Money Manager to invest for their account, the Client should carefully review the selected investment services. Should their objectives change, Clients should reevaluate their participation in these investment services and notify the Money Manager in writing of any change.

Any investment program entails the risk of loss. While we make every effort to keep these losses small, there have been numerous loss periods in the past and there will be others in the future. It must be stressed that investment returns, particularly over shorter time horizons, are highly dependent on trends in the various investment markets. XYZ's investment management services are suitable only as long-term investments, and should not be viewed as short-term trading vehicles.

If the Client is subject to ERISA, the Client hereby agrees to be bound by the terms of the *ERISA Supplement to the Agreement.*

Client Signature   Date

Notes

[1] H.R. Rep. No. 1280, 93rd Cong., 2d Session 302.

[2] The pension trustees who breached the fiduciary duties of this plan were jointly and severally liable for more than $2 million plus interest, costs, and legal fees. *Katsaros vs. Cody* (DC E NY, 27 December 1983).

[3] The fact that trustees may have acted with good intentions or in good faith is no defense if their conduct did not meet the objective standard. *Donovan vs. Mazzoia* (DC N CAL, November 1981).

[4] ERISA Sec. 502(1). See also, "Report to the Secretary of the Task Force on enforcement (9-90), relating to the ERISA Enforcement Strategy Implementation Plan.

[5] See *PBGC v. LTV* (110 S. Ct. 2668, 1990).

[6] Donald B. Trone and William R. Allbright. *Procedural Prudence.*

[7] *Changes are Needed in the ERISA Audit Process to Increase Protection for Employee Benefit Plan Participants.* Department of Labor, Office of Inspector General (November 1989).

[8] *Marshall v. Teamsters Local 282 Pension Trust Fund,* 485 F. Supp 986 (E.D. NY 1978); *Freund v. Marshall & Ilesly Bank,* 485 F. Supp 629 (W.D. Wisc. 1979); *Brock v. Berman,* 673 F. Supp 634 (D.C. Mass 1987); *Donavan v. Guaranty National Bank,* 4 E.B.C.1686 (S.D. W. Va. 1983); and *Brock v. Citizens Bank of Clovis,* 841 F.2d 344 (10th Cir. 1988) but cf. *Withers v. Teachers' Retirement System of the City of New York,* 447 F. Supp 1248 (S.D. NY 1978); *Sandoval v. Simmons,* 622 F. Supp 1174 (D.C. Ill. 1985); and *Davidson v. Cook,* 567 F. Supp 225 (E.D. Va. 1983), aff'd mem., 734 F2d 10 (4th Cir. 1984).

[9] H.R. Rep. No. 1280, 93rd Cong., 2d Sess. 302 at 304 (1973).

[10] 10 E.B.C. 2290 (S.D. Ga. 1989) aff'd 895 F 2d 729 (11th Cir 1990).

CHAPTER
20

Look into the Future

Judging the success of separate accounts at this stage is like judging a sky-diver before he/she reaches the ground. So far so good! But it's still low on the investor's financial education curve. Even as the education process expands, the financial advisor remains indispensable for the foreseeable future, and that's good news.

The bad news is that you are going to have to expand your service levels to compete in what is becoming a very crowded market. The original consultants who delivered separate accounts were stockbrokers who pioneered the charge into the fee side of the business. They generally have operated, from the investment perspective, as one of a group of professionals (certified public accountants [CPAs], lawyers, insurance agents, financial planners) who coexisted competitively with each other, while servicing the investor. Today, as the battle for control of the investor's assets has heated up, the gloves have come off. *All* of these various professionals are vying for the role of general contractor or master advisor. There are no educational hurdles, bar exams, or professional designations required to enter the financial advisory business other than obtaining a broker's or a Registered Investment Advisor (RIA) registration. Now these non-investment-oriented professions have started to enter the investment consulting arena. The separate account can be a good fit for tax-savvy advisors (CPAs, insurance agents, and financial planners). What they might lack in investment experience, they make up for in ability to advise on the integration of the separate account into the investor's overall financial and personal life strategy.

If you are planning to service the high-net-worth investor, you are going to have to become a master advisor and implement an umbrella strategy. The umbrella strategy is the multiproduct service solution put in place to satisfy investors' financial objectives. The successful master advisor will also have to integrate tax management, financial planning, trust, and legal services into his/her umbrella strategy.

Who holds the edge, the RIA and registered financial advisor at a full-service financial services firm, or the independent RIA? Both have their positives and negatives.

The employees of large Wall Street firms can boast about brand identity, access to product, and tremendous institutional-quality firm support and research. The independents can hang their hats on "best of breed," and conflict-free advice. What you do not see much of anymore is the sole practitioner, a lone advisor working with an assistant. To compete effectively as a master advisor, a broad array of experience is required. No one individual can master it all. This applies both to the Wall Street, as well as the independent, advisor. Regardless of the method of conducting their business, there will be a consolidation of advisors into professional consortiums to be able to provide one-stop shopping for the high-net-worth investor.

Problems

Investors still haven't been able to determine who gets paid what. Each firm has incredibly complex payout structures and product pricing grids. Plus, how do you address the whole issue of proprietary versus independent separate account management? Most of the wirehouses have substantial in-house or proprietary asset management capabilities. If these large institutional firms adopt the new control account model within a larger umbrella strategy, is it really necessary or smart for them to use independent nonaffiliated money managers? Excluding independent managers would dramatically increase product margins, as there would be no requirement to share a normalized asset management fee. Also, why share asset management fees with a firm that may eventually build its own distribution and compete with you? It's like letting the fox into the henhouse or selling weapons to your enemy.

Eliminating the availability of independent money managers could dramatically impact the historical culture of these firms, especially the independent nonwirehouse firms. It would also bring more inherent risk into the process for the firm. If the firm's proprietary asset management services underperform, they run the risk of losing the high-net-worth investor to a competitor with more diversified offerings—whereas, if an outside manager underperforms, the situation may be resolved by just changing asset managers.

The temptation will be to create a superfirm strategy, eliminating independent managers. In the long run, however, culture and competitive pressure will keep the independent managers in the mix.

The odds favor that the only way a wirehouse will be able to maintain its market share in the investment management business will be to take its product offering outside its captive salesforce and offer it through other channels and distribution networks. This will have tremendous political ramifications for the captive salesforce, but may be the best strategy for the wirehouse.

The current separate account back-office infrastructure will be extinct in 2010! That's a bold statement, but the one obstacle that could stop the growth of the separate account industry in its tracks is operational infrastructure. There are no standard operating procedures for managed accounts, no guidelines to follow; each sponsor must establish its own rules. This whole separate account picture looks very similar to the mutual fund industry in the late 1970s and early 1980s. Mutual funds, due to IRAs and later, 401(k)s, were becoming extremely popular. Even though there was far less than $1 trillion in funds, demand was picking up. (Mutual funds did not exceed $1 trillion until 1987.)

Each mutual fund complex had its own rules and procedures regarding new accounts, terminations, data distribution, and so on. As you might remember, in the early 1980s the wheels came off. The financial records of the mutual funds were out of balance. The third-party resellers of the funds had different records than the fund companies. Checks were eventually sent to investors based on what they said they had. It was almost a meltdown for the fund industry. Only when industry standards were created with consistent operational platforms and applied technology did the mutual fund industry become a model of efficiency. And only then did the focus shift to pure investment management offerings and profitability and distribution.

If the separate account industry gets hit with the same type of demand as mutual funds before there is industry-wide standardization of systems and processes, it will make the mutual fund industry look like a day at the beach. Separate accounts, due to the very things that make them popular, also make them a bear to administer.

The Achilles' Heel of Separate Accounts

The root of the problem goes back to how separate accounts evolved. Separate accounts are one of the very few retail financial products that originated within the broker-dealer community. Most products, such as mutual funds, annuities, real estate investment trusts (REITs), insurance, hedge funds, and so forth, originate at the product manufacturer level and are then offered to the broker-dealer salesforce to be distributed. For example, a money manager decides to create a mutual fund. They pick a custodian, determine the fee structure, hire shareholder record keepers, and so on. Then they take the completed product to the mutual fund department of the broker-dealer and convince and compensate them to distribute their funds.

Not so in the separate account industry. The broker-dealer created the product. They selected themselves as custodian and trade executor. They hired money managers to work for them; they established all the administrative rules. These broker-dealers saw the value in separate accounts long before the institutional money managers, so they firmly took the role of lead dog and created a product that was offered within their own distribution network. Because each broker-dealer was unique, there was very little cross-breeding or distribution outside of the specific broker-dealers. But, like the movie line in *Jurassic Park,* "Life finds a way," separate accounts are cross-breeding. In many cases now, the same money managers managing the original proprietary separate accounts are now being hired by different broker-dealers. Advisor-brokers changed firms and took their clients with them, necessitating that the investment manager be able to offer the same services, but through a different broker-dealer. As a result, many smaller broker-dealers were required to build the infrastructure to offer separate accounts. And more financial advisors became exposed to these service offerings, causing a rapidly accelerating increase in demand for separate accounts. In short, all of a sudden there was a population explosion! This is a train wreck waiting to happen.

The largest separate account managers participate in upward of 50 sponsor programs. That means they have to:

- Reconcile their portfolio management system with 50 different custodians.
- Deal with 50 different new account procedures.
- Deal with 50 different termination policies.
- Deal with 50 different billing systems (the author's challenge to any manager is to confidently state that they know they are being paid correctly by all sponsors).
- Place trades for the same stock at 50 different broker-dealers (Who goes first?).

- Have 50 trade error accounts.
- Have 50 different ways to receive cost data on securities transferred in.

The list goes on and on. It becomes very clear why there are so few managers participating in the separate account industry relative to the mutual fund industry, at least at this time.

Perspective of an Investor Who Wants to Comparison-Shop

It's not much better from the perspective of the investor who changes broker-dealers or wants to compare different broker-dealer programs. There are no standard databases showing all sponsor offerings and no standard pricing formats. The same manager may be offered by multiple sponsors, but they manage the money using a different style at each firm. Some sponsors accept stock transfers; others do not. And the managers' fees may vary among the different sponsors.

Let's look at the process of an investor changing from Sponsor A to Sponsor B, but wanting to retain the same manager. First, the investor has to instruct Sponsor A to terminate the account. Sponsor A (depending on which one) will either automatically liquidate the account or just turn off the management of the account. Because Sponsor A bills quarterly in advance, the investor must wait to get a pro rata fee refund. Next, the investor must go to Sponsor B and open a new brokerage account.

Sponsor B requests an automated customer account transfer (ACAT) of all the securities in the account. (This assumes that Sponsor A did not liquidate the account, creating a taxable event for the client.) While the investor waits three to six weeks for the securities to transfer, the back office checks to see if Sponsor B has the same manager and the same style. If Sponsor B does have the same manager, then the account is reopened with the manager, who must reenter all the cost data. The investor is billed a pro rata inception fee, probably at a different rate than that of Sponsor A. The whole process can take four to eight weeks. Meanwhile, the account is left unmanaged the whole time. If Sponsor B does not have the same manager, the investor then must search for a manager that is similar in style with similar performance results and fees. This adds just more time to the overall process, when all the investor really wanted was to change brokerage firms or financial consultants.

The investor usually comes away with a very bad taste in his/her mouth. A mutual fund transferring from Sponsor A to Sponsor B takes approximately one to three days. There is no interruption in management, and the fees remain the same.

Perspective of an Advisor-Consultant

The advisor perspective is very similar to that of the client, the investor. Advisors generally feel as if they are constrained by the sponsor. They are dependent on the sponsor's menu of offerings, and it is very difficult, as well as risky, to change firms.

The Winner in the Current Infrastructure

The clear winners in the current infrastructure are the large, traditional sponsor/broker-dealers. They control the gate keys to the inventory of investment management offerings and will protect them vigorously. The lack of account portability is a major positive for them.

How Does the Separate Account Industry Reinvent Their Infrastructure?

The separate account industry is going to have to take a lesson from all of the other financial products in the financial consulting industry. Separate accounts are the only product in which distribution is tied to the custody of the assets. Look at mutual funds as the model. Each money manager deals with only one physical custodian of the assets. That custodian, combined with a shareholder recordkeeper, transfers at net asset value (NAV) regularly between any firm that is distributing their funds. The separation by custodian of the physical dollars from distribution is the key to building a scalable infrastructure for separate accounts. Virtually every financial product that amasses large dollars operates in this fashion, with the exception of separate accounts.

Each money manager should have one single custodian for all separate account assets. That custodian should be distributing managed account value (MAV) to any sponsor firm who wants to distribute their investment management capabilities. It can be argued that distributing only an MAV to the sponsor distribution firm would be a step backward for separate accounts, in that the advisor and investor could not see the underlying holdings. That is true, but the Internet technology exists to click on the MAV and get see-through access into the holdings of the account each day.

Having the money manager determine the custodian of the actual assets is a radical departure from the separate account industry norm. It will be met with resistance from the large traditional sponsors, but all the other parties to separate accounts should welcome it with open arms.

Current Operational Nightmares Melt Away

Central custodianship determined by the money manager starts to melt away many of the problems we previously identified. Money managers no longer have 50 sets of administrative procedures; instead they have just one. They will be able to trade in blocks at any firm for best execution as they do in mutual funds. They need only to reconcile the portfolio management system to one custodian. They can track their billings and receivables. They can reduce their error accounts. All these things should dramatically reduce their operational expenses, improving their bottom line.

The advisor and investors will enjoy greater freedom as accounts become portable in the same fashion as mutual funds. Going from Sponsor A to Sponsor B will take days rather than weeks with no interruption in management. The portfolio manager at the money manager would not even be aware of the MAV transfer from Sponsor A to Sponsor B.

Once separate account managers start to select common custodians as they have in mutual funds, common operating procedures for separate accounts will be established just as they are in the mutual fund industry or the annuity industry. This will make data aggregation much easier, allowing for greater and more consistent information on separate accounts. Small sponsors will find it much easier and substantially less expensive to build sponsor programs. It will be much more of a plug-and-play model, as it is in the mutual fund industry, rather than the closed-architecture system it is today.

The only party that will feel pain is the large traditional sponsor. In effect, they will be giving the keys to the fiefdom to all of the members, allowing them to come and go. At first, this sounds scary but, in reality, they have some of the best quality programs in the industry. They may find that an open-architecture platform may attract more assets rather than less. When Schwab first introduced the mutual fund supermarket, the big wirehouses resisted offering no-load funds. Demand from the salesforce finally made them cave in. Today, they sell more mutual funds than they ever did in the past and are getting paid fees on the no-load funds they resisted in the past.

The money managers centralizing custodianship may not be the only solution to scalability, but it is the only proven successful model. Experimenting with anything else as volume turns up dramatically will be very risky. Today's major mutual fund families who are entering the separate account market are the logical candidates to drive this process. They do not have legacy systems to retool; it is a similar process to the administration of their funds, and they have the marketing muscle to force the issue.

What Do You Do—Lead or Follow?

The financial services landscape is changing daily. Even though separate accounts have a 25-year history and their roots go back 100-plus years, the industry is in its infancy. At this stage, just as in any other industry, seat-of-the-pants flying with limited visibility is required to bring the industry to maturity. There have, and will continue to be, a few crashes along the way, but the winners will be amply rewarded for the risks taken.

At maturity, separate accounts will take their place alongside mutual funds and insurance as the core products of the financial services industry. Their flexible, customizable features make them a natural vehicle to transport the high-net-worth baby boomers into retirement. The separate account as a core control account will complete the investors' solution to the puzzle. The separate account is the only puzzle piece that can alter its shape to fit almost any remaining opening.

Technology will change the way money is managed. For the past 25 years, asset management has been about beating the illusive intangible market. The debate between index funds and actively managed funds has raged on for those 25 years, and rightly so. Active managers have proven that they cannot consistently beat the illusive market index. All the technological advances of the past 25 years, while perhaps helping marketing, communications, and administration, have not really improved performance. Separate accounts have the opportunity to change this by replacing this legacy by starting to manage the money through the eyes of an individual investor, to work in the world of absolute dollars and specific securities rather than total return and pooled assets, while accomplishing the mission of satisfying specific investor needs with the highest probability of success.

The opportunity still exists for you to be a leader in the separate account industry. All the components are almost in place. The horses are lining up at the gate. It is time to make a major commitment—or to sit in the stands and watch the race.

About the Authors

Larry Chambers is a freelance writer and author with over 30 books and 700 investment-related articles. Chambers started at EF Hutton & Co. as a stockbroker, where he achieved an outstanding track record and was placing clients in separate accounts in the mid-1970s. In 1979 he was named one of the top 20 brokers and was a member of the Blue Chip Club and Associate Vice President. He attended University of Utah, received both Bachelor's and Master's of Science Degrees, and was elected to the Phi Kappa Phi honor society.

Chambers is also a Tiburon Strategic Advisors Fellow. He is an advisory board member for the *Journal of Retirement Planning,* associate editor for the *Journal of Investing,* on the board of advisors for *Personal Financial Planning Monthly,* and the business and economics columnist for the Honor Society of *Phi Kappa Phi Forum.*

Ken Ziesenheim is currently a managing director of Thornburg Investment Management Company, the manager and advisor for Thornburg mutual funds, and serves as President of Thornburg Securities Corporation, the distributor of Thornburg Funds. Prior to joining Thornburg in mid-1995, Ken was Senior Vice President of Mutual Fund Marketing at Raymond James & Associates. Ken also previously held a variety of other positions at Raymond James, including Senior Vice President of Financial Planning and Financial Services, President of Planning Corporation of America (wholly owned insurance marketing subsidiary), and First Vice President of Sales for all Raymond James offices outside of the state of Florida.

Ken's education background includes a degree in Business Administration from Stetson University, a Juris Doctor from Baylor University, and a Master of Laws Taxation from the University of Denver. In addition, he is a Certified Financial Planner and a Certified Mutual Fund Specialist. Ken also attended the Securities Industry Institute at Wharton from 1985 to 1987.

Prior to his affiliation with Raymond James, Ken was a practicing lawyer. He continues to maintain both licenses to practice law in Texas and Colorado (inactive).

Ken currently serves as a Trustee for the National Endowment for Financial Education (NEFE) and was elected chairman for 1994. He also has been elected to serve as an arbitrator for the National Association of Securities Dealers (NASD) and the American Arbitration Association (AAA). He is a past director of the National Board of the International Association for Financial Planning (now the FPA) and a past director, president, and chairman of the board of the Tampa Bay Chapter of the IAFP. Ken resides in Sebring, Florida, with his wife, Diane, and three Weimaraners, Mamie, Chili, and Zadie.

Peter Trevisani, Director of separate accounts at Thornburg Investment Management MBA in finance from Columbia Business School, B.A. from Boston College. ptrevisani@thornburg.com 505.954.5218 (Office)

The Firm Profile

Thornburg Investment Management, Inc., is a privately held investment management company based in Santa Fe, New Mexico. The firm advises the Thornburg family of mutual funds and manages separate portfolios for select institutions and individuals. Sister companies manage specialty Real Estate Investment Trusts.

Thornburg Investment Management was founded in 1982 by Garrett Thornburg. In 1984, the firm created and offered one of the first limited-term municipal bond mutual funds in the United States, and began earning its reputation for disciplined yet creative value investing in both fixed income and equities. Today, Thornburg Investment Management manages over $4 billion in mutual fund assets and separately managed portfolios.

Index